SINGAPORE
The Little Red Book

SINGAPORE
The Little Red Book

Photography by
Luca Invernizzi Tettoni

Talisman

Published in 2009 by
Talisman Publishing Pte Ltd
52 Genting Lane
Ruby Land Complex 1
#06–05 Singapore 349560
Tel: +65 6749 3551
Fax: +65 6749 3552
Email: customersvc@apdsing.com
www.talismanbooks.com.sg

ISBN 978-981-08-1468-7
Printed in Singapore

Copyright © 2009 Talisman Publishing Pte Ltd
Photos © 2009 Luca Invernizzi Tettoni www.tettoni.com
Introduction and captions by Kim Inglis www.kiminglis.com

All rights reserved. No part of this publication may be reproduced, stored in a retrieval system or transmitted in any form by any means, electronic or mechanical, including photocopy, recording or any information retrieval system, without prior permission of the publisher.

Introduction

In many ways, Singapore is a microcosm of the many and varying cultures found in Asia. Everywhere you look, you see a different face, another style of dress, a different building: it's a layered country, full of contradiction, yet homogenized in a way no other country has seemingly achieved.

With the exception of a plethora of foreign or overseas workers, every person is a Singaporean, yet they may have originated as far afield as India, China, Indonesia, Malaysia and the Middle East. Their religions include Taoist, Buddhist, Islamic, Christian; their languages reflect their diversity, with many dialects from China intermingling with Bahasa and, of course, the lingua franca, the lilting "Singlish"; and their religions (or non religions) are freely practised or ignored.

It's a country of immigrants. Back in the early 1800s, it was home to a few original fisherfolk; these were superceded by British colonists, who developed the small island into a thriving port, thereby attracting labourers from India, Sri Lanka and China, Chinese merchants, Middle Eastern traders, and many others. These people settled, had families and prospered. It is their ancestors who make up the modern Singaporean population.

As the years passed, the city-state developed, modernized, expanded and, with independence, became a forward-thinking country with soaring skyscrapers, efficient communication and technology, and a standard of living envied by many.

Yet, it isn't these trappings of modernism that you remember about Singapore. It's much more likely to be a fascinating emporium, a little temple, some religious festival or a street-corner meal. It could be the maze of alleyways in Chinatown, a thriving market in Little India, the majesty of a neo-Palladian civic building, an exotic jungle flower. For, as the waves of immigrants came to this tiny island, they brought with them something from home—be it a memory, a fragment of culture, or a

photograph. Then, building from these, they recreated these in Singapore: in the form of clan houses, temples and mosques, rituals and customs, meals–and more.

As a result, the sights, sounds and systems so entrenched in Singapore life are often more "real" than their counterparts in their country of origin. The bazaar in Little India seems more "Indian" than the one in Old Delhi; a Taoist temple is more authentic than one in southern China; the Padang or cricket pitch better tended than the green in an English village.

Similarly, a new identity has been forged: bastardized Indian, Chinese and Malay dishes are now considered examples of "Singaporean food", idiosyncratic phrases have entered the lexicon, very particular local customs have developed. In the same way that Caesar salad is served in Italian restaurants worldwide (but never in Italy!), Singapore is home to numerous imitations that have evolved into a kind of hyper-reality.

There's nowhere else like it. In a word, Singapore is unique.

This book showcases some of these particularly Singaporean sights: the contrasts and contradictions as well as the parallels. We include people, art, architecture, religion, flora and fauna, shopping, food–the everyday and the extraordinary. Modern and traditional, old and new, young and old. The lifeblood of the country flows through these pages.

At the end, there are short captions explaining the images; but, in general, it's a visual book. Arranged according to picture flow as opposed to editorial logic, it invites you to take a little bit of Singapore home. There's unity in its diversity, just as there's unity in the images in this little book.

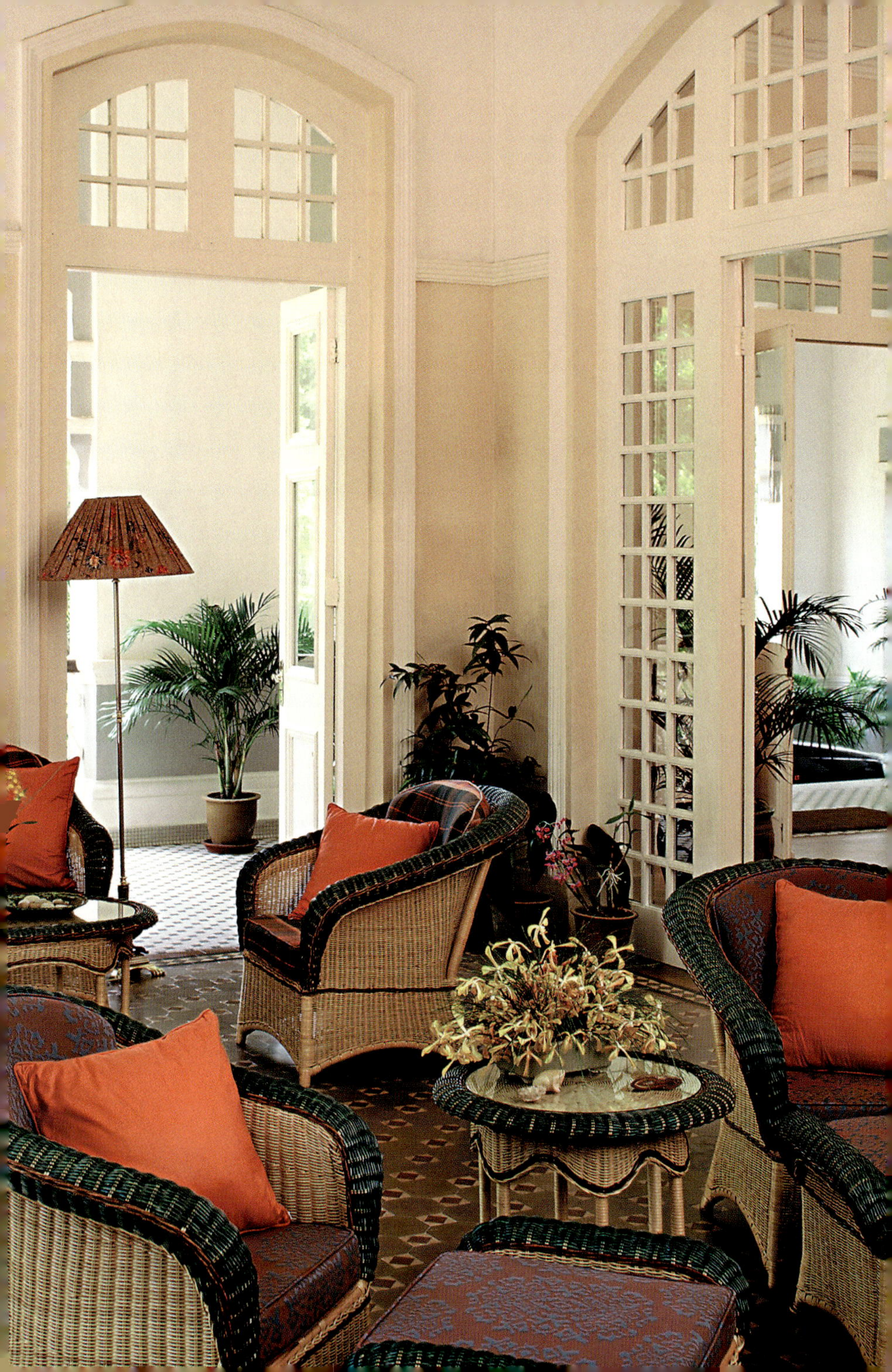

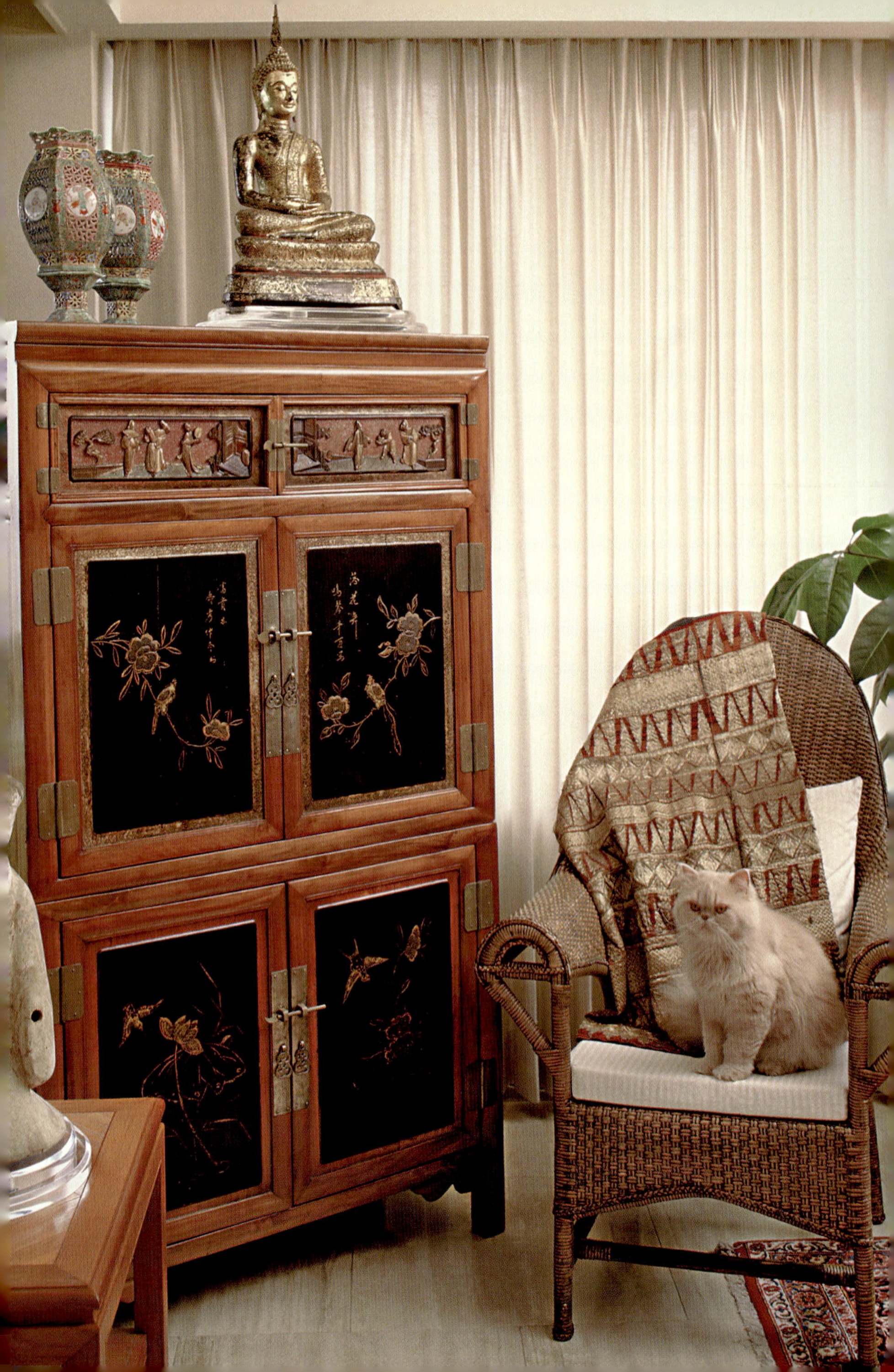

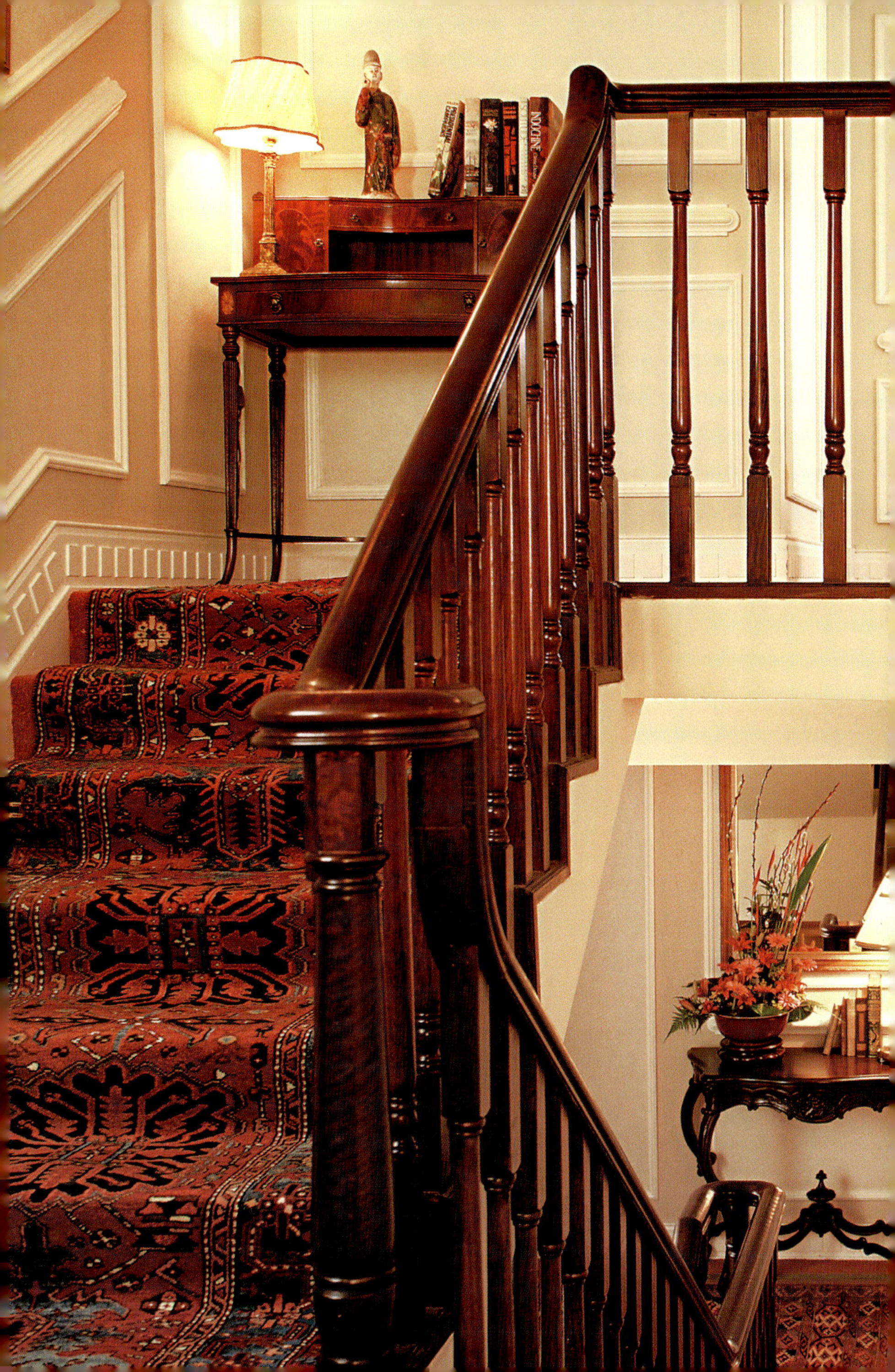
INDOCHINE

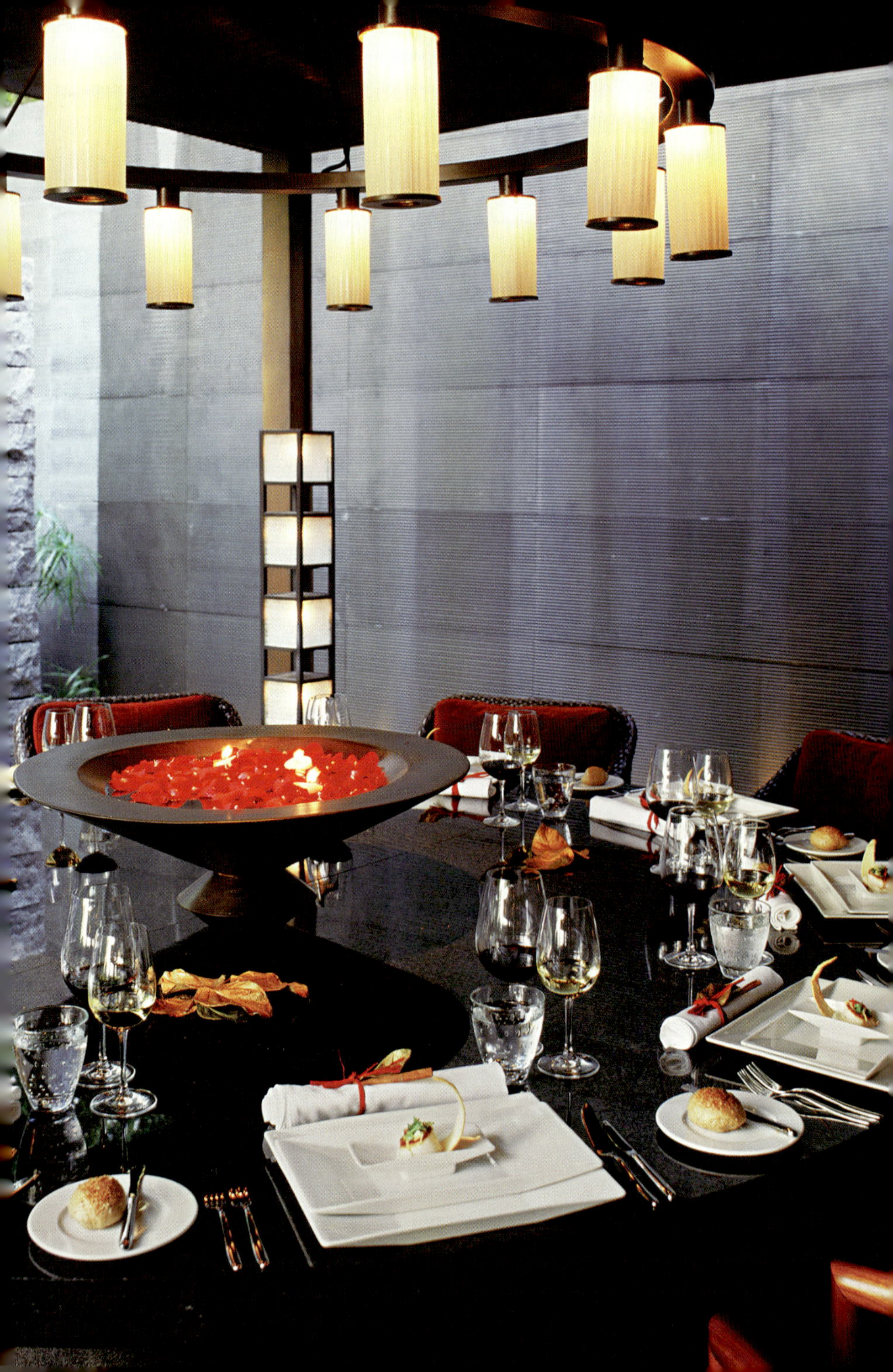

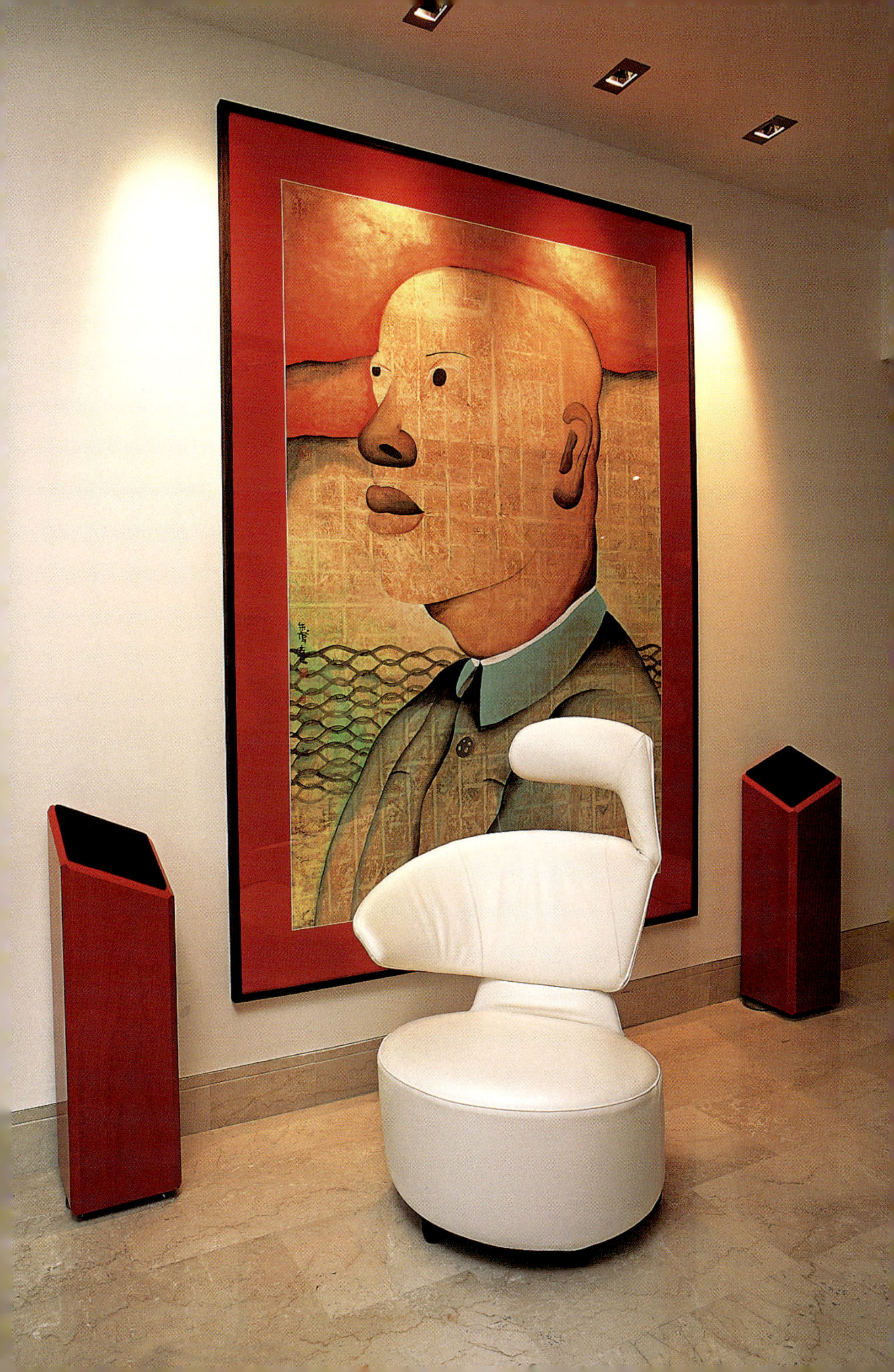

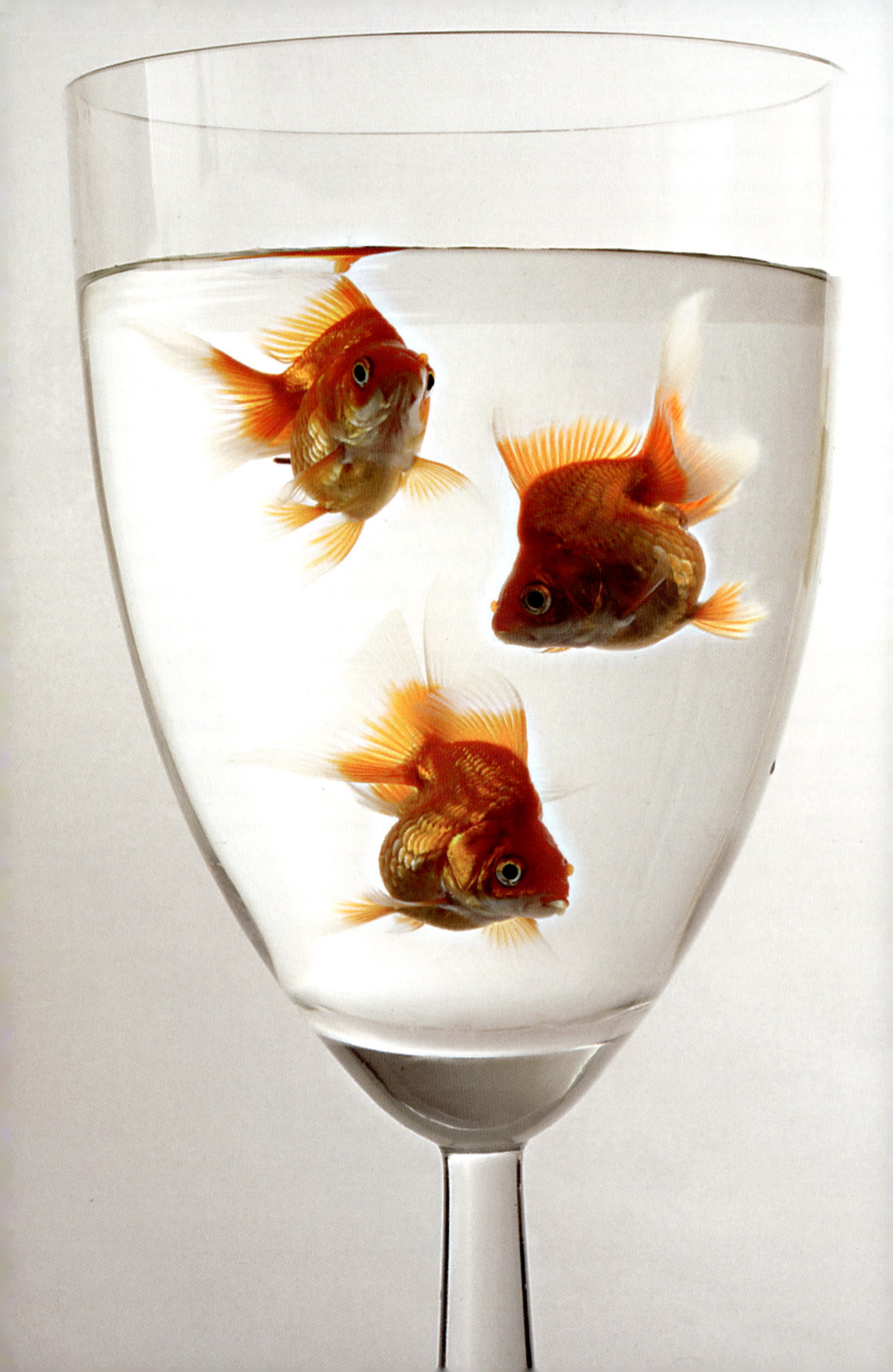

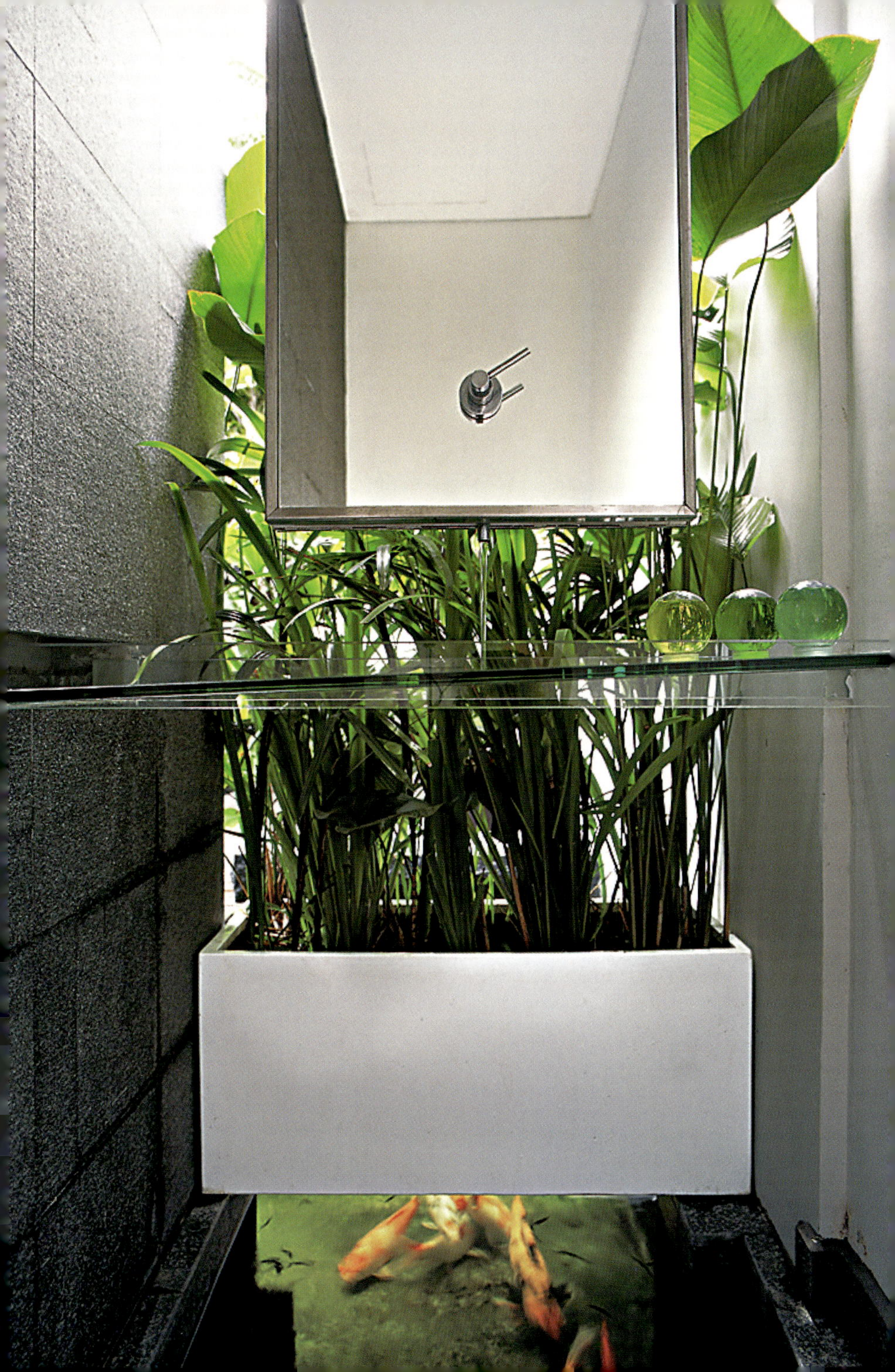

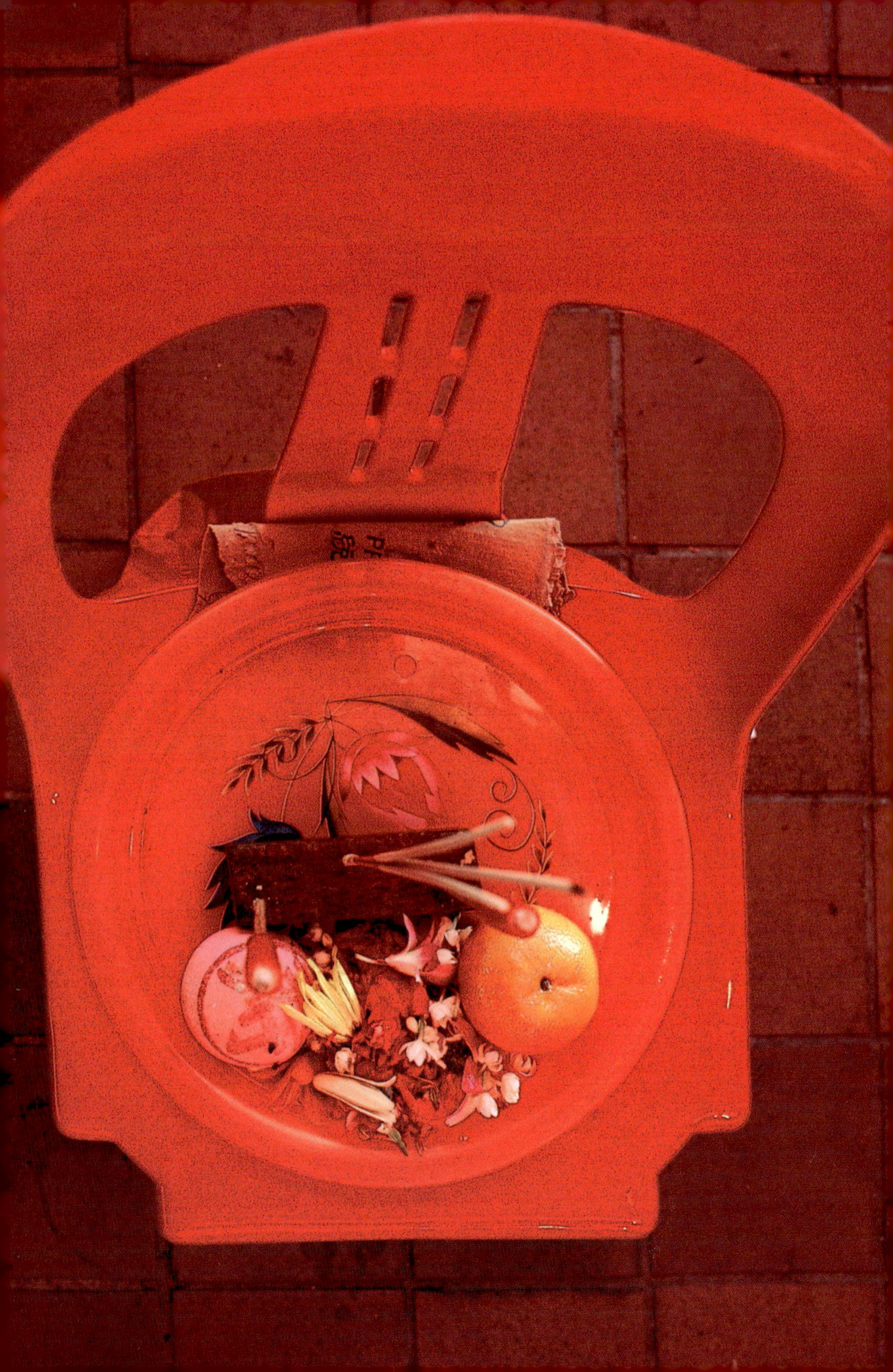

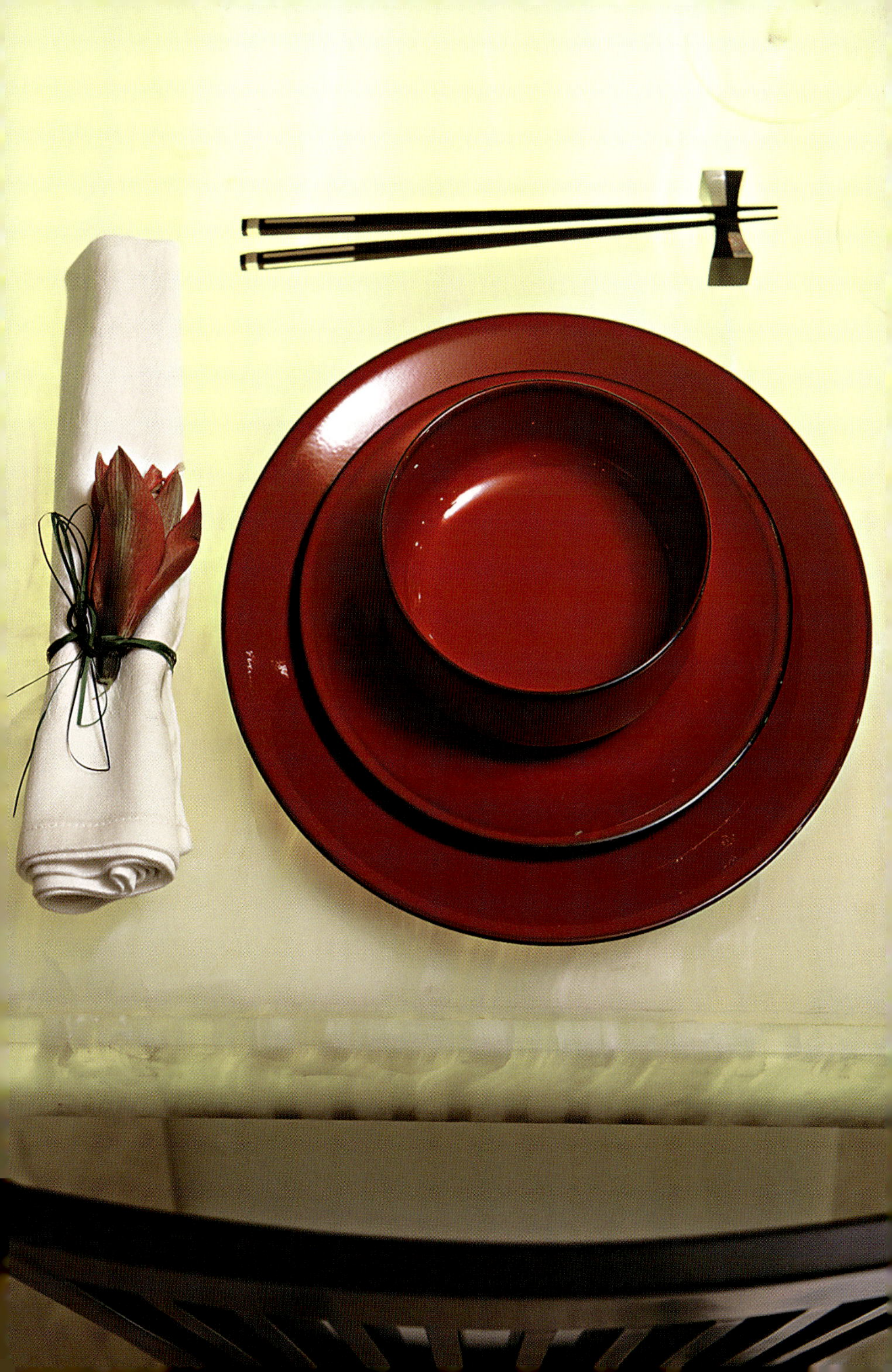

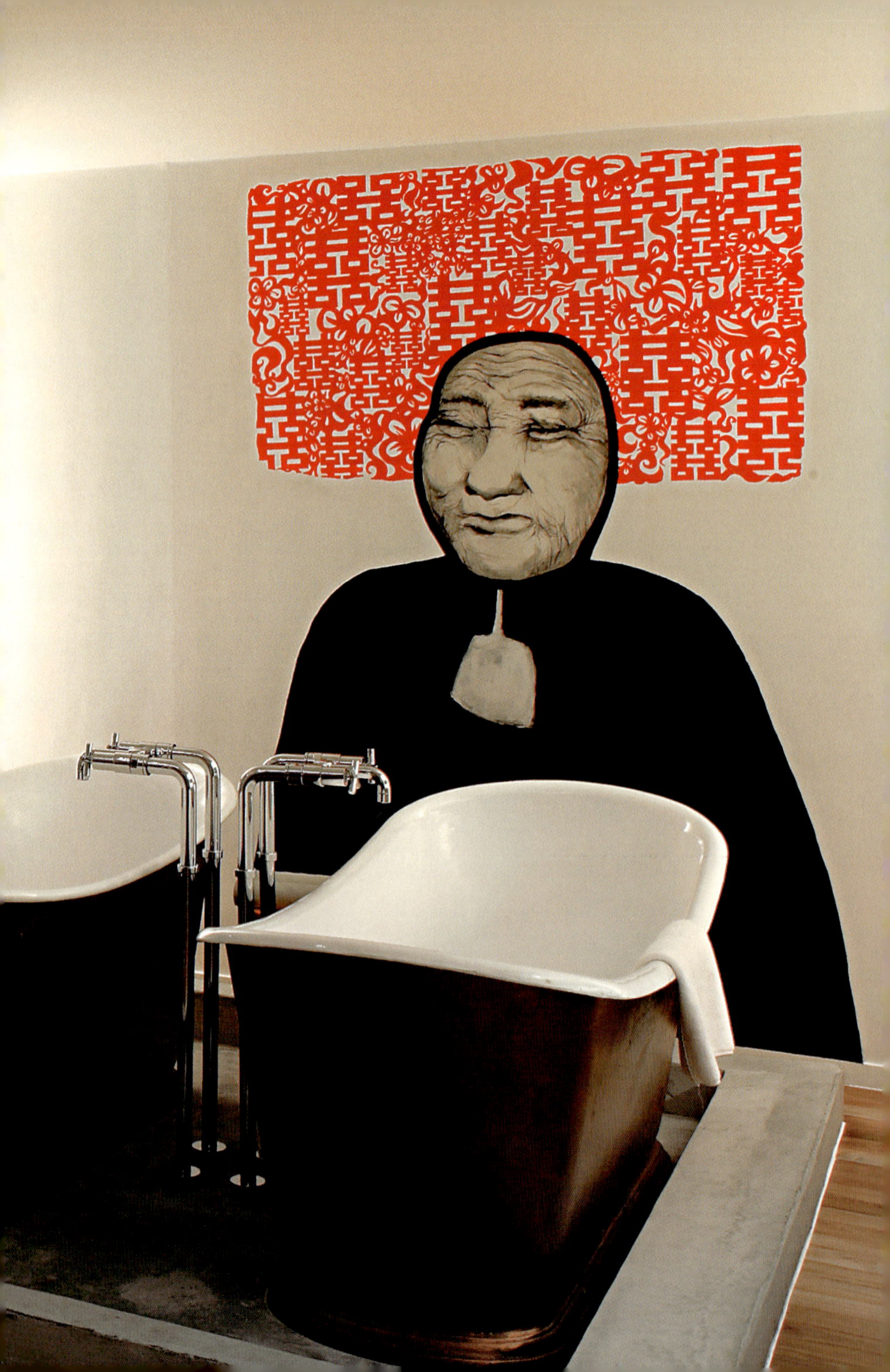

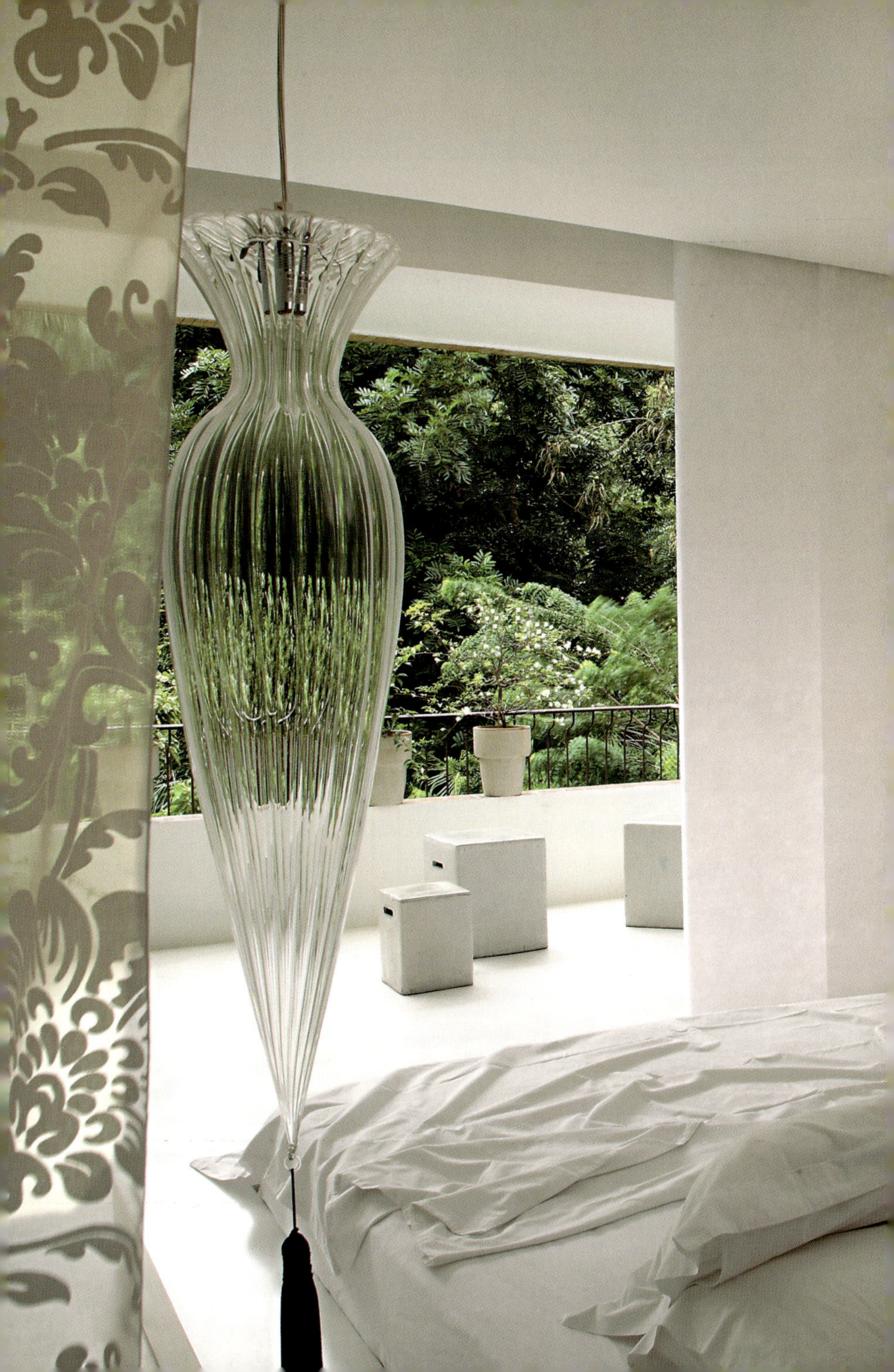

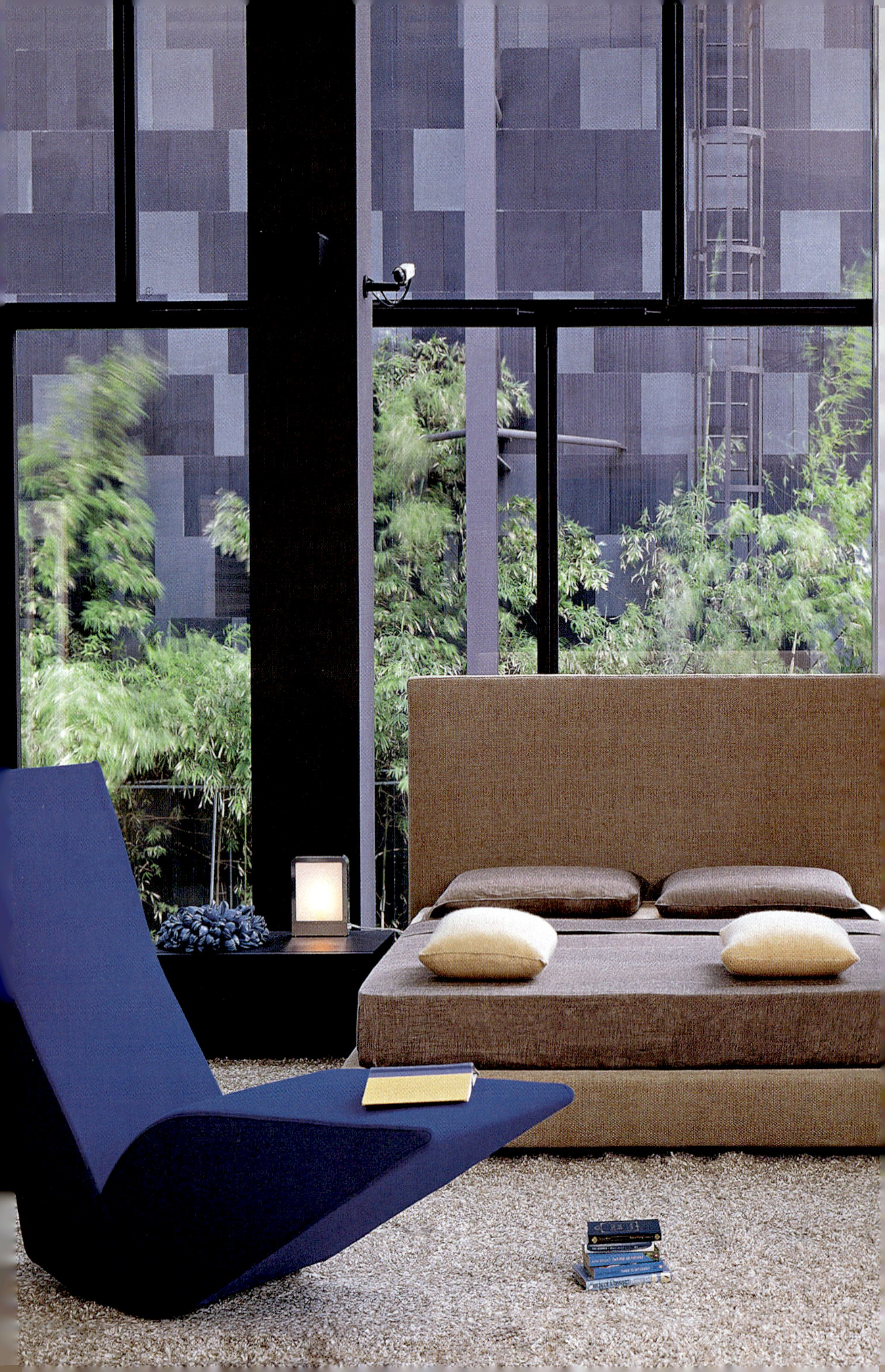

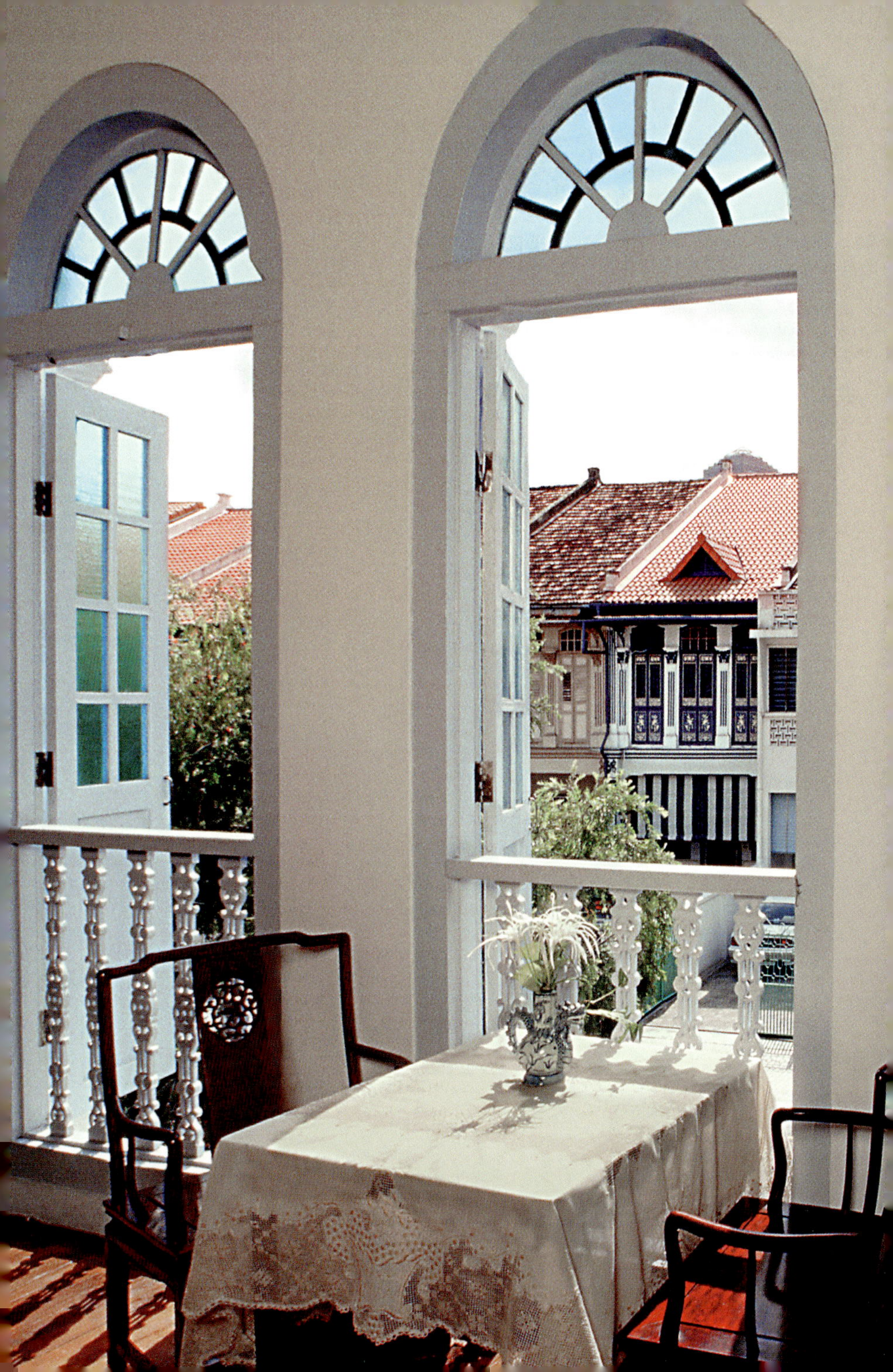

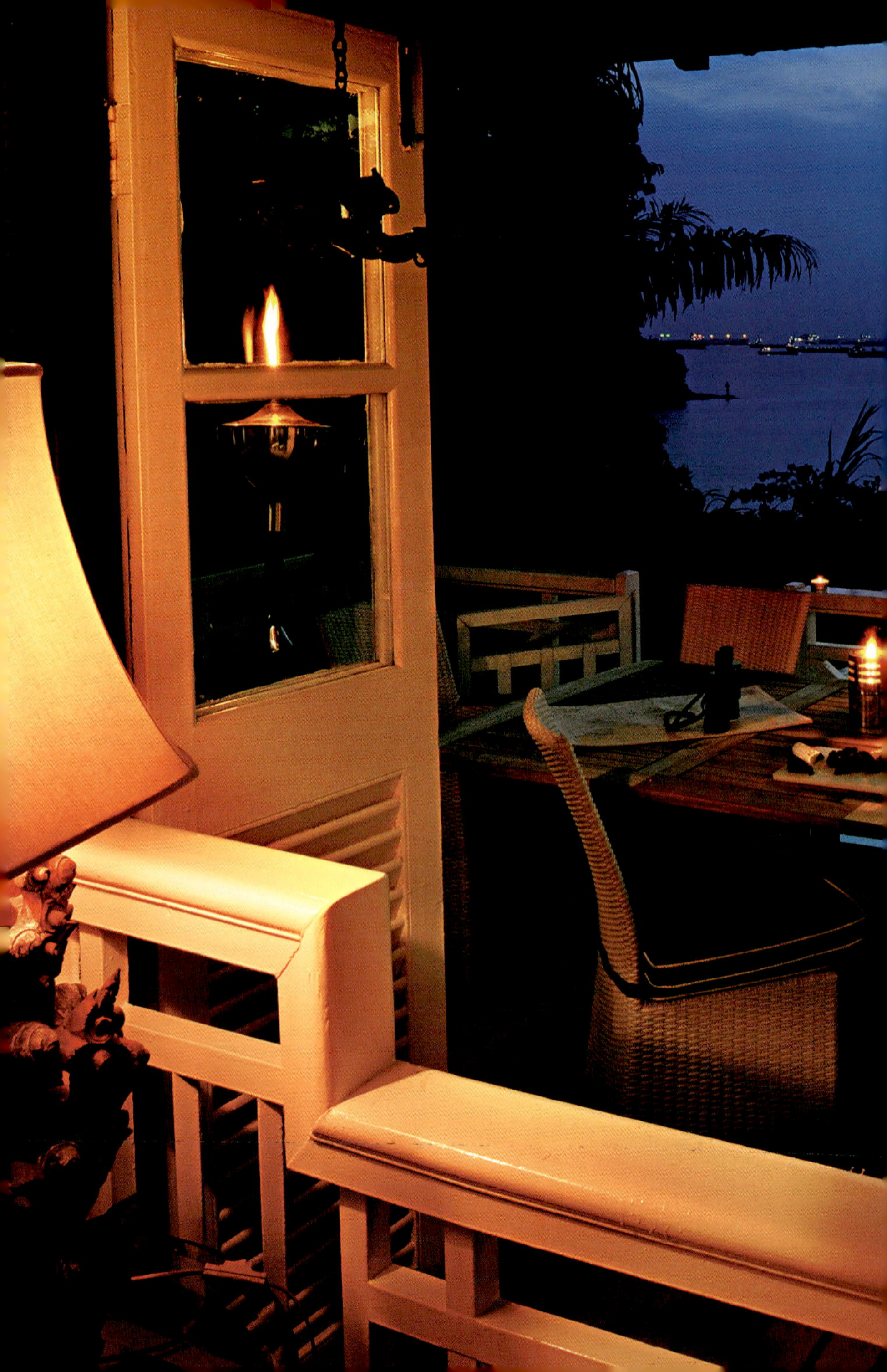

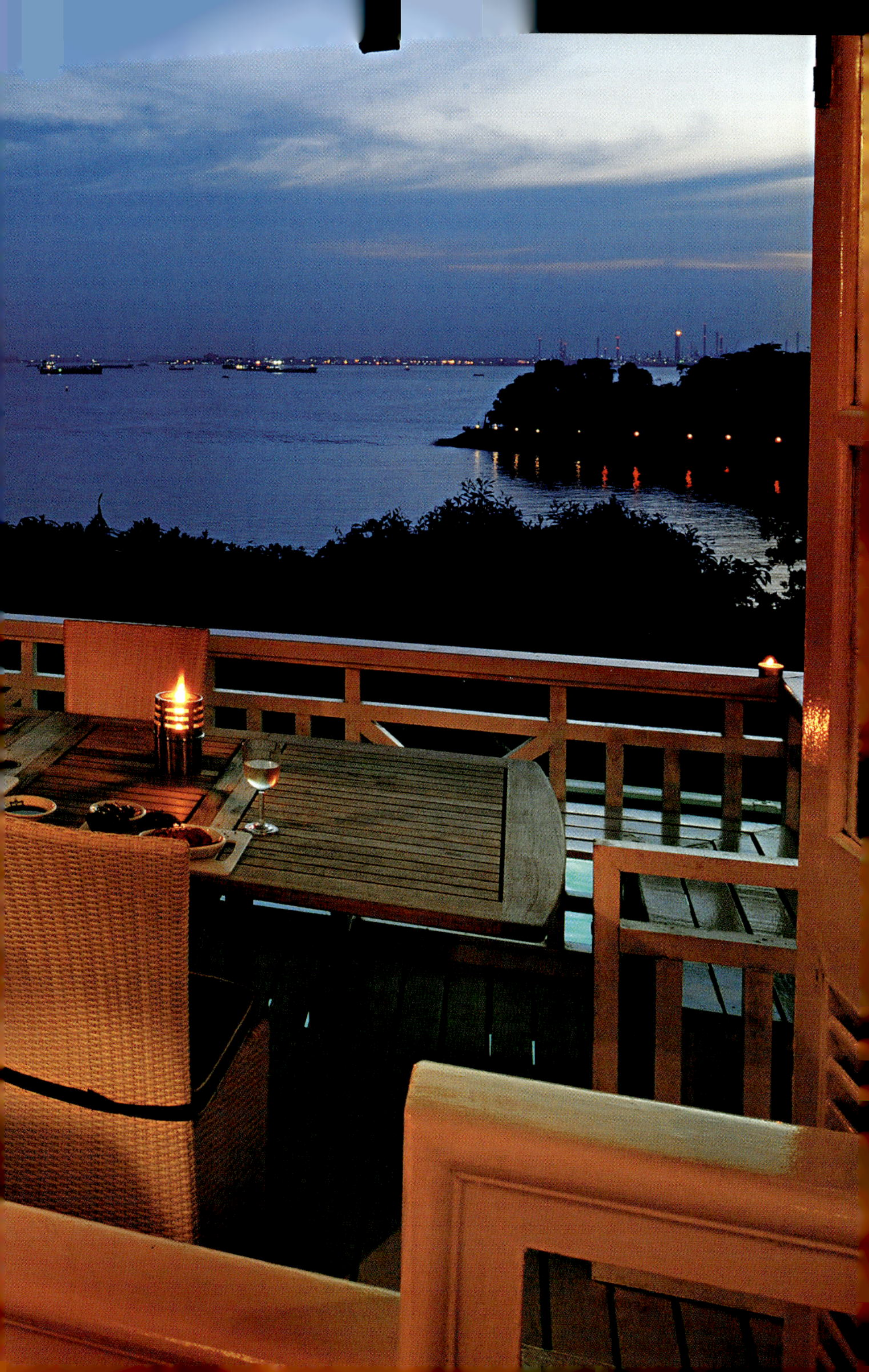

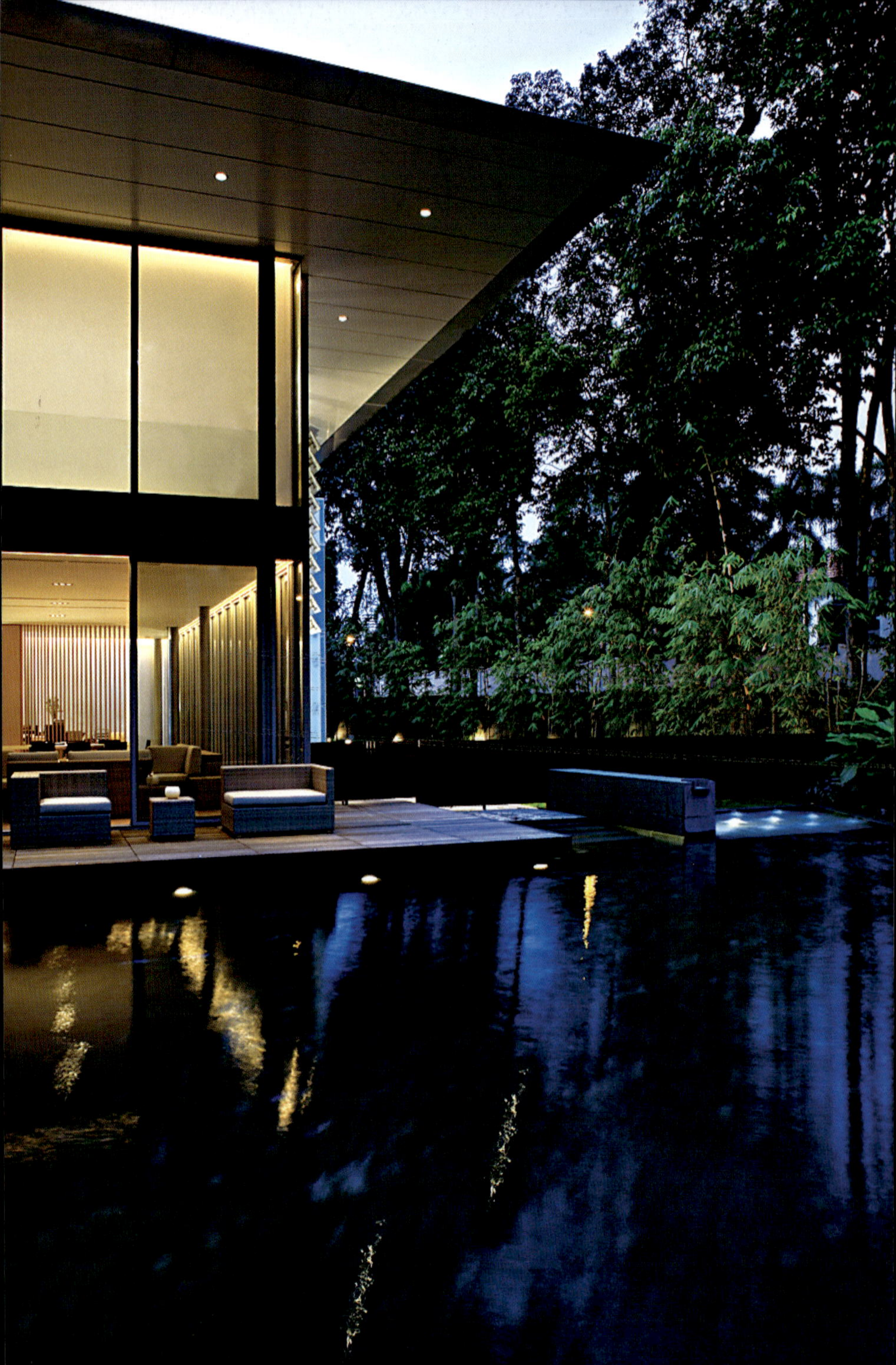

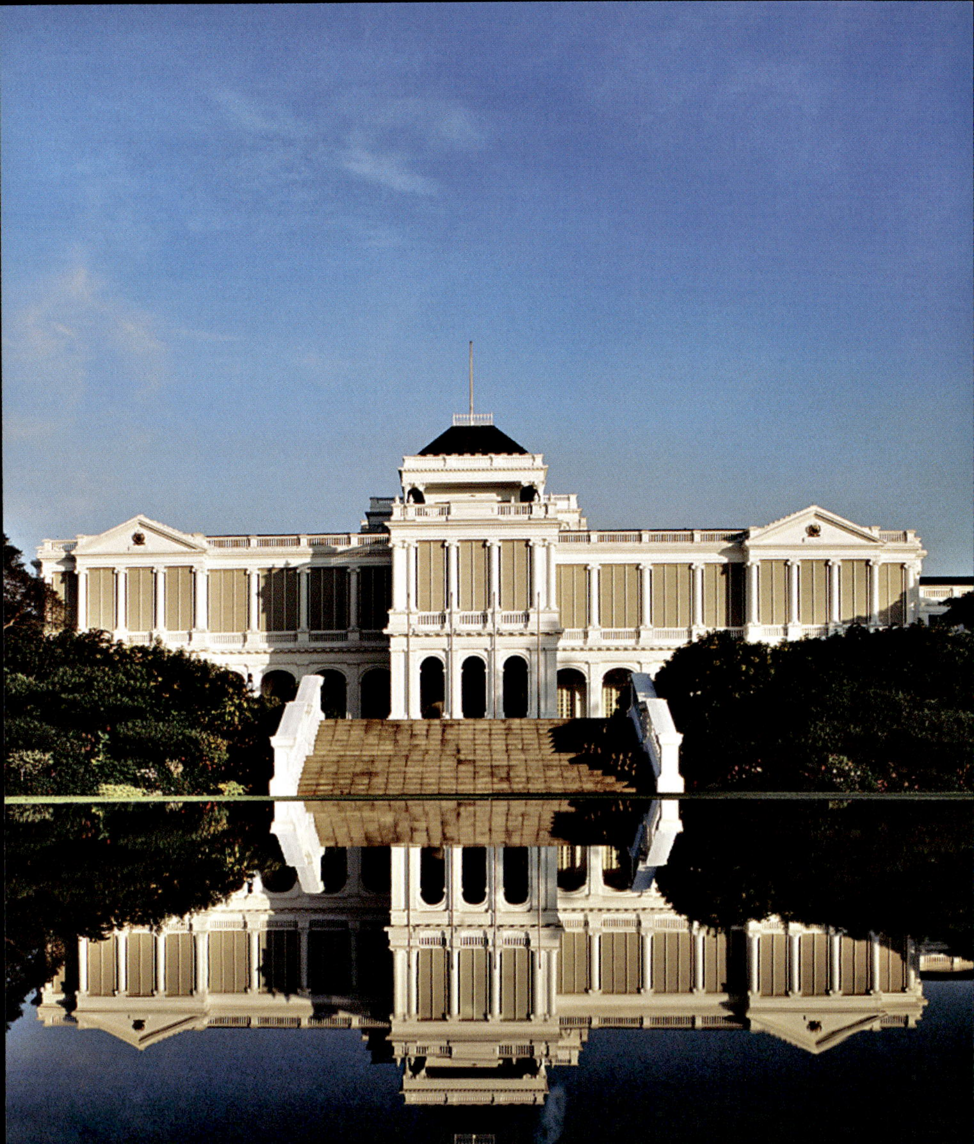

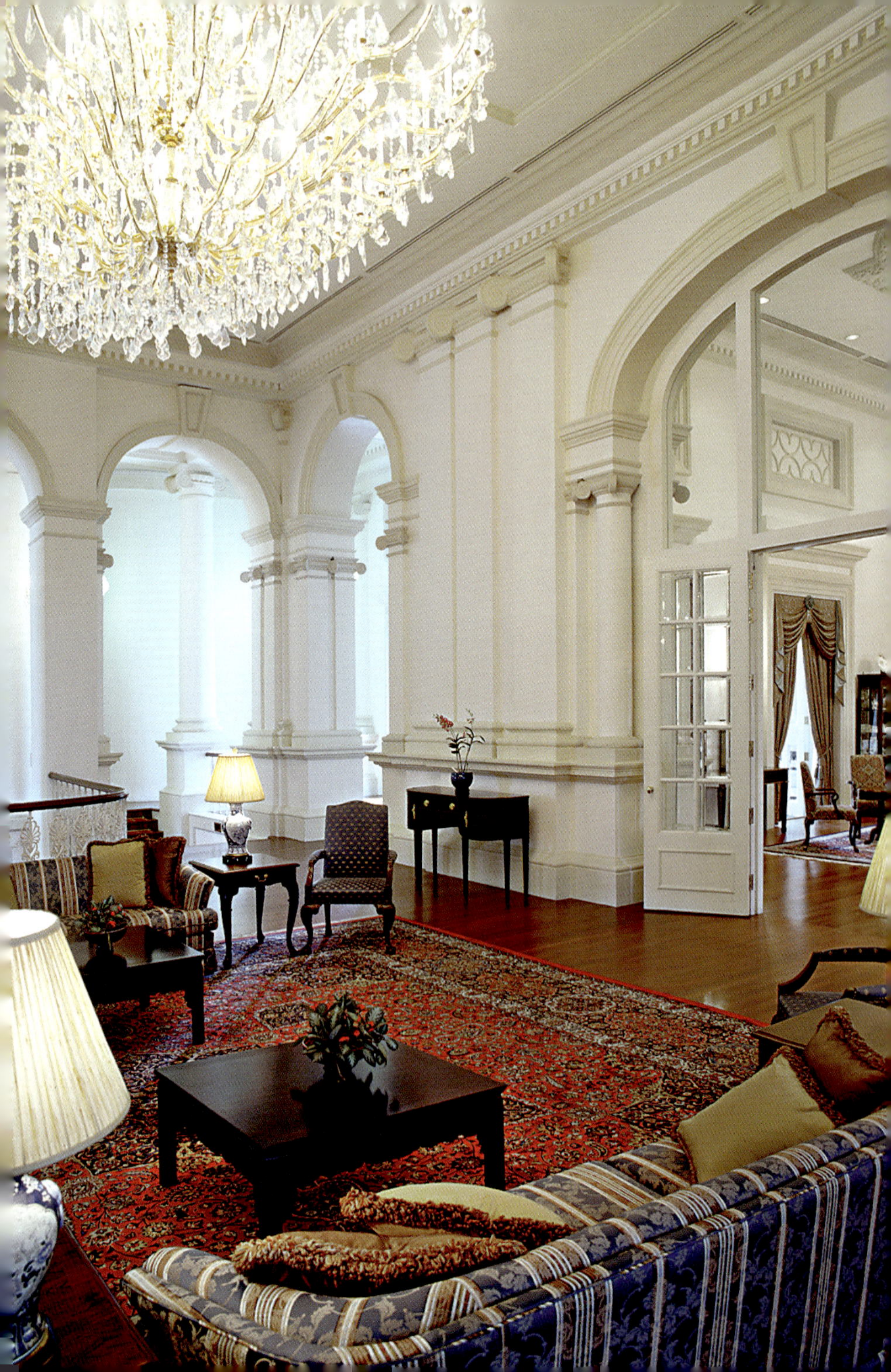

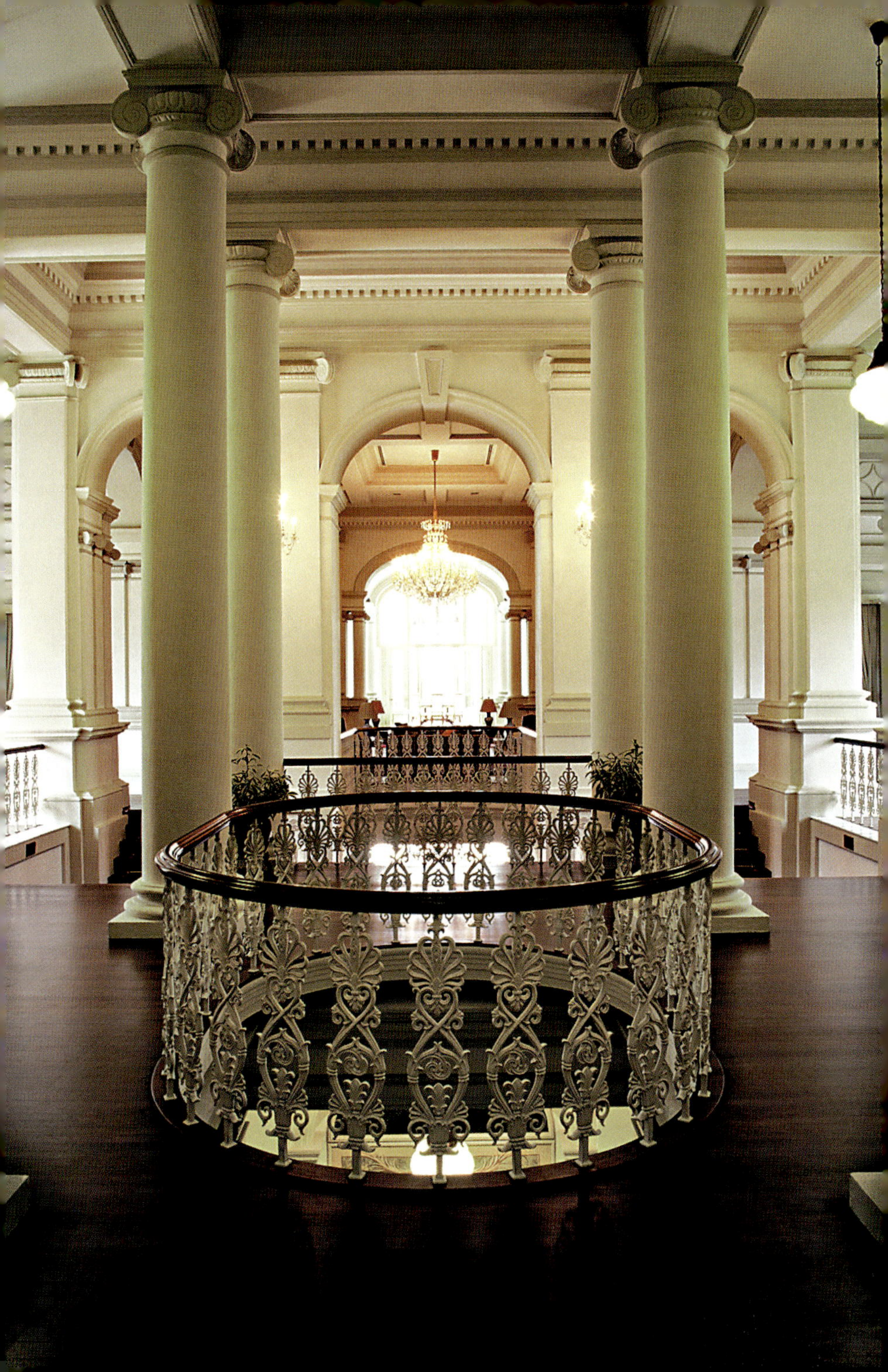

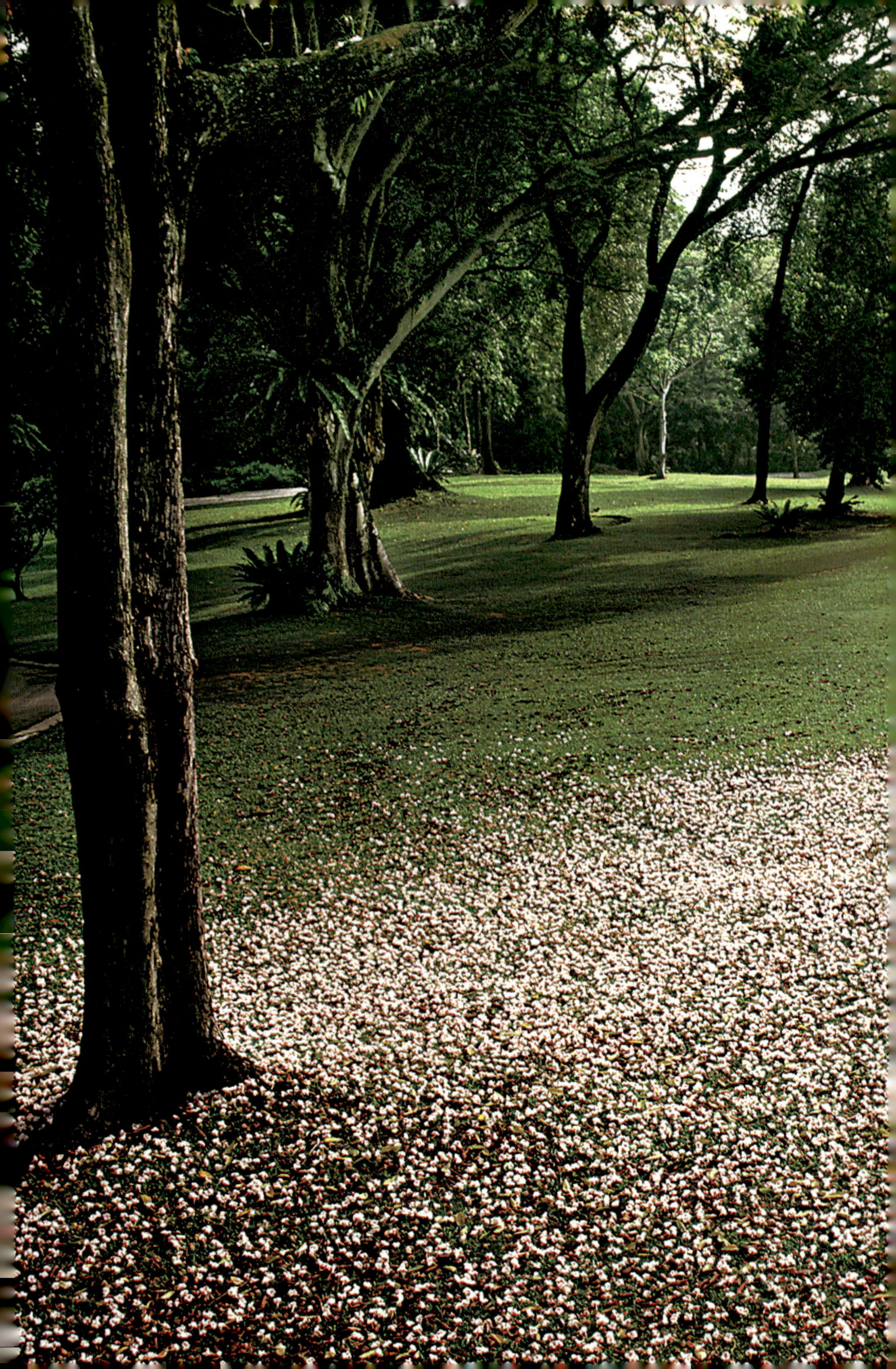

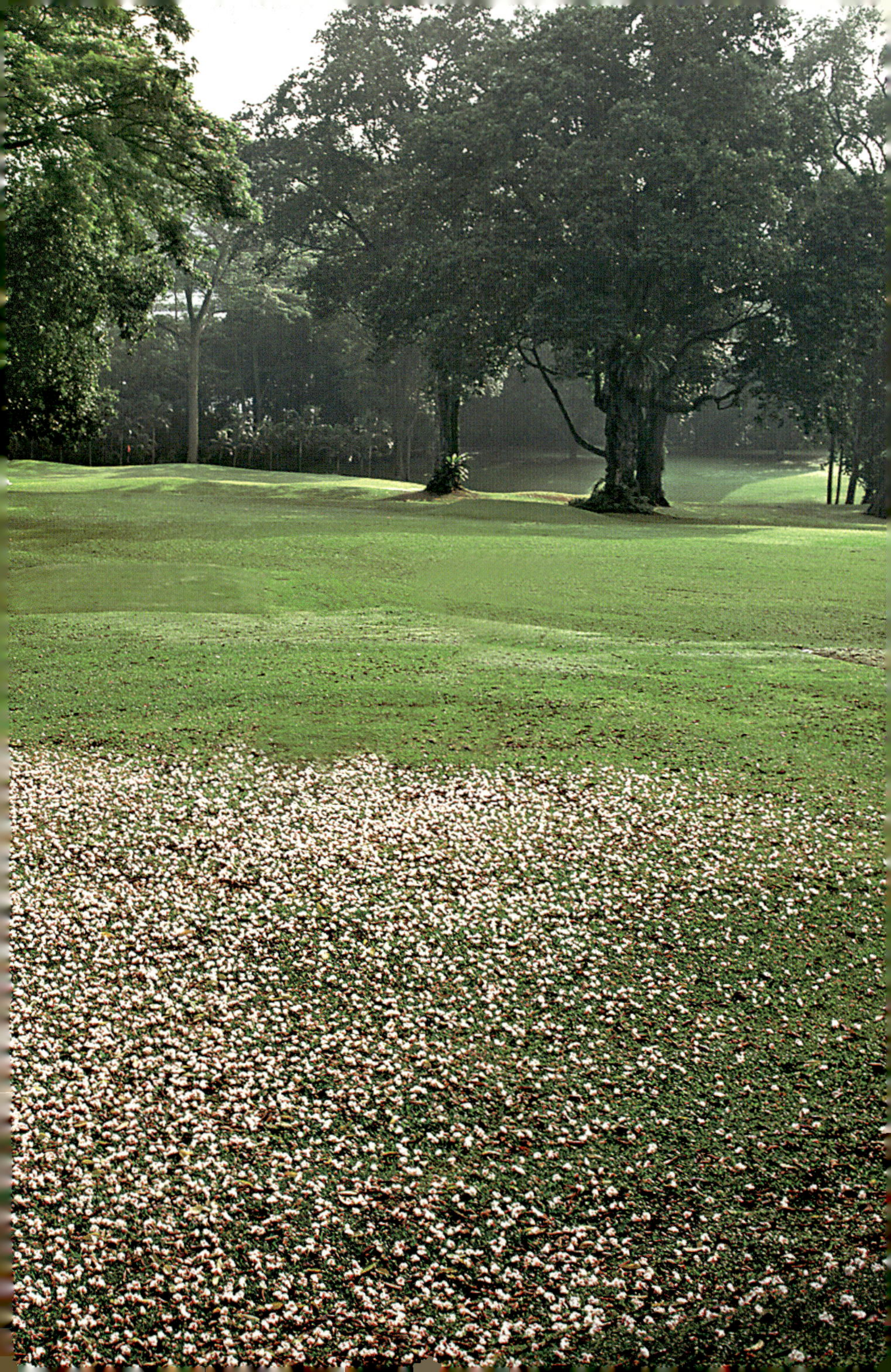

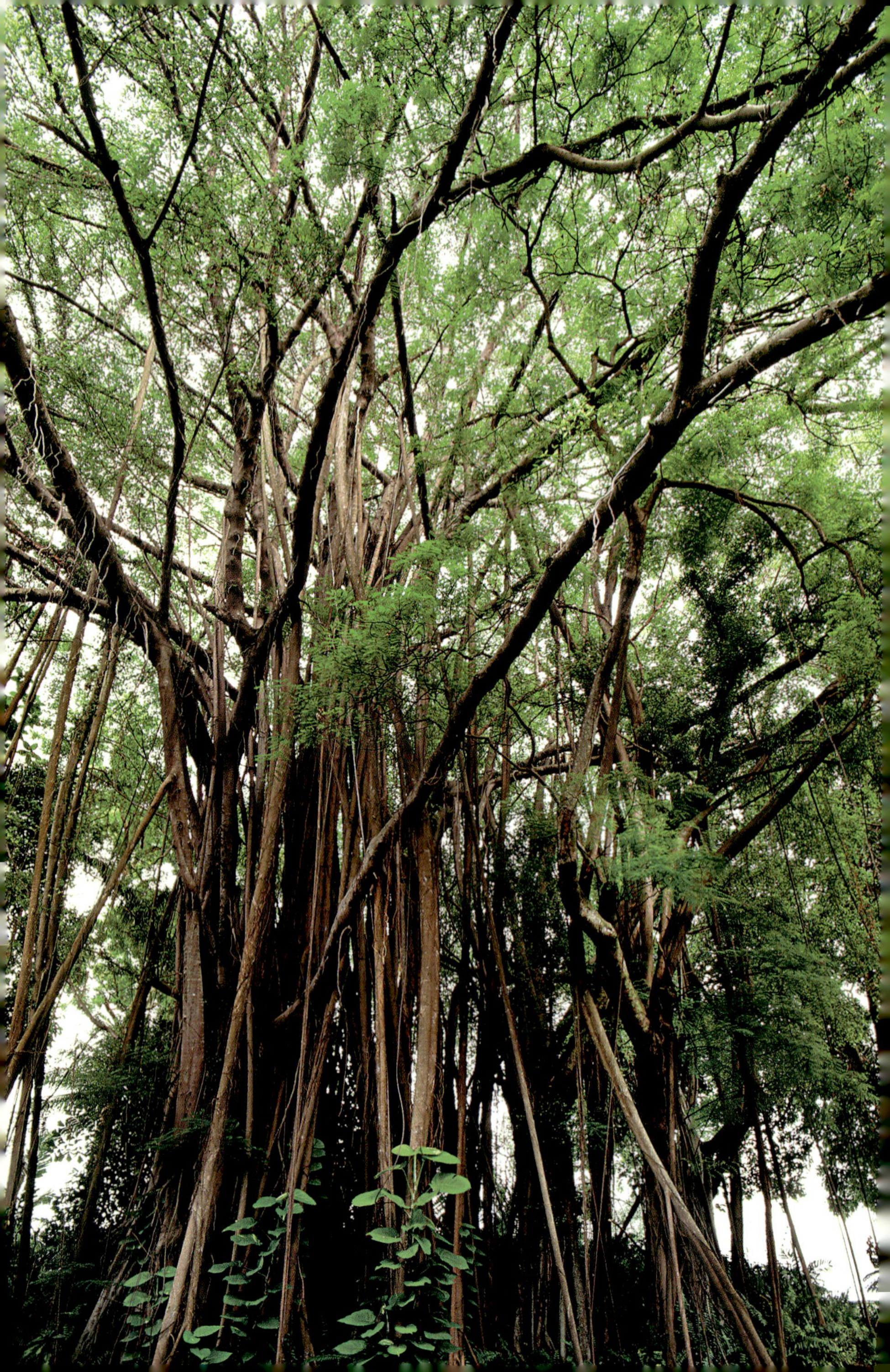

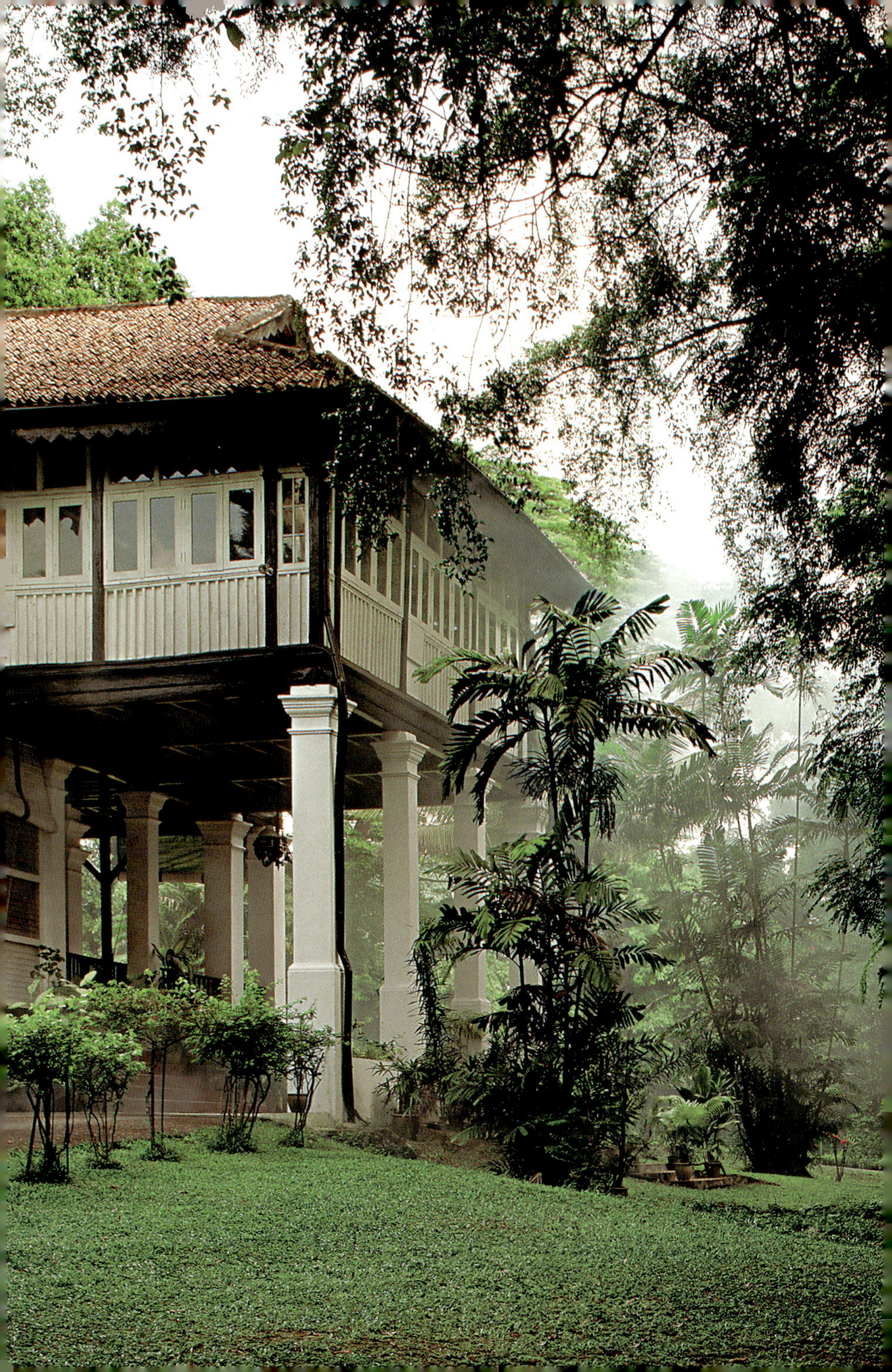

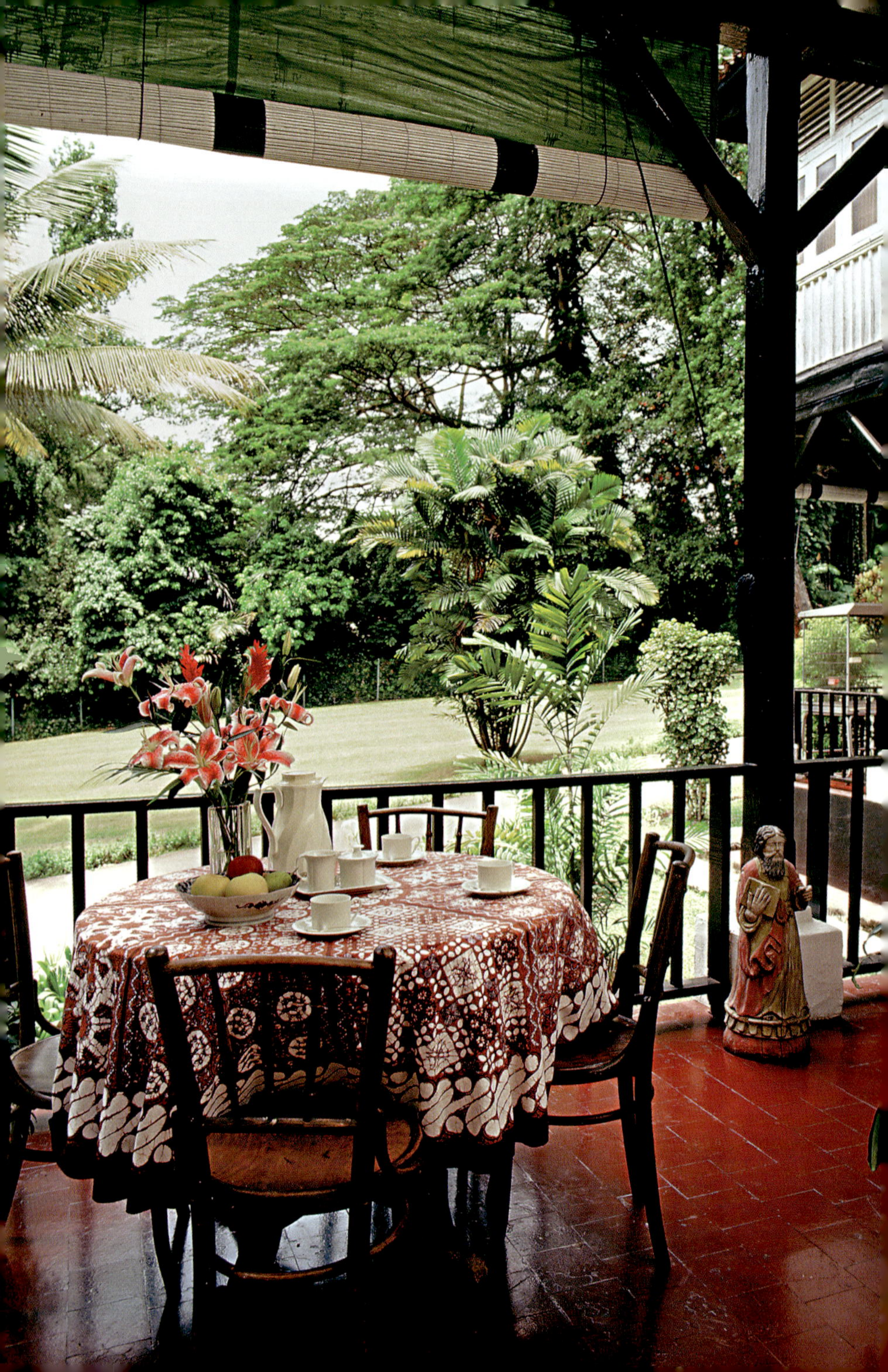

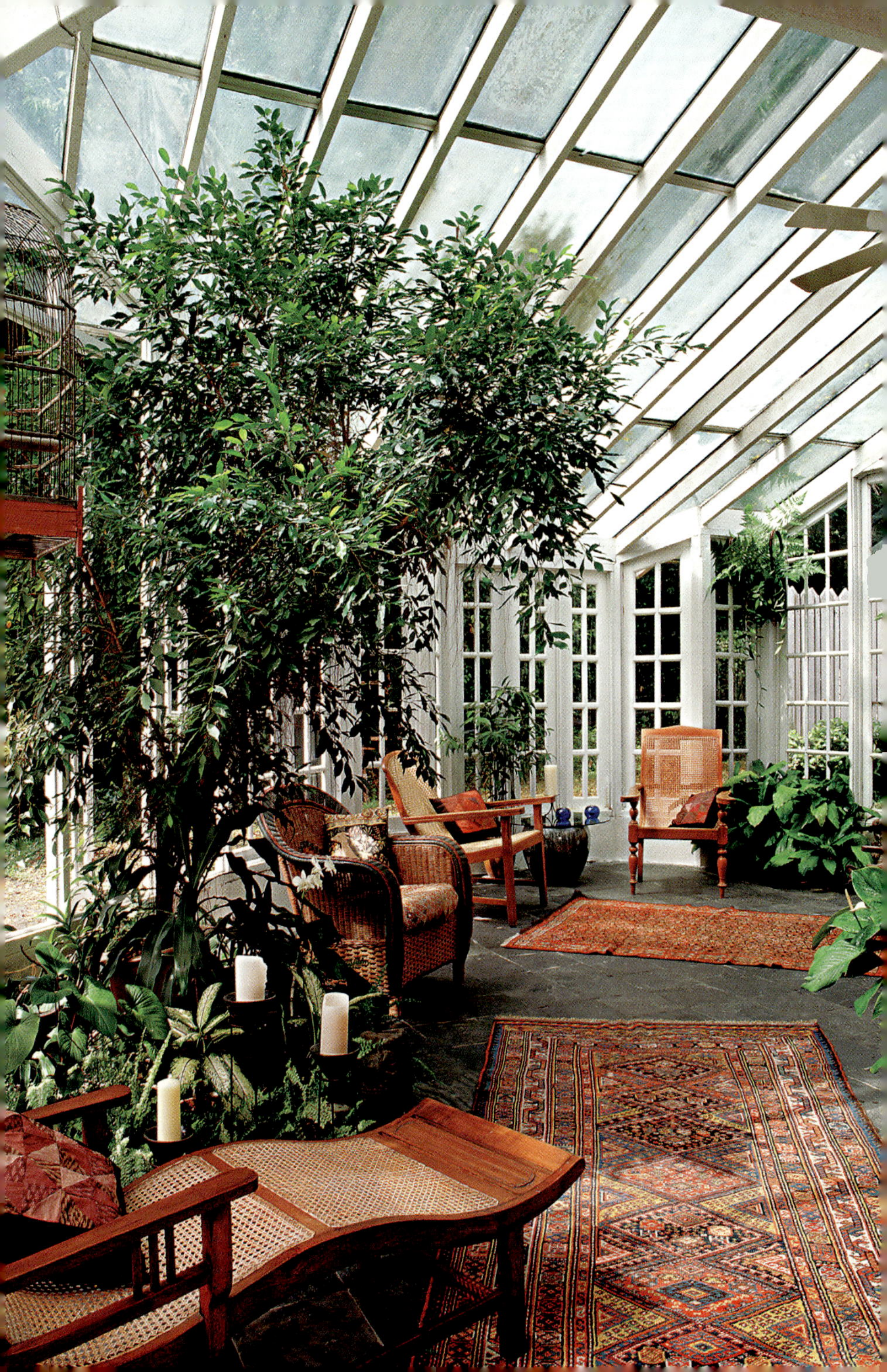

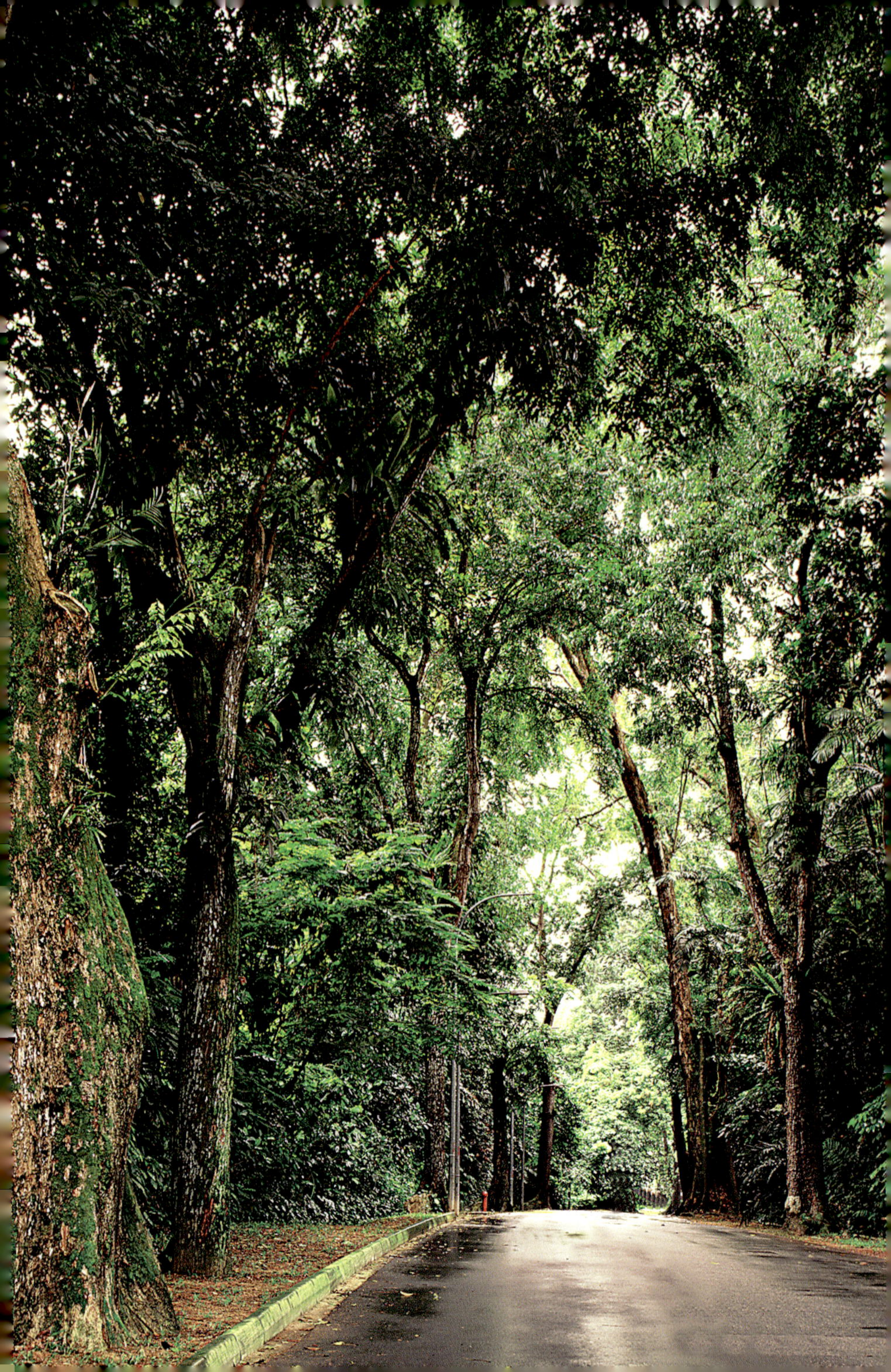

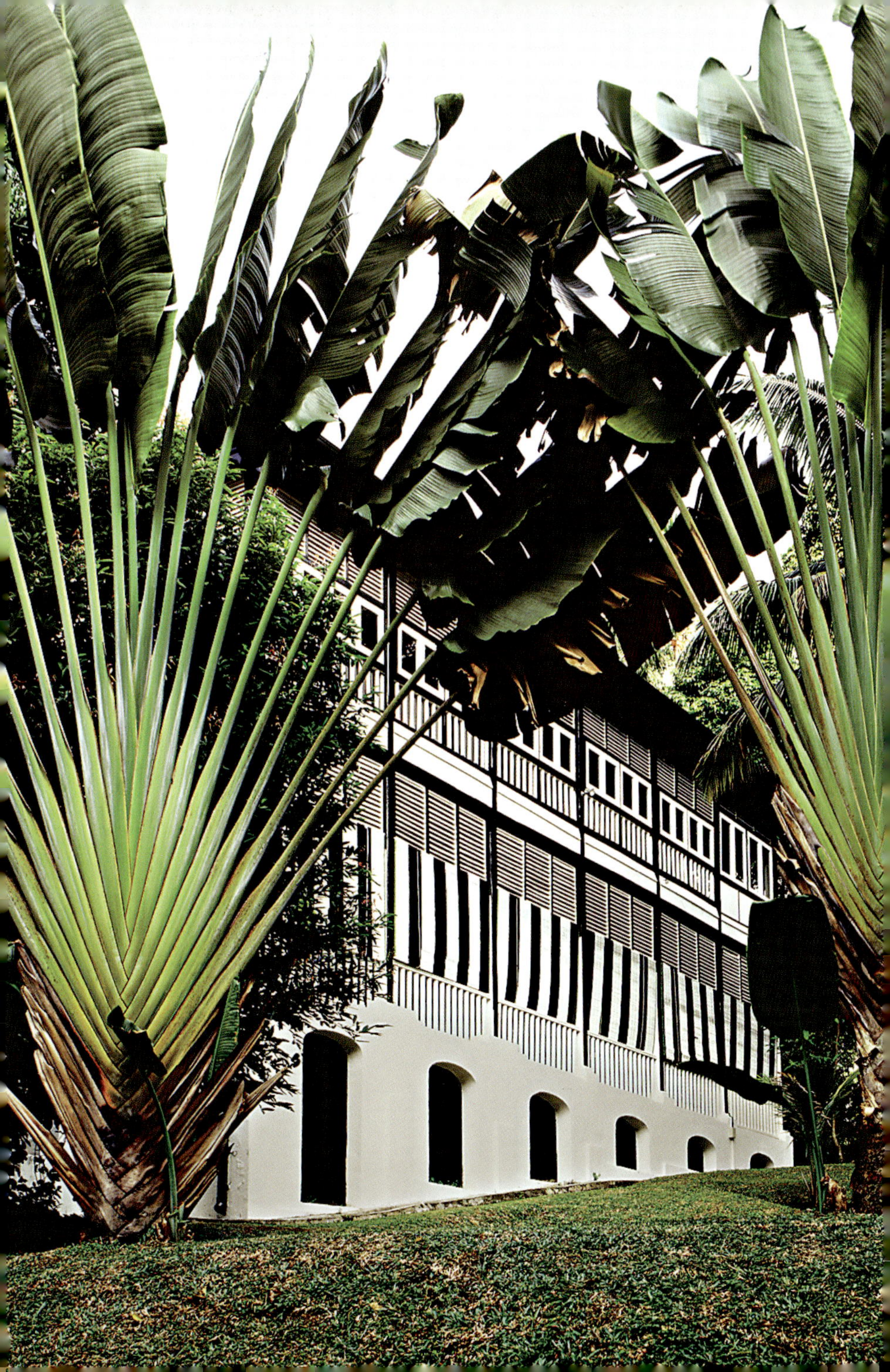

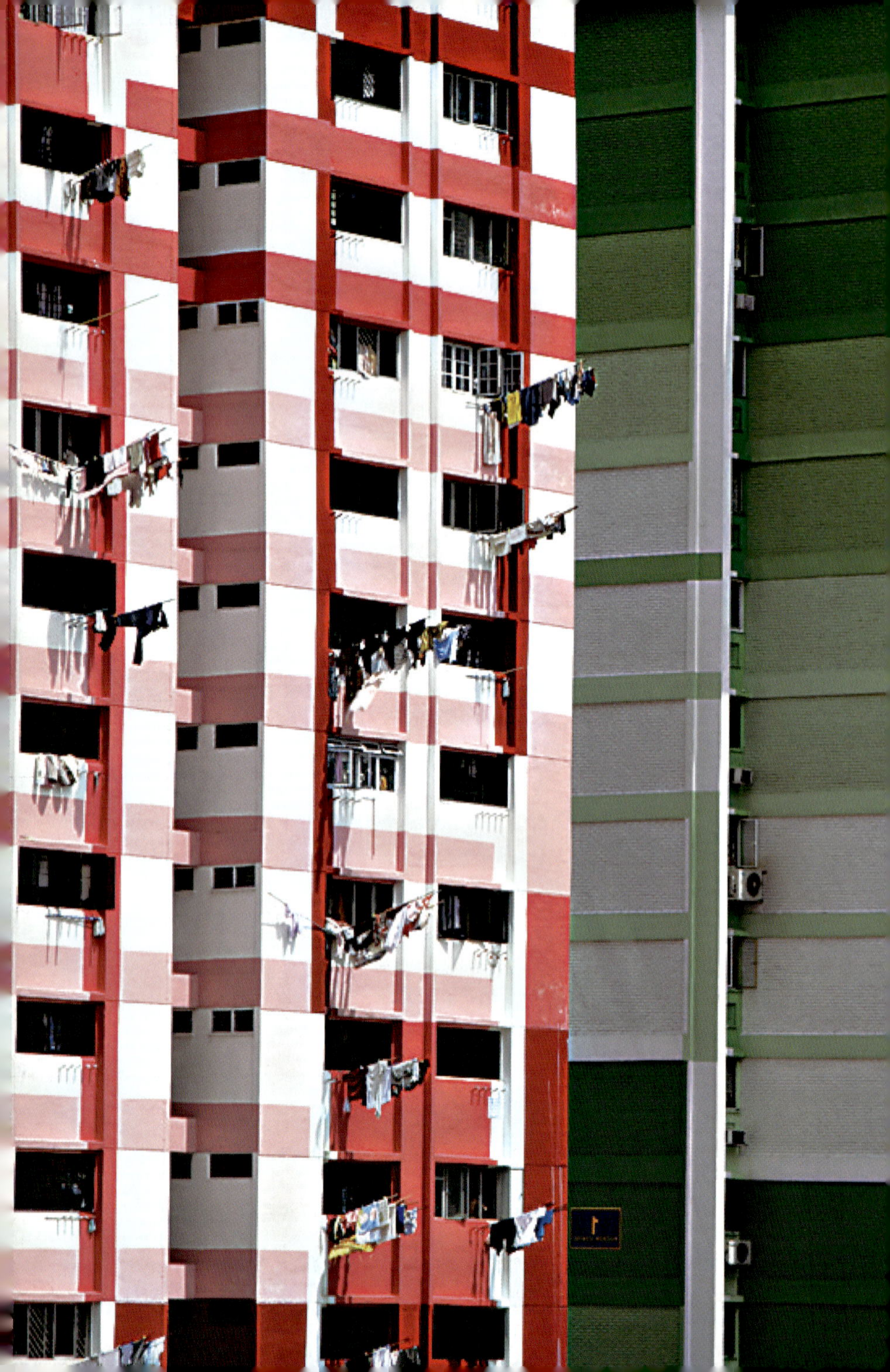

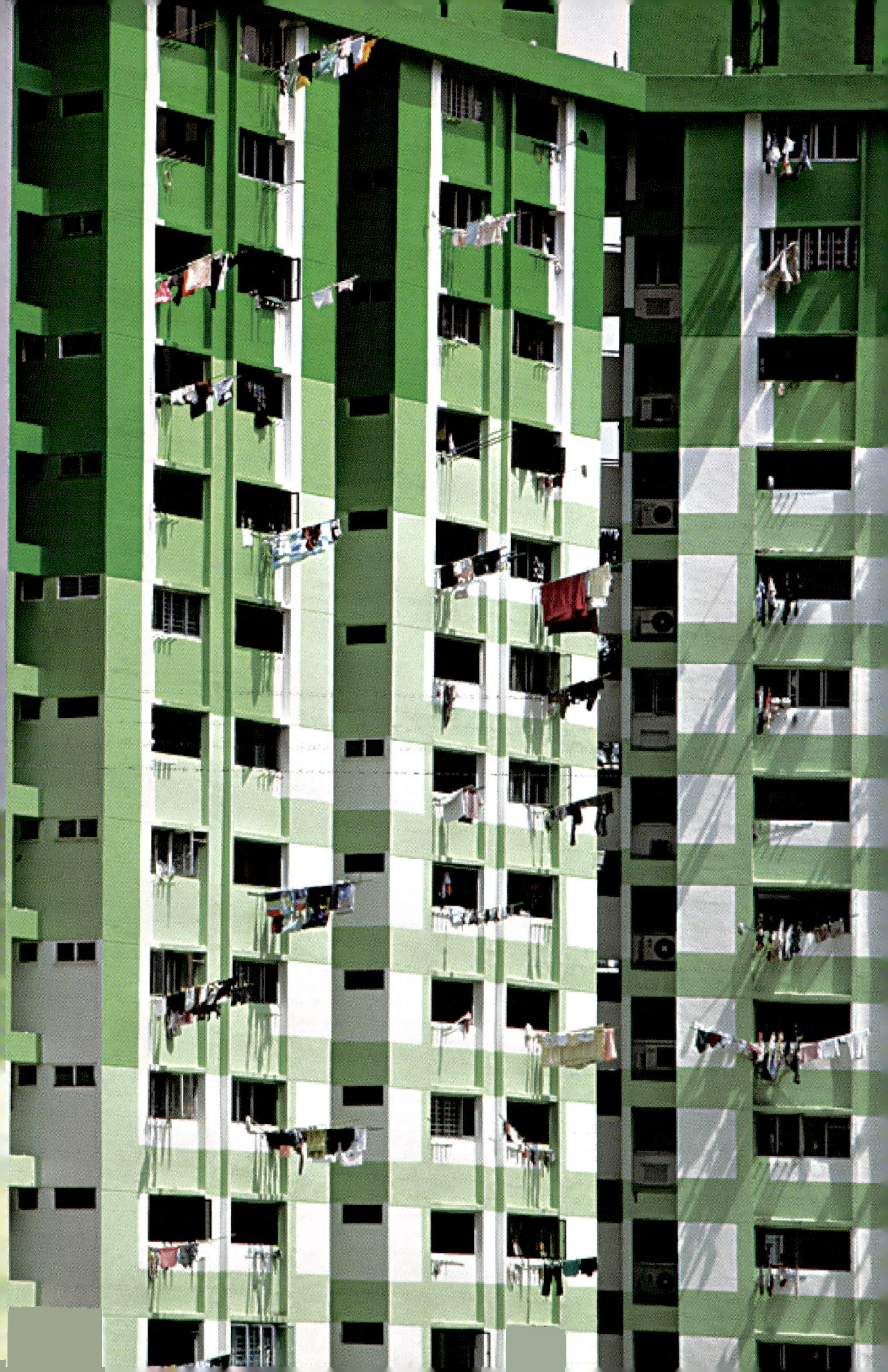

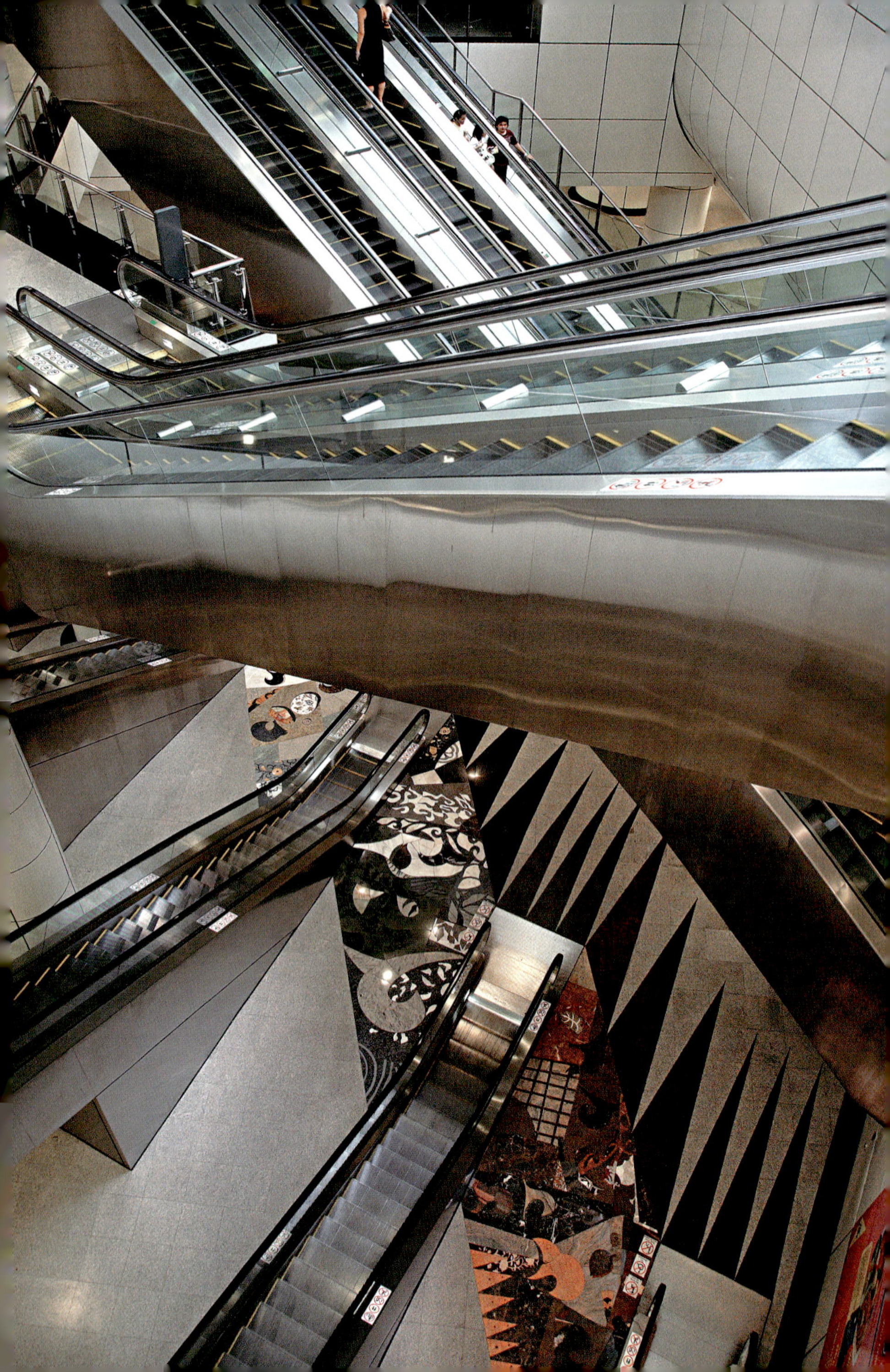

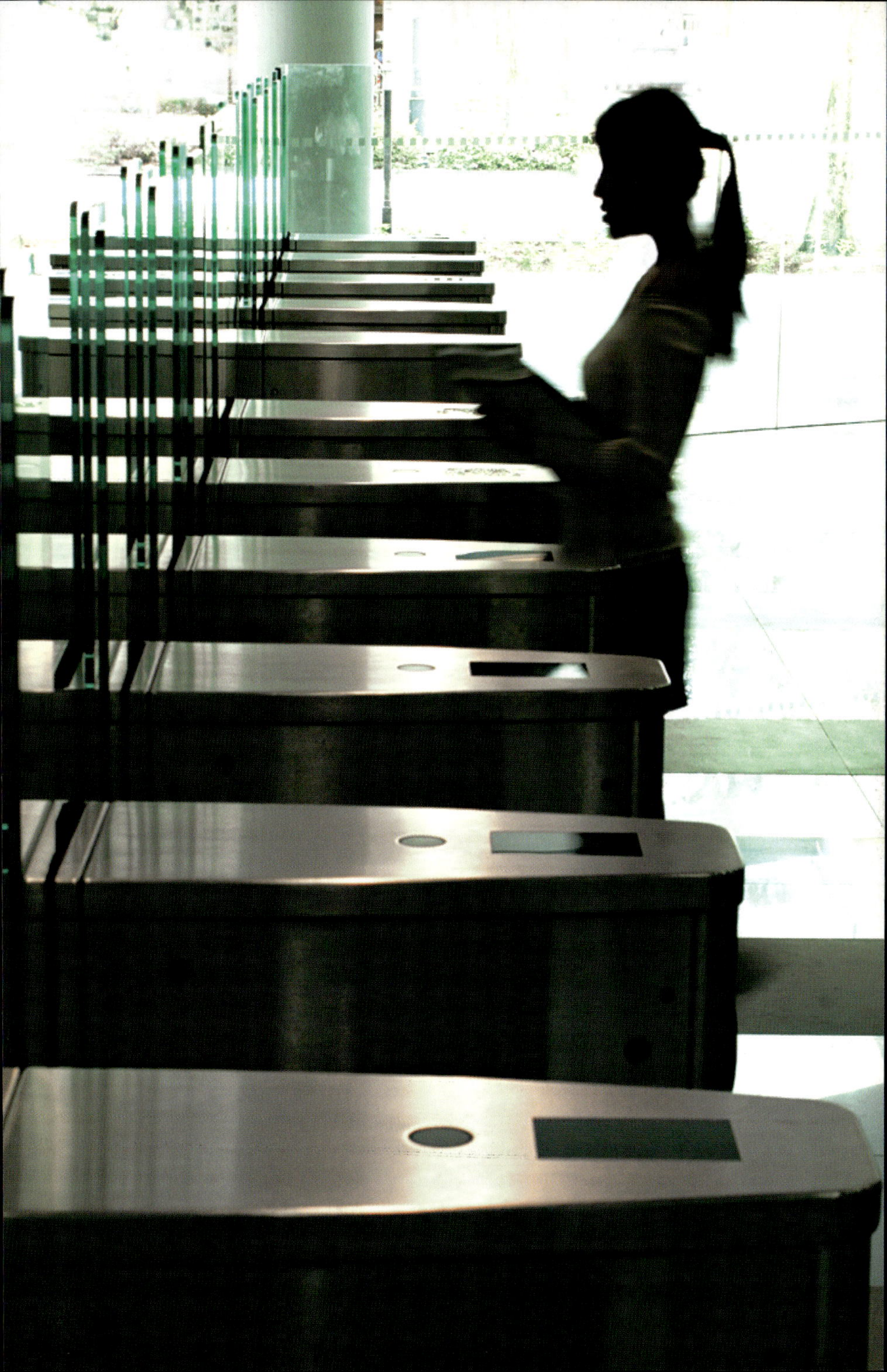

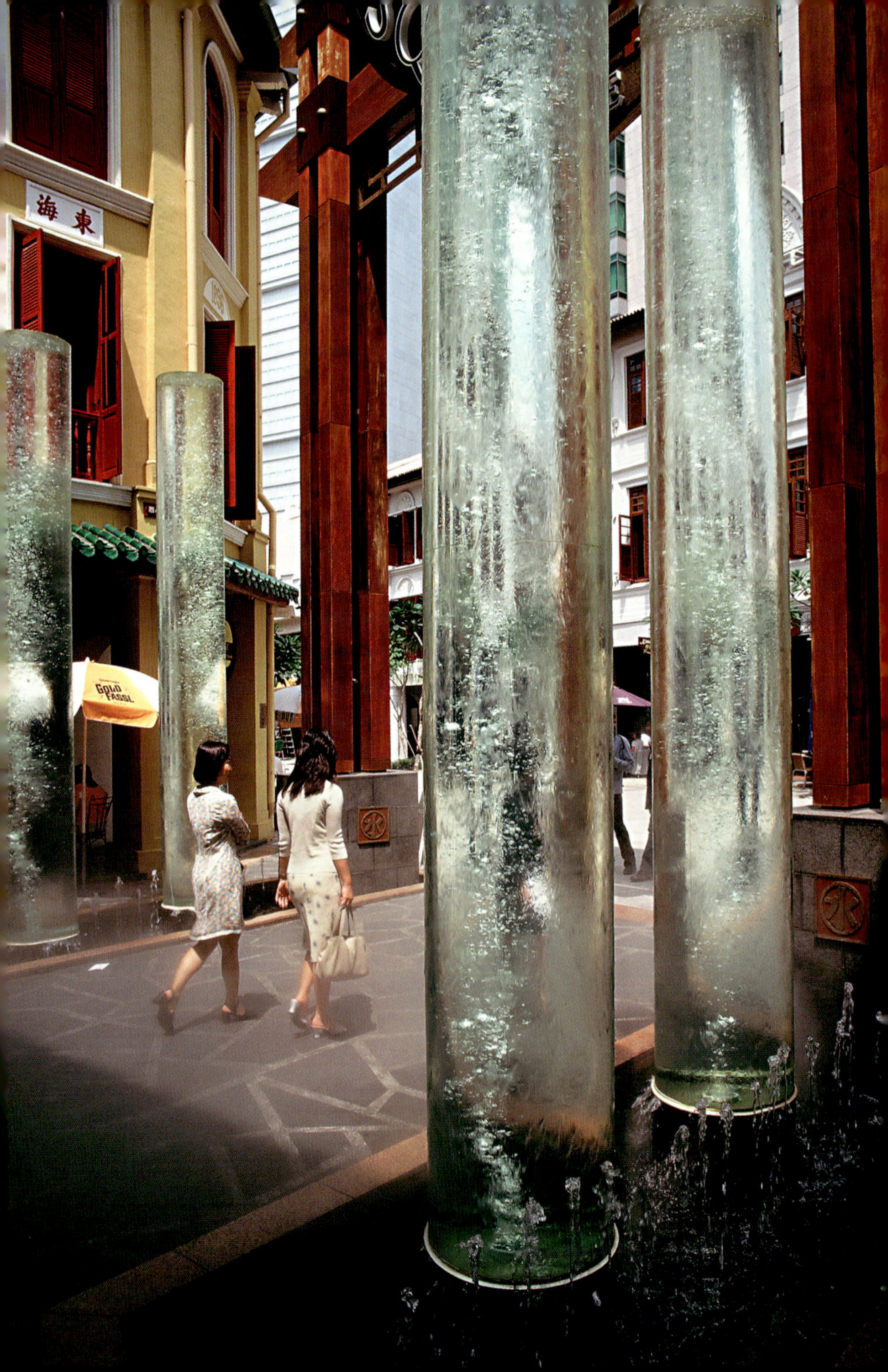
GOLD FASSL

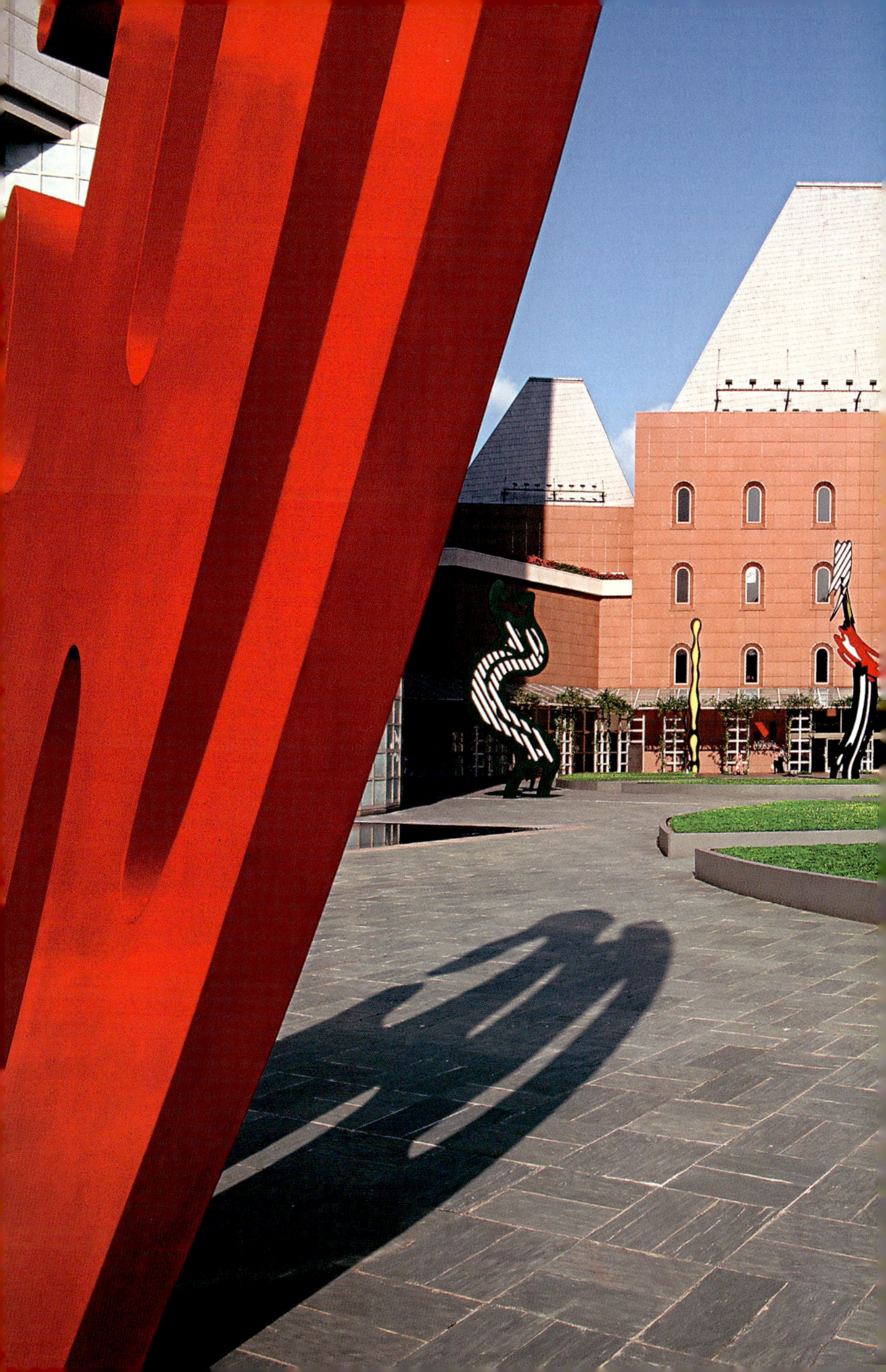

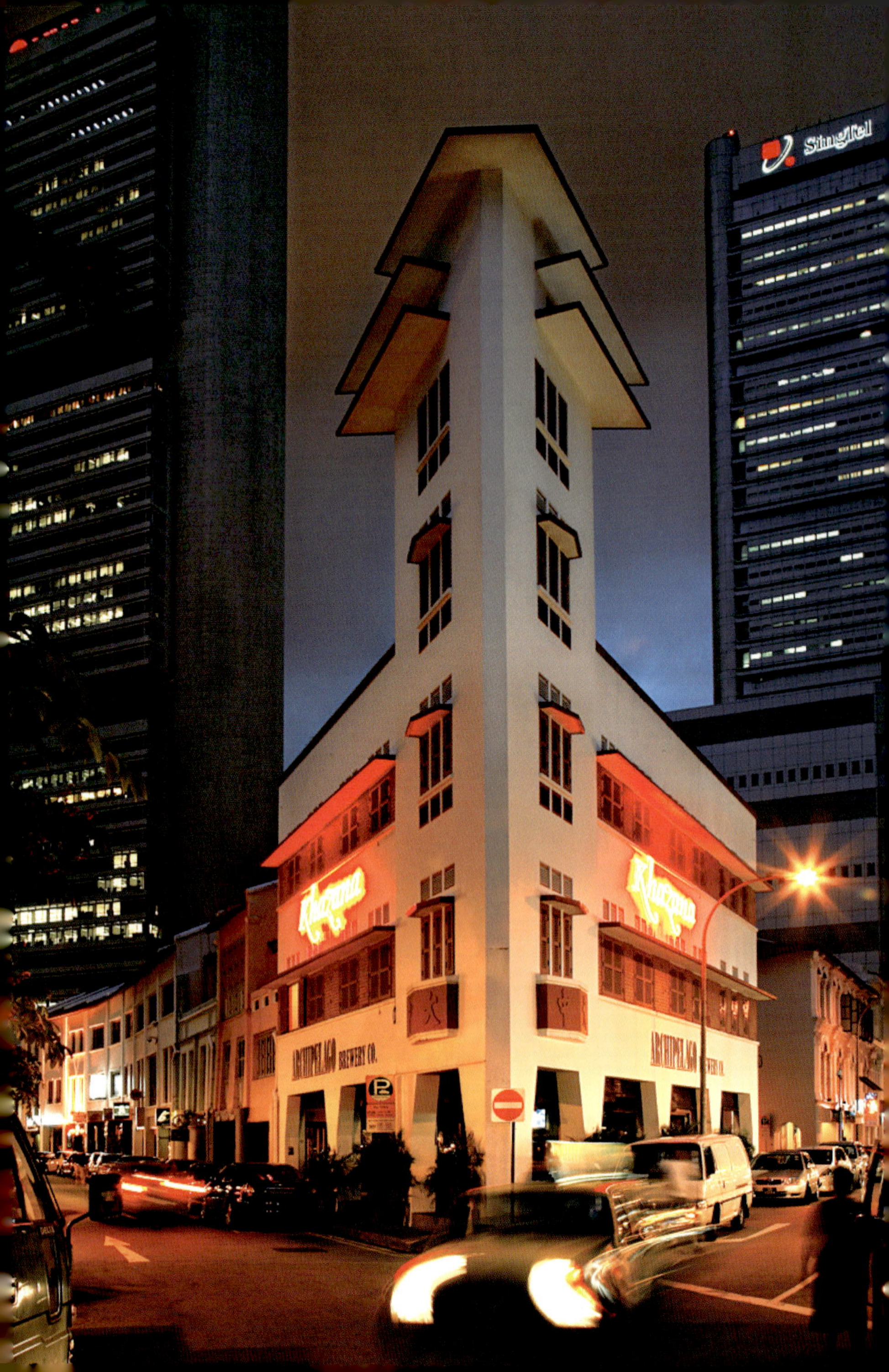
SingTel
Khazana
ARCHIPELAGO BREWERY CO.

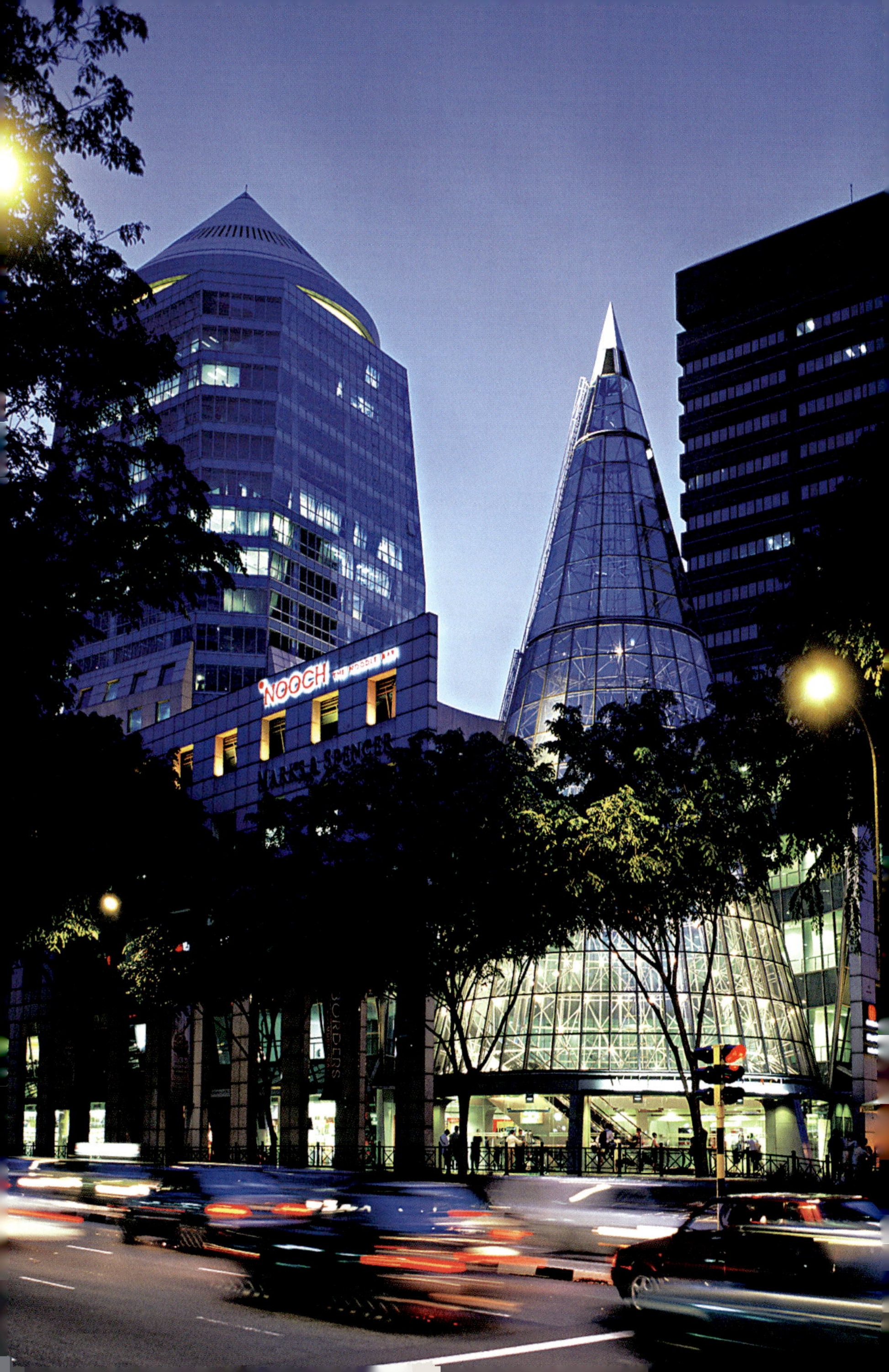
NOOCH
MARKS & SPENCER
BORDERS

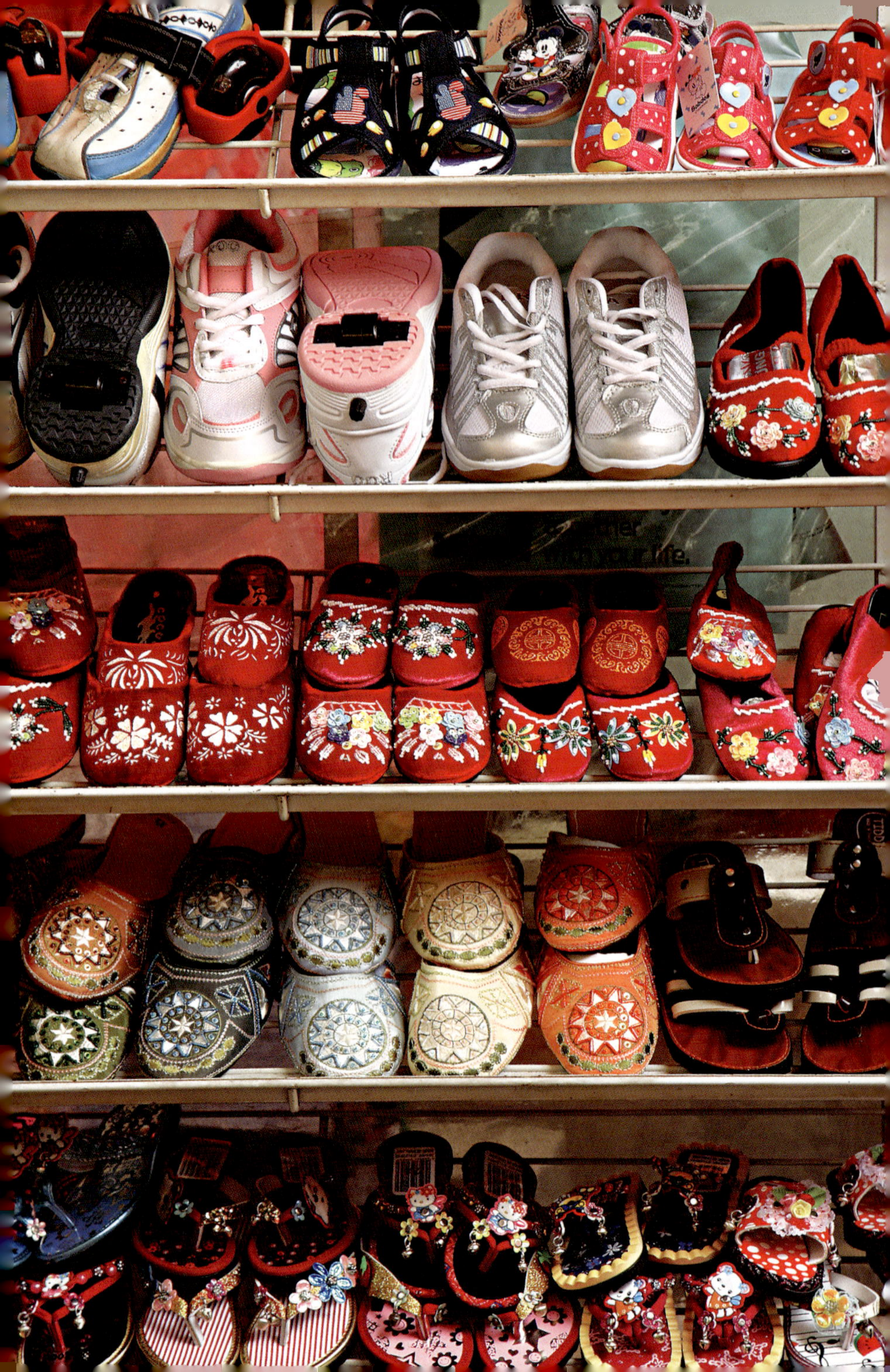

东方艺术汇集五楼

The Best Of Oriental
Art & Antiques
At Level 5

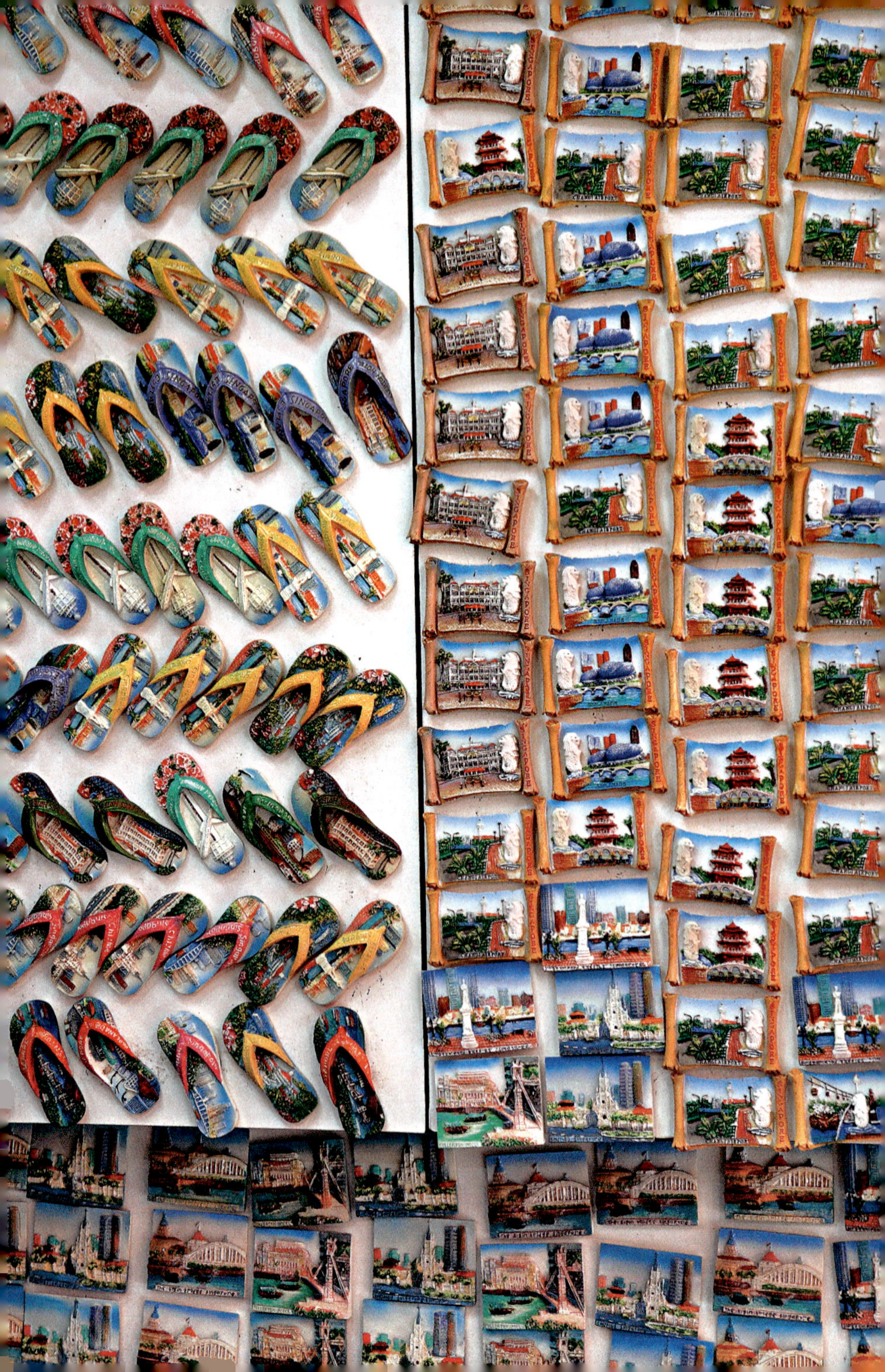

3 For $10

3 For $10

2 For $10

2 For $10

3 For $10

3 For $10

1 For $10

1 for $6
Any 2 for $10

GIFTMASTER

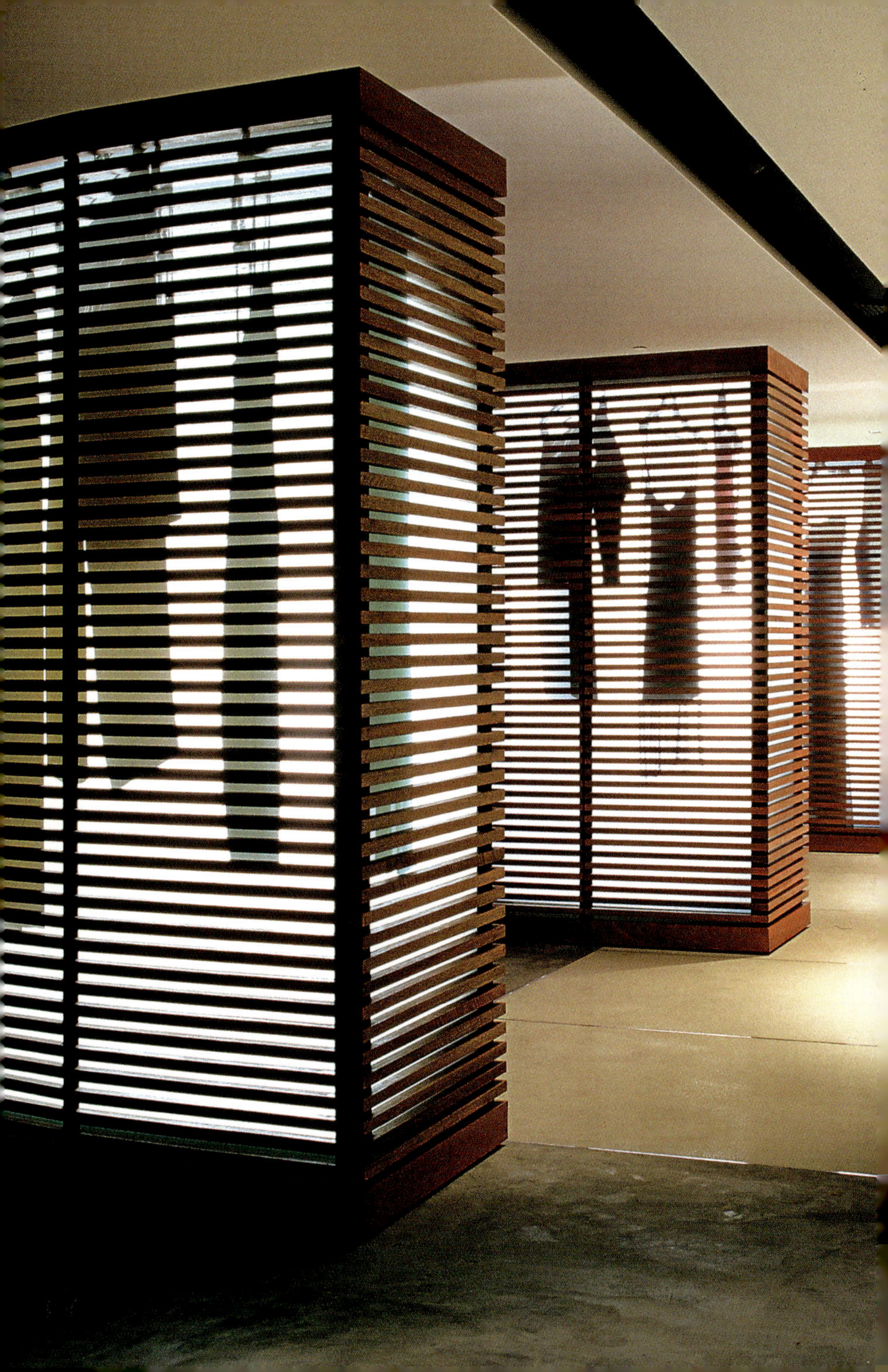

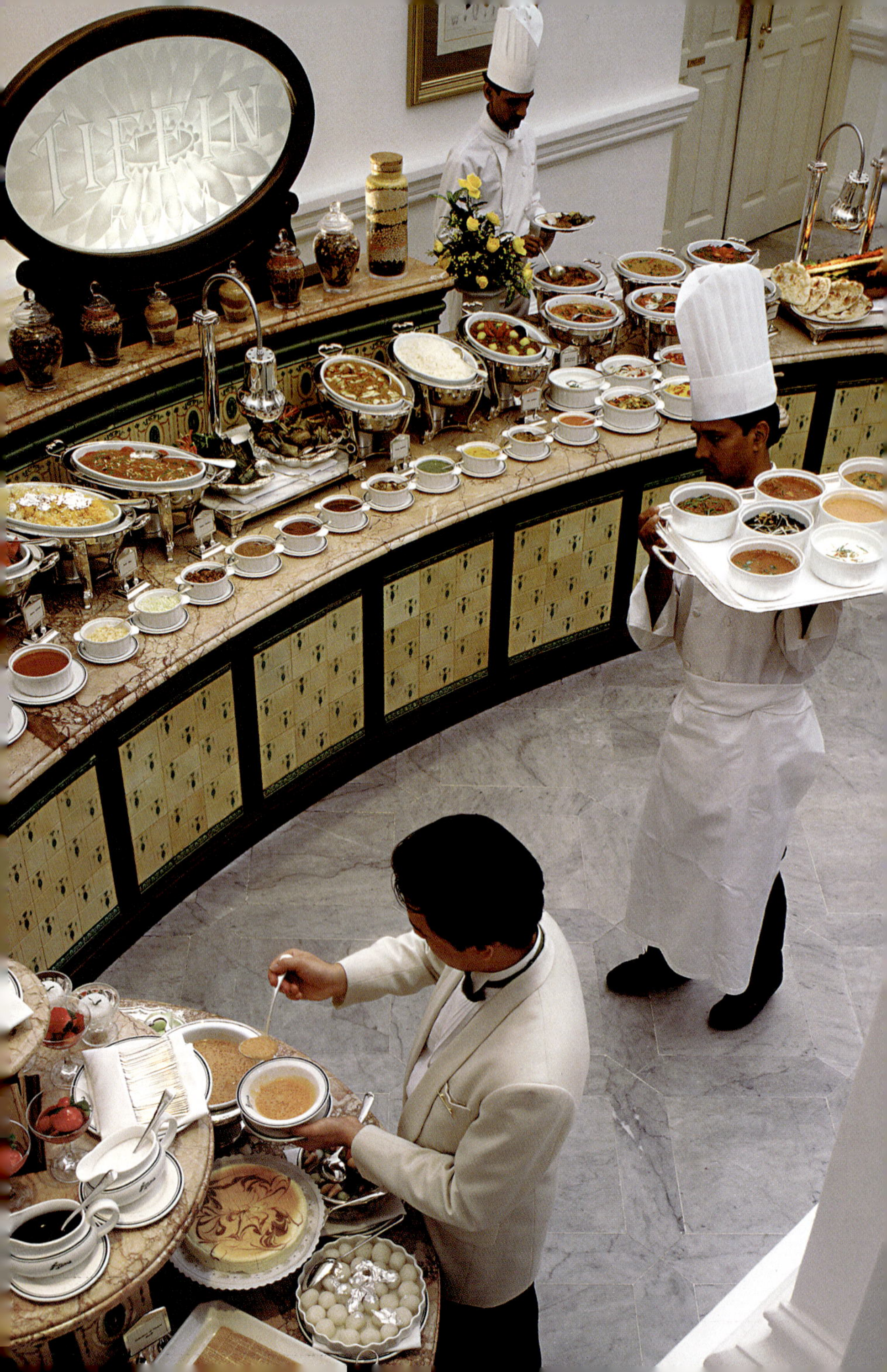
TIFFIN
ROOM

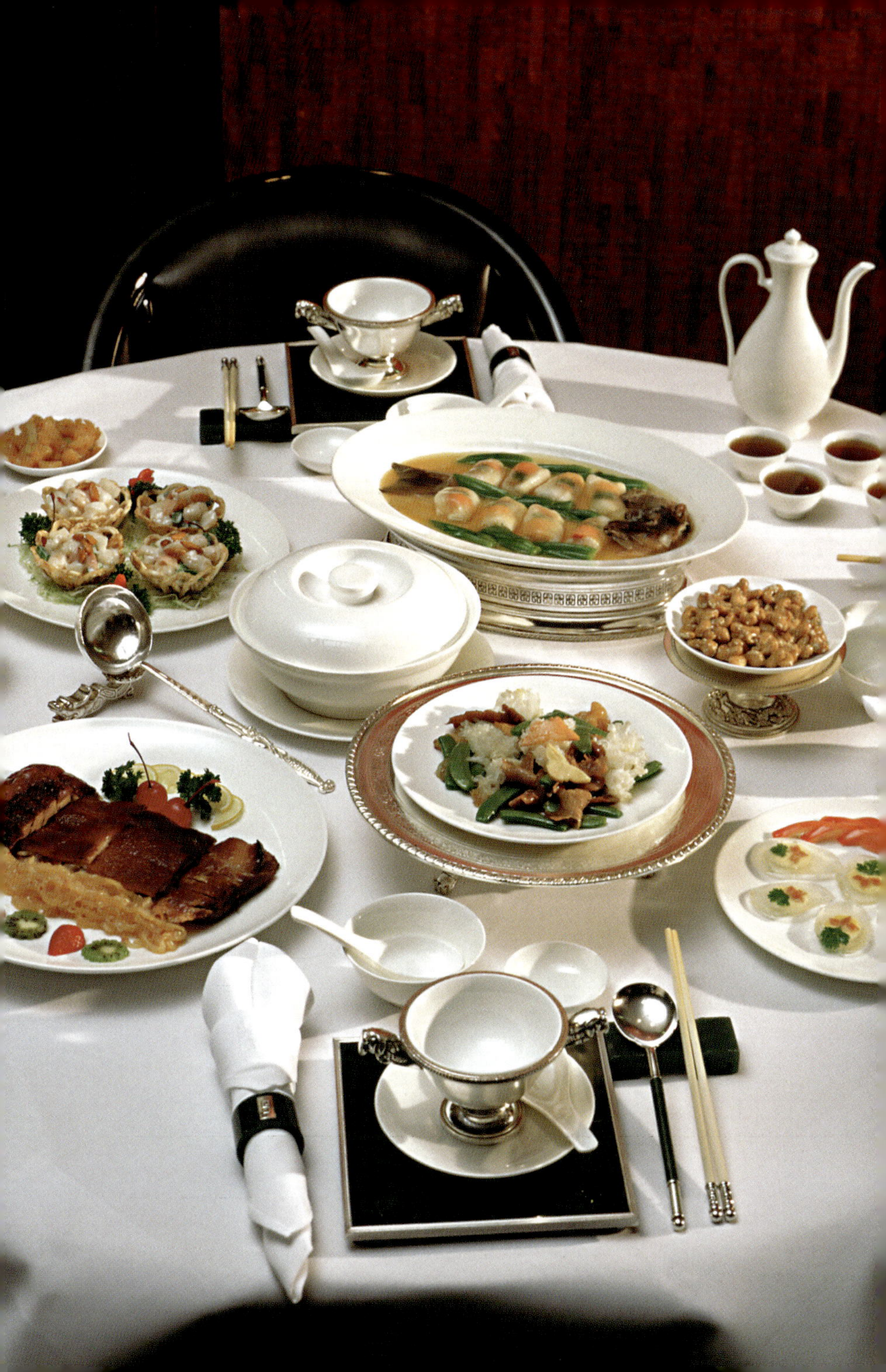

UNADDRESSED LETTERS
SIR FRANK ATHELSTANE SWETTENHAM.
MALAY

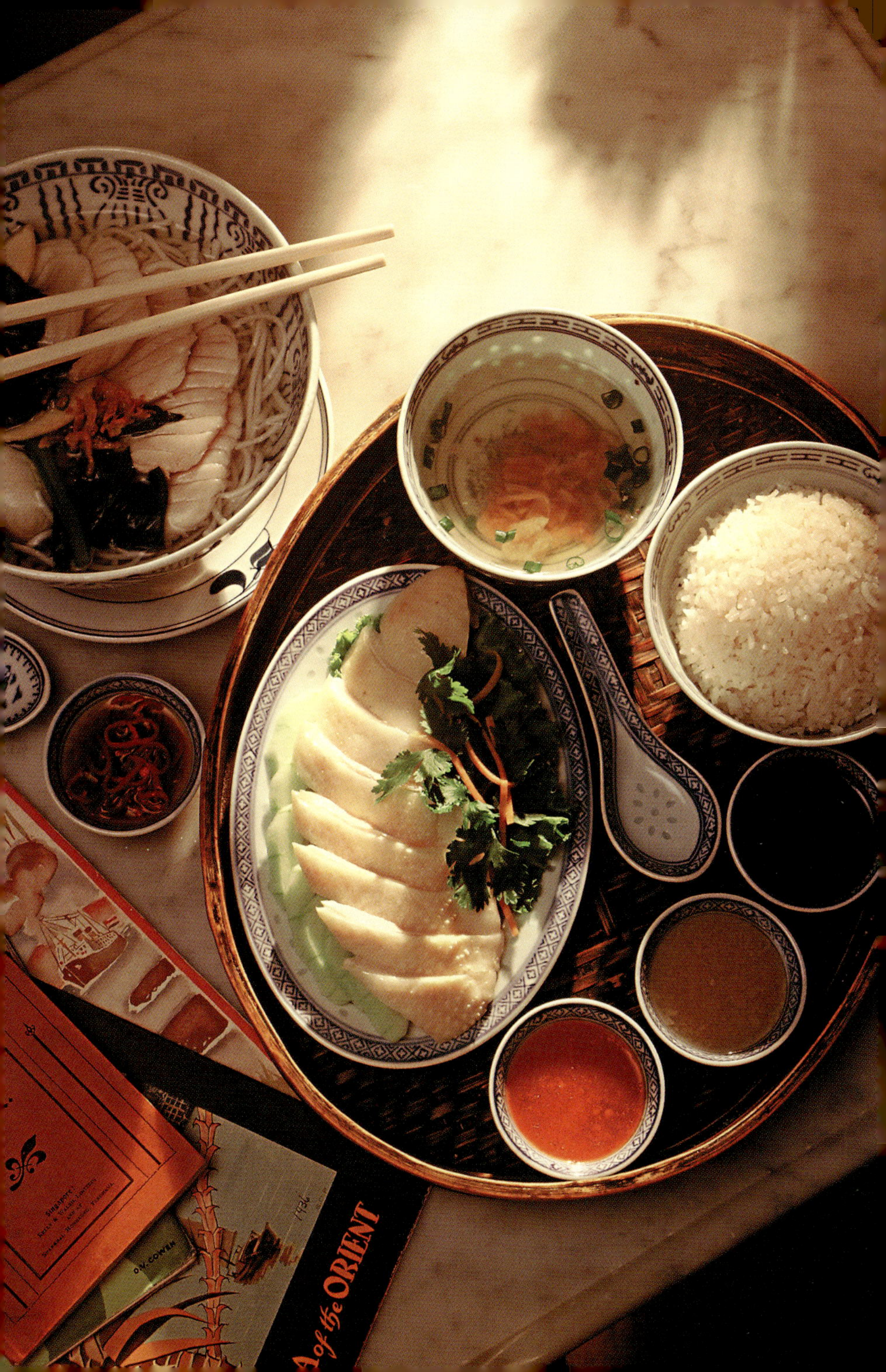
of the ORIENT

PAGODA
宝塔

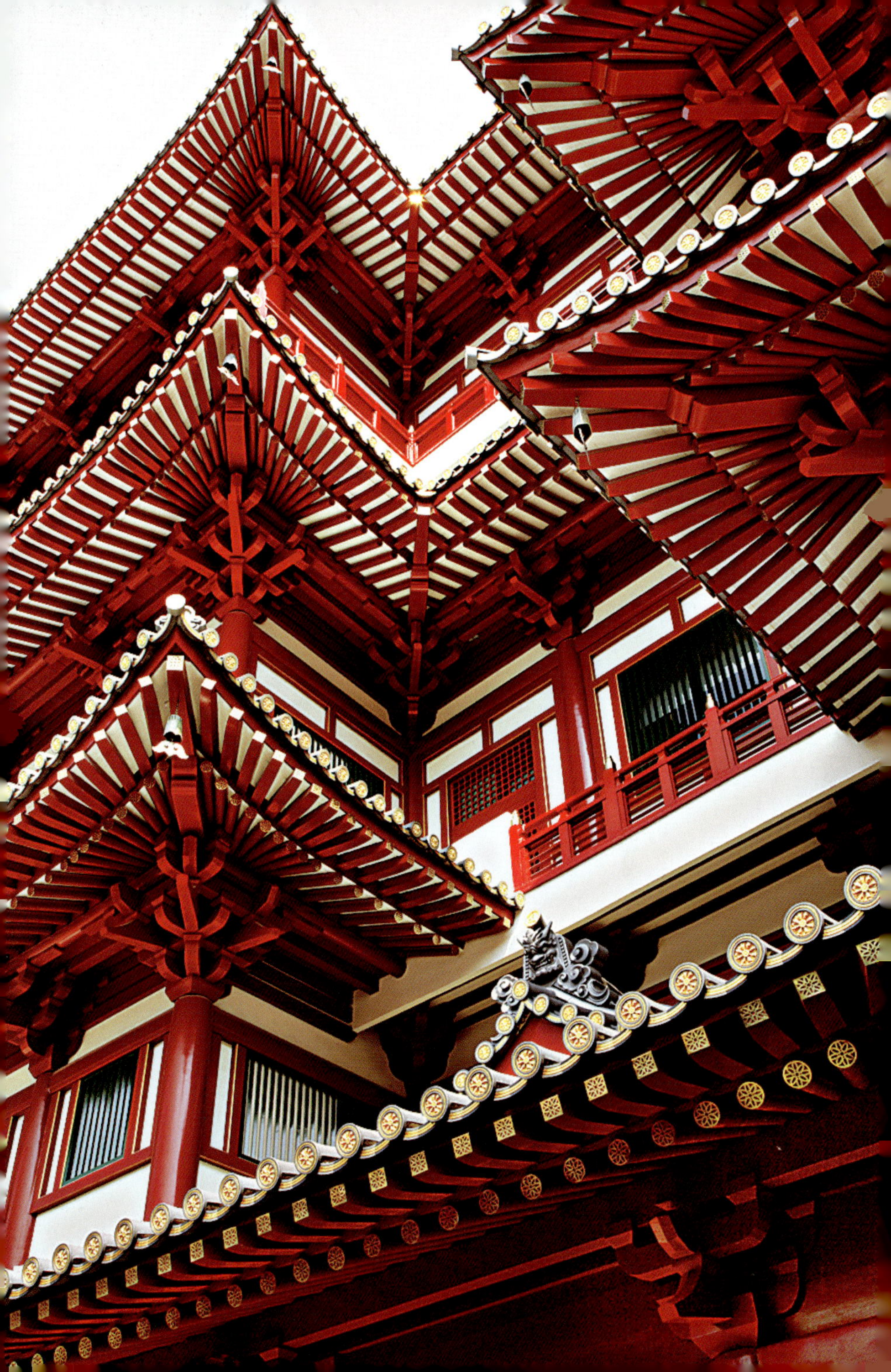

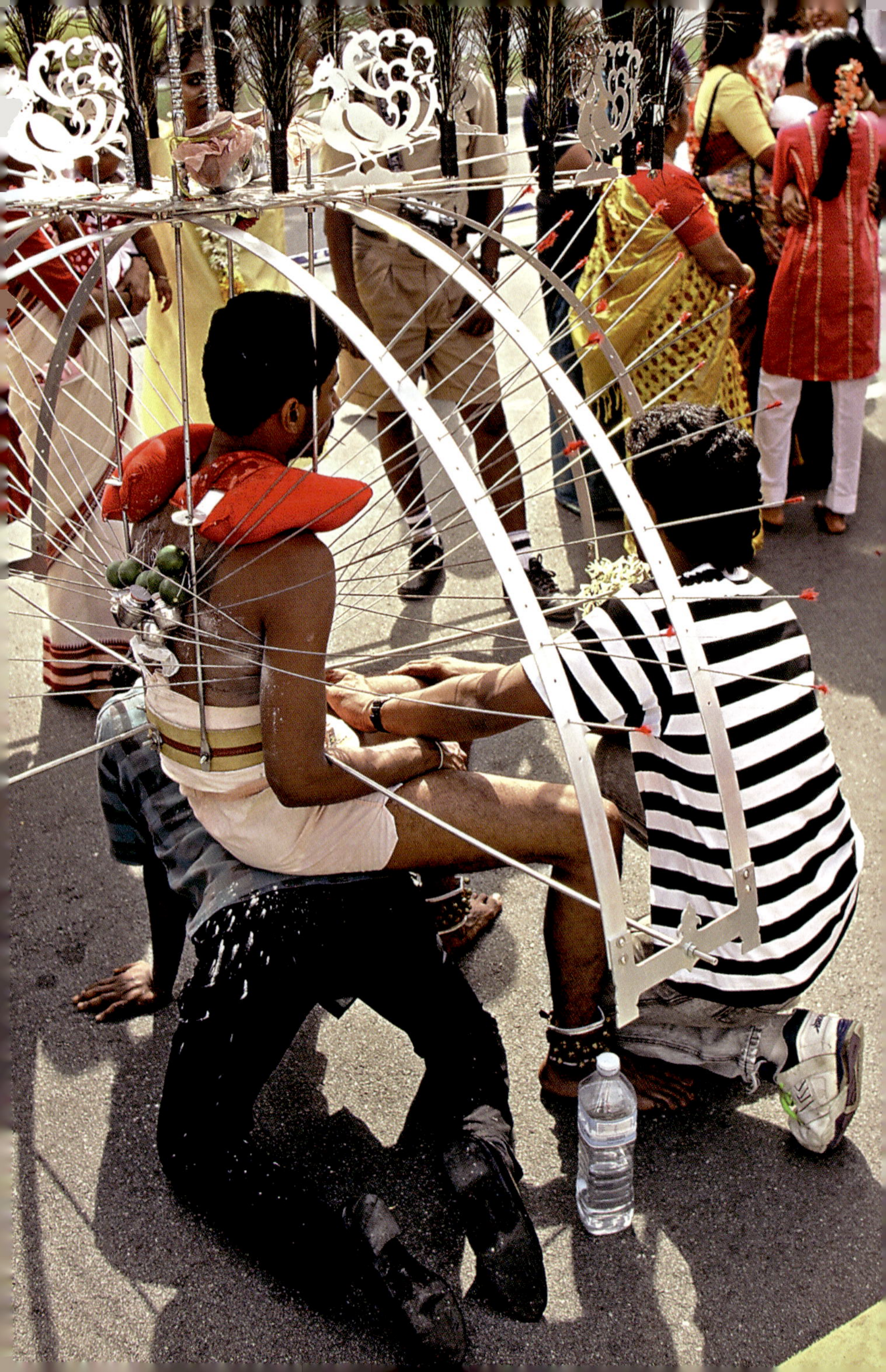

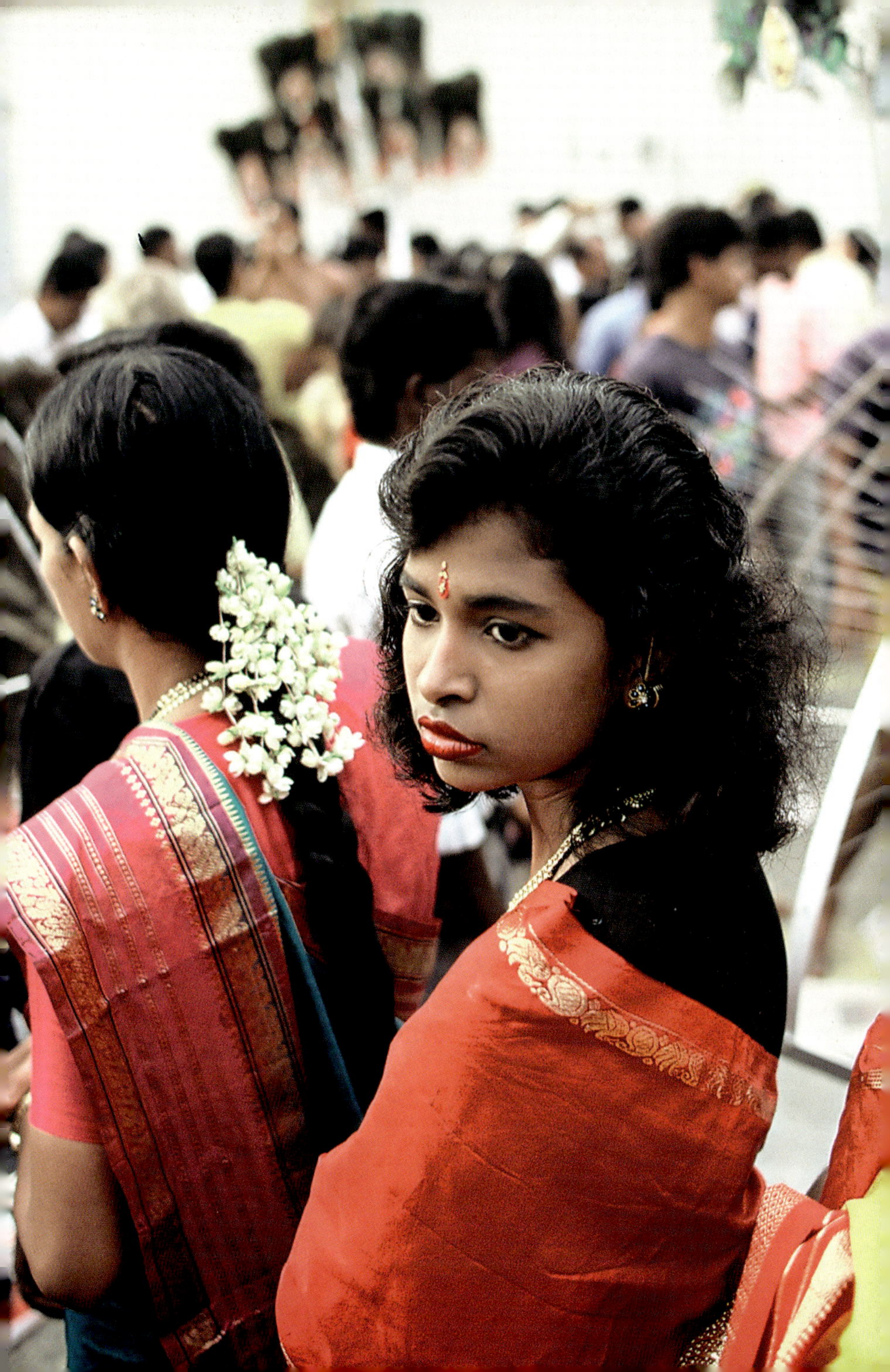

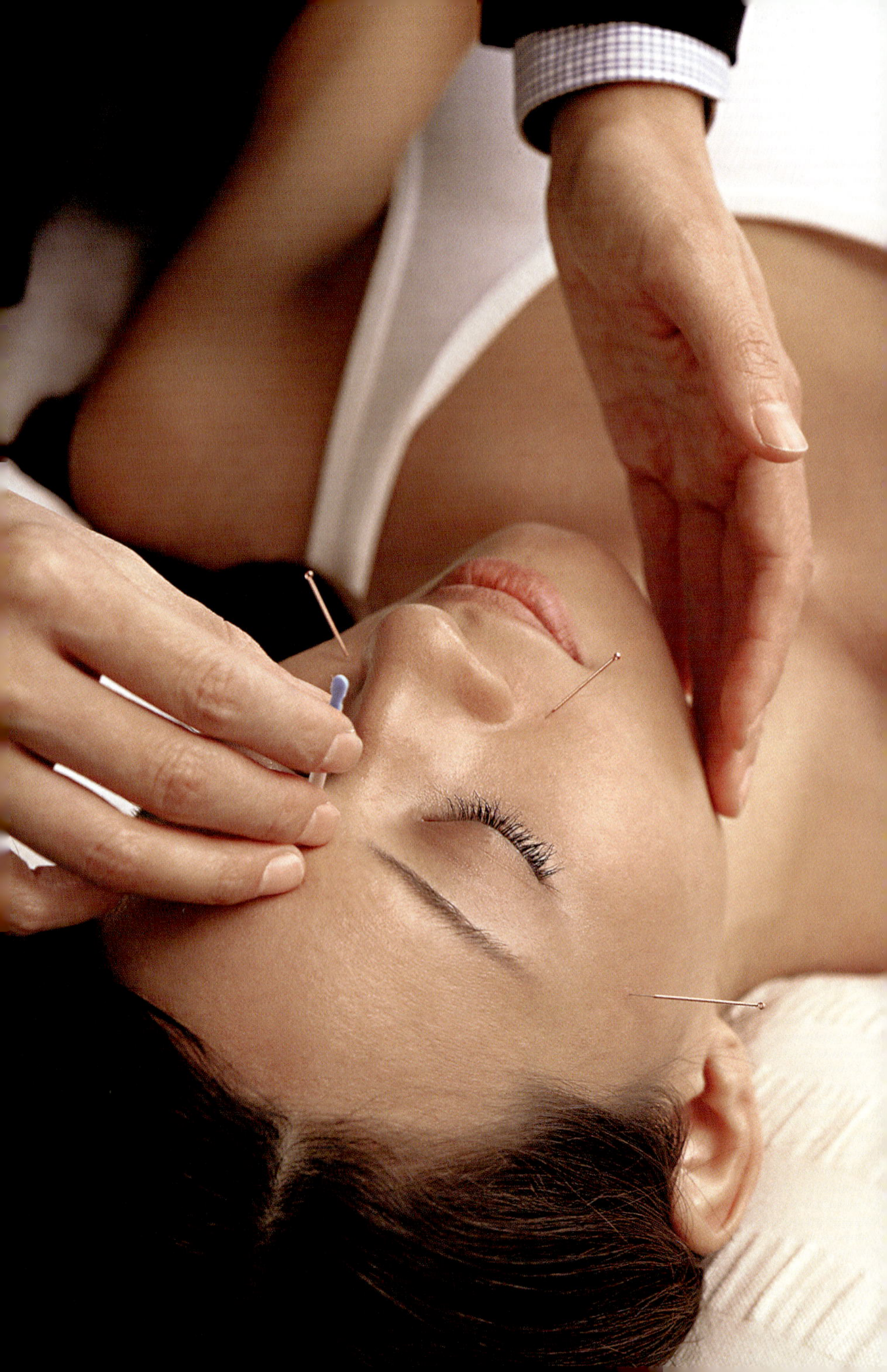

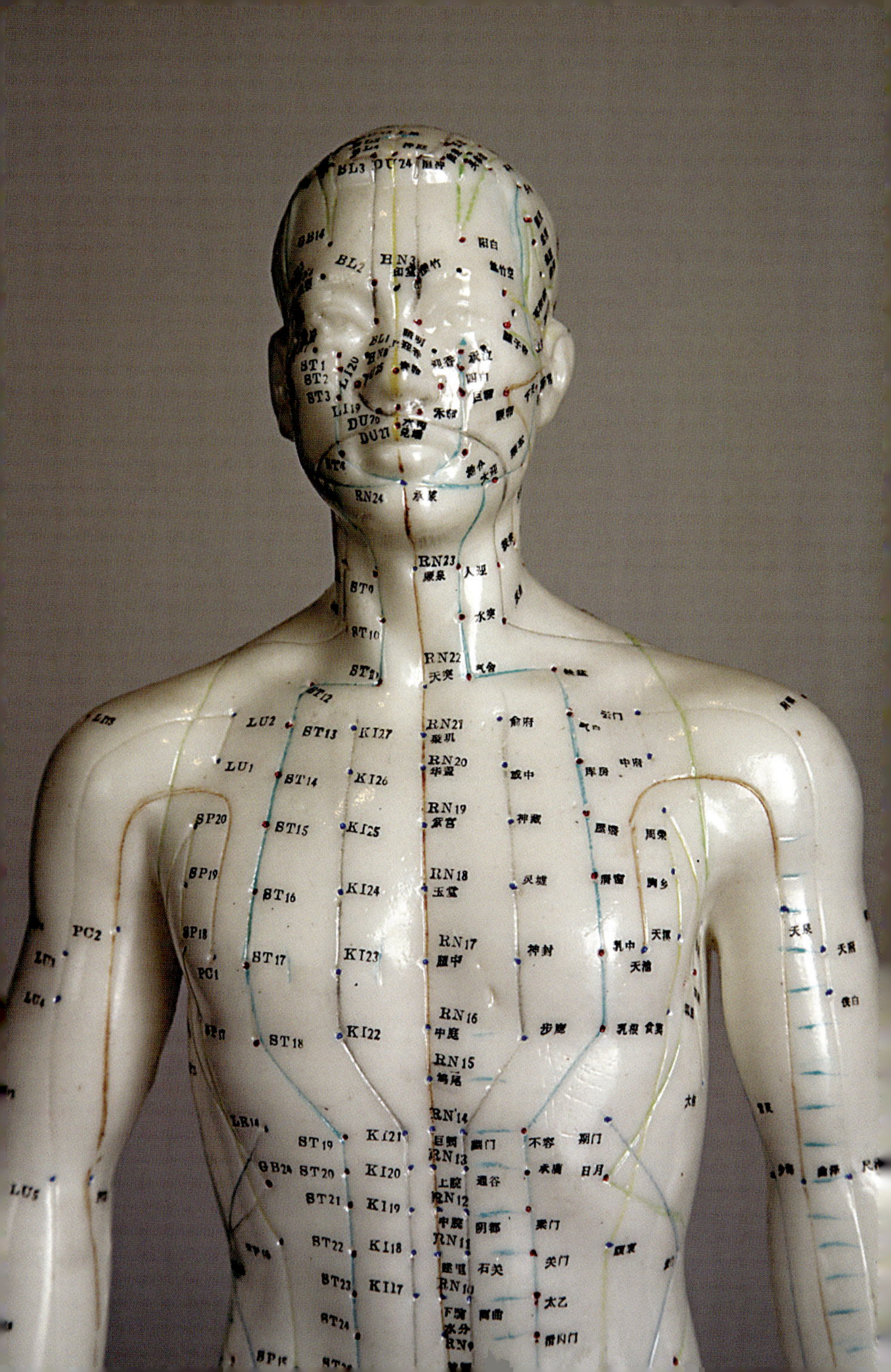
BL3
DU24
BL2
RN3
阳白
ST1
ST2
ST3
LI20
LI19
RN24
承浆
RN23
廉泉
人迎
ST9
水突
ST10
RN22
天突
气舍
ST11
ST12
LU2
ST13
KI27
RN21
璇玑
俞府
云门
气户
LU1
ST14
KI26
RN20
华盖
彧中
库房
中府
SP20
ST15
KI25
RN19
紫宫
神藏
屋翳
周荣
SP19
ST16
KI24
RN18
玉堂
灵墟
膺窗
胸乡
PC2
SP18
ST17
KI23
RN17
膻中
神封
乳中
天溪
天池
天泉
天府
PC1
侠白
ST18
KI22
RN16
中庭
步廊
乳根
食窦
RN15
鸠尾
LR14
ST19
KI21
巨阙
幽门
不容
期门
RN13
GB24
ST20
KI20
上脘
通谷
承满
日月
ST21
KI19
RN12
中脘
阴都
梁门
LU5
ST22
KI18
RN11
建里
石关
关门
ST23
KI17
RN10
下脘
商曲
太乙
ST24
水分
滑肉门

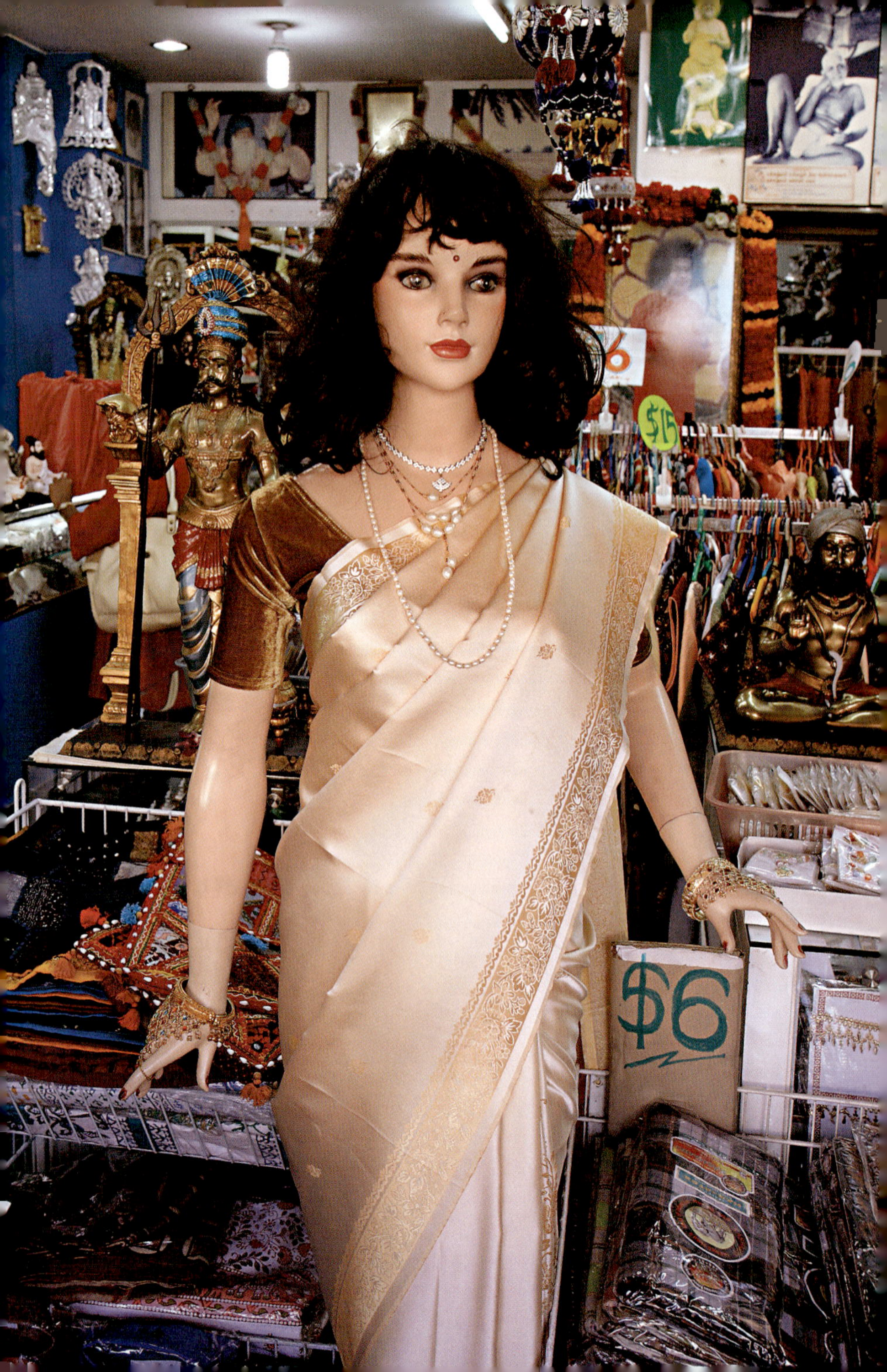
$15
$6

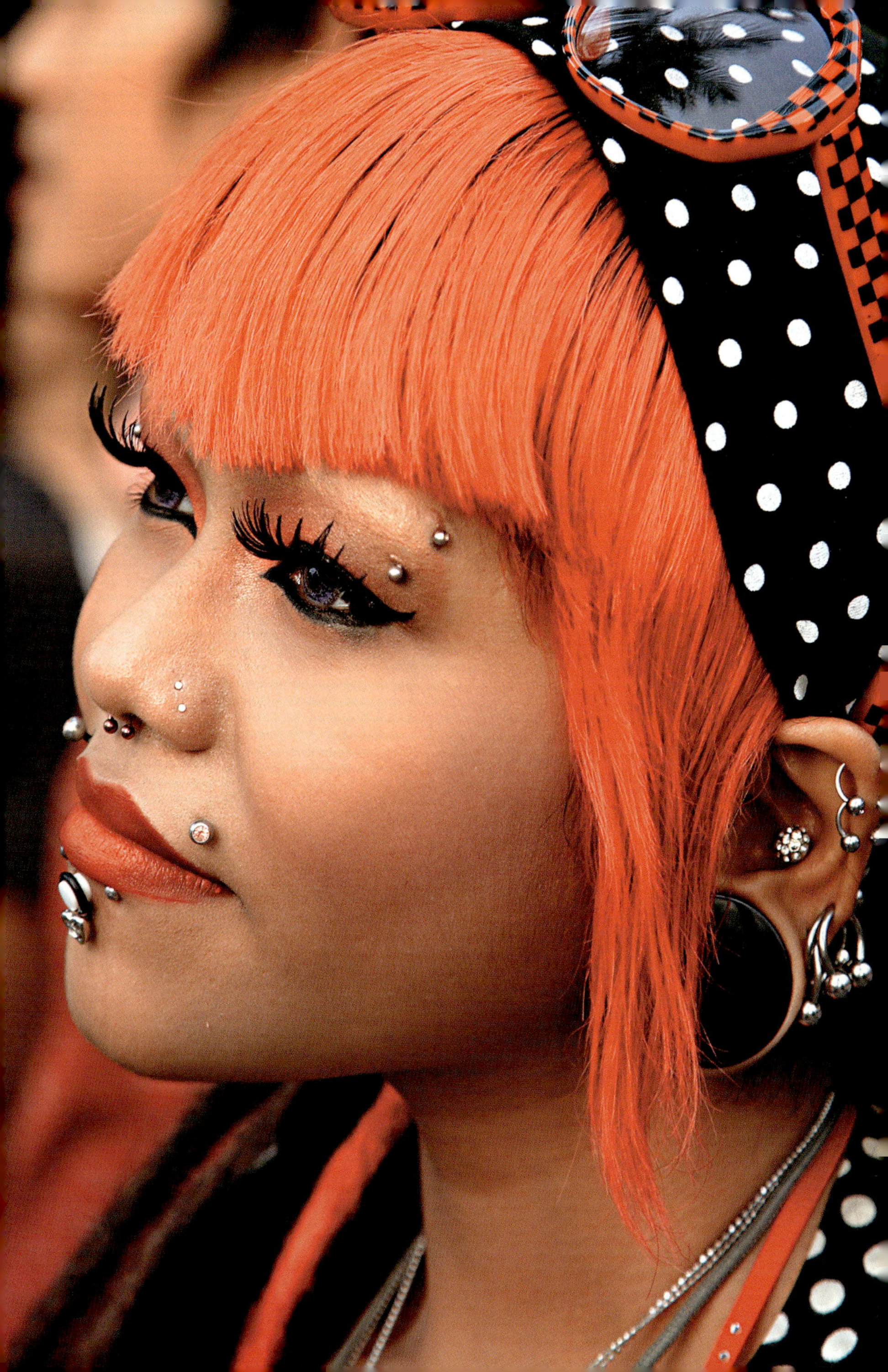

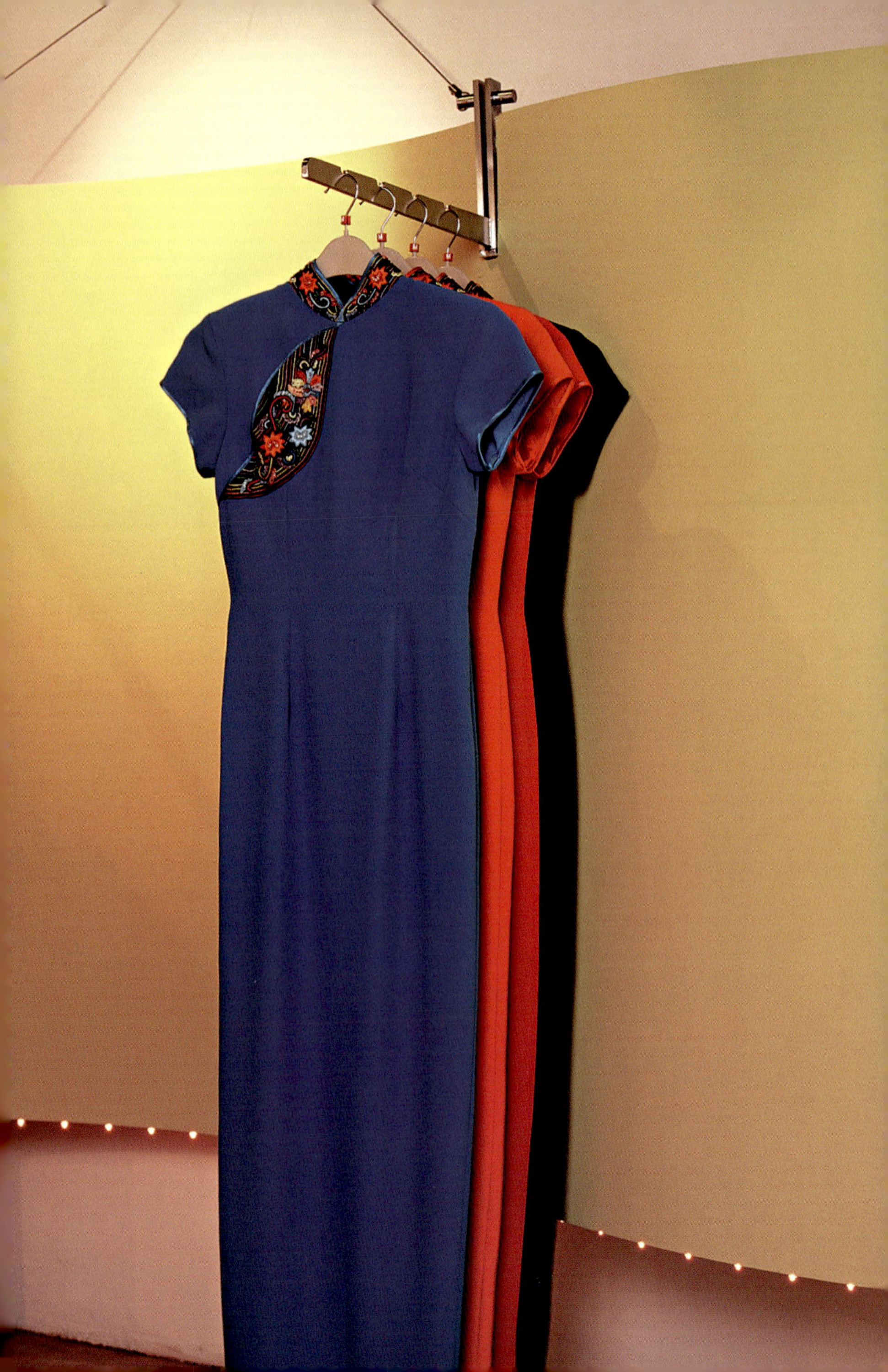

生意興隆

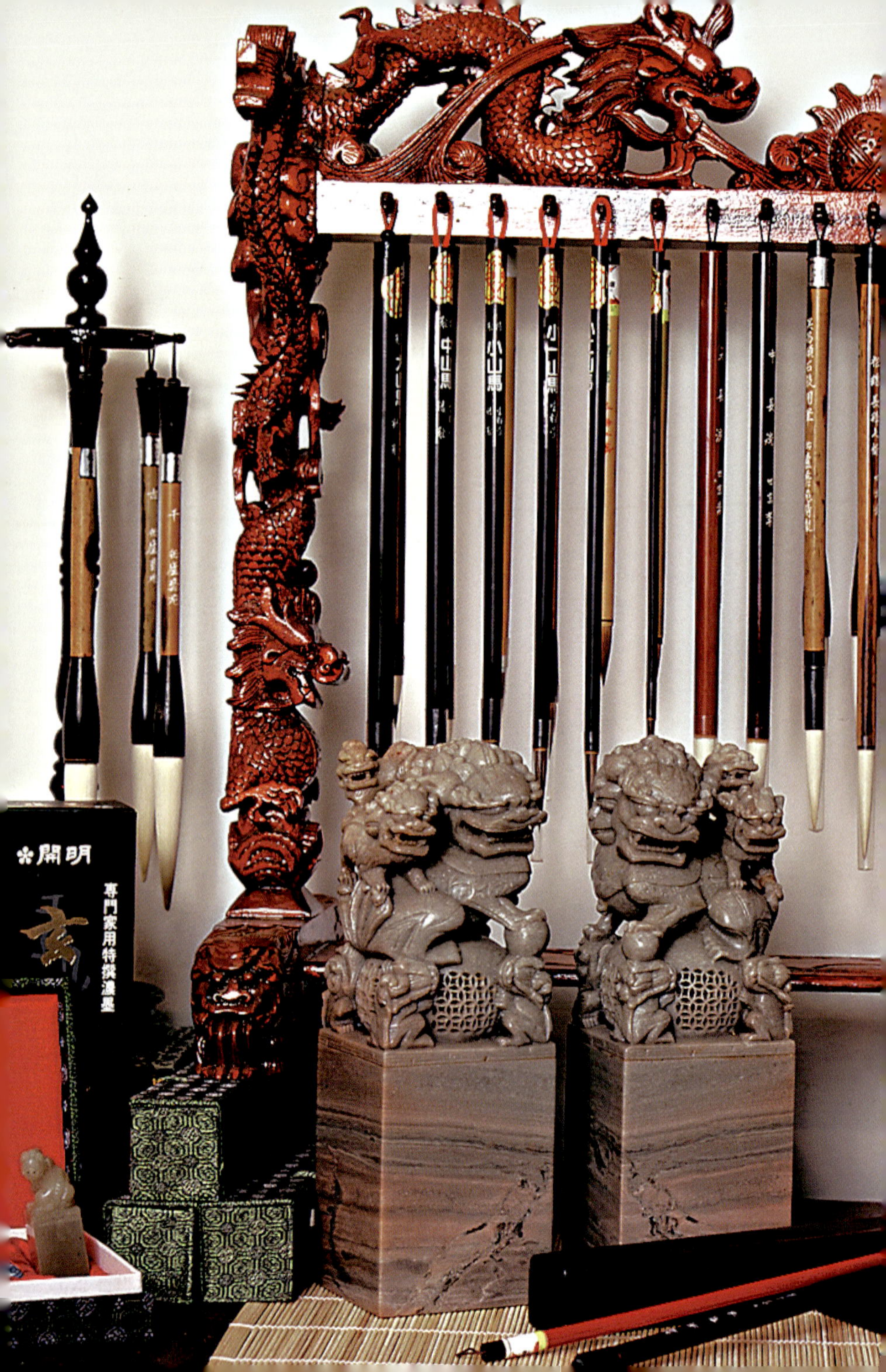
中山馬
小山馬
開明
玄
專門家用特撰濃墨

阿彌陀佛

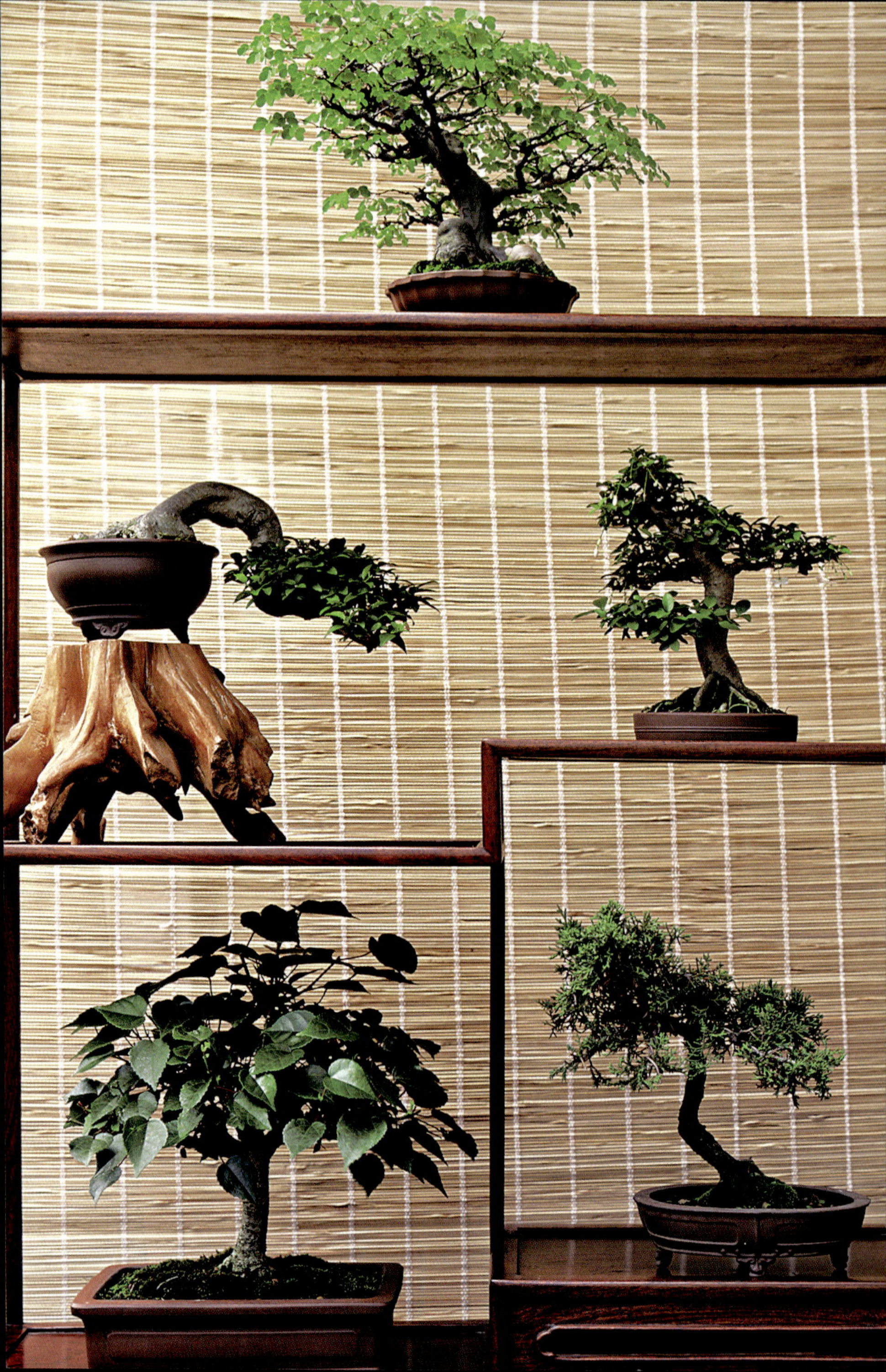

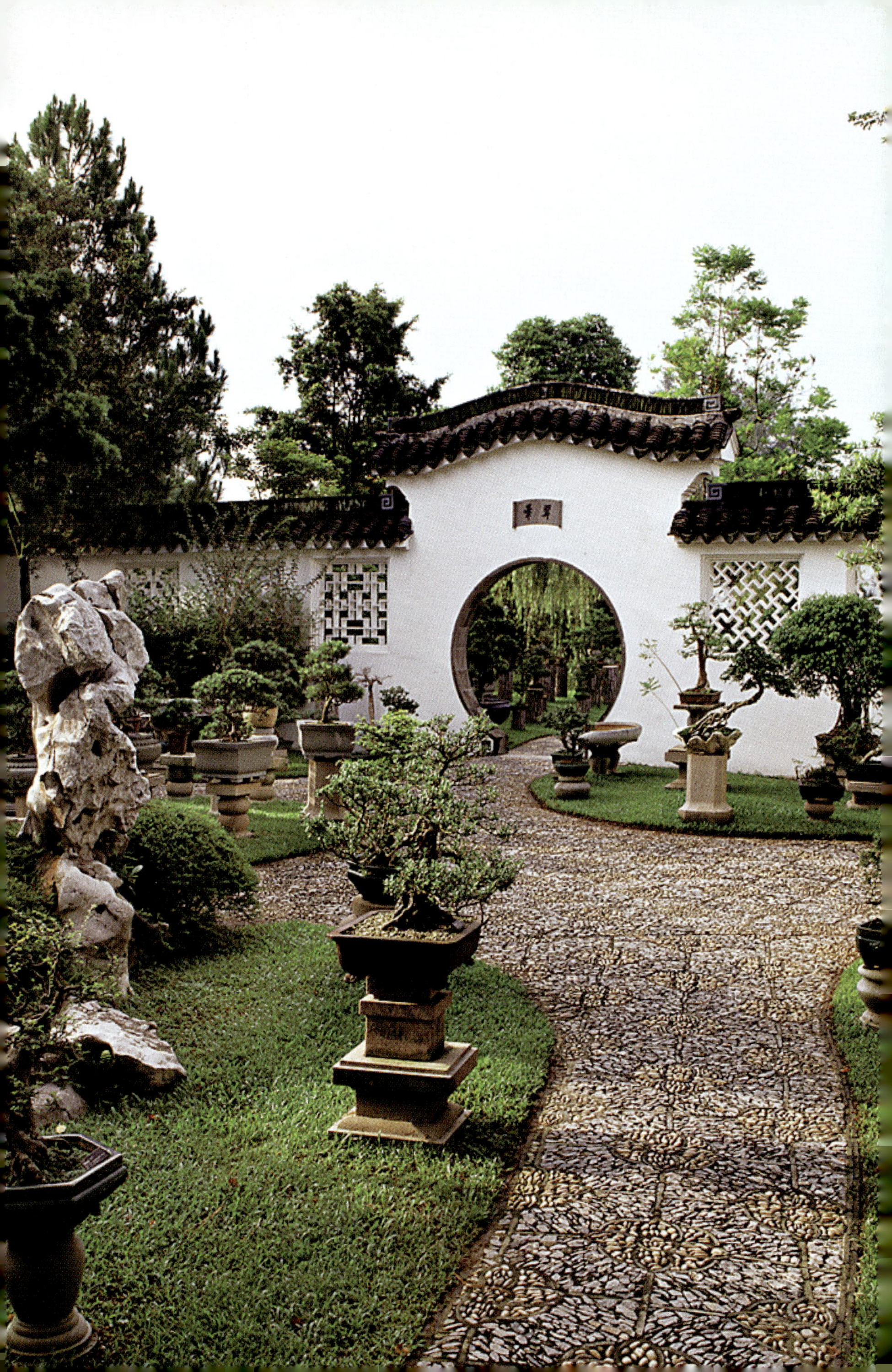

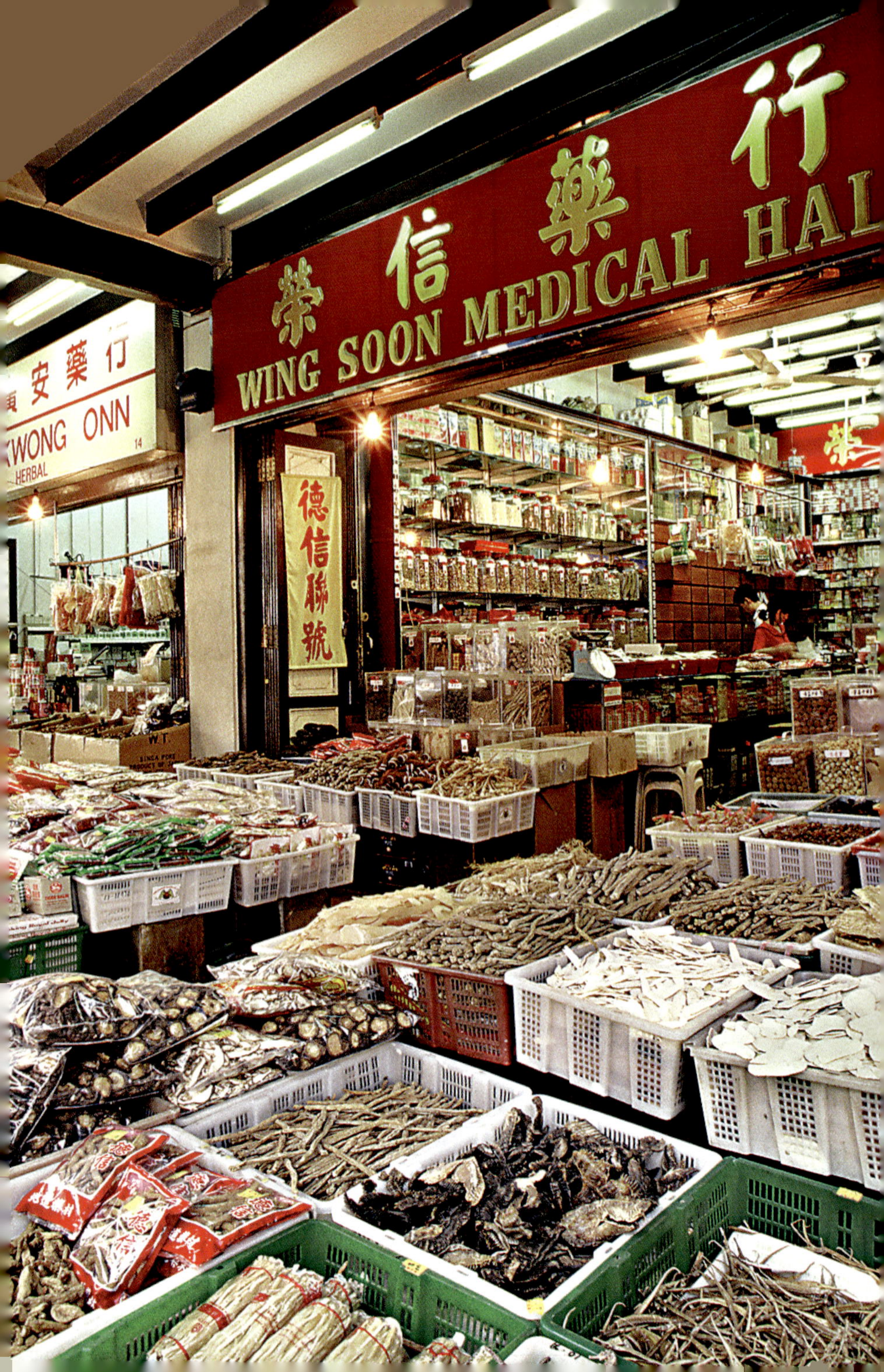
榮信藥行
WING SOON MEDICAL HAL
安藥行
KWONG ONN
HERBAL
德信聯號

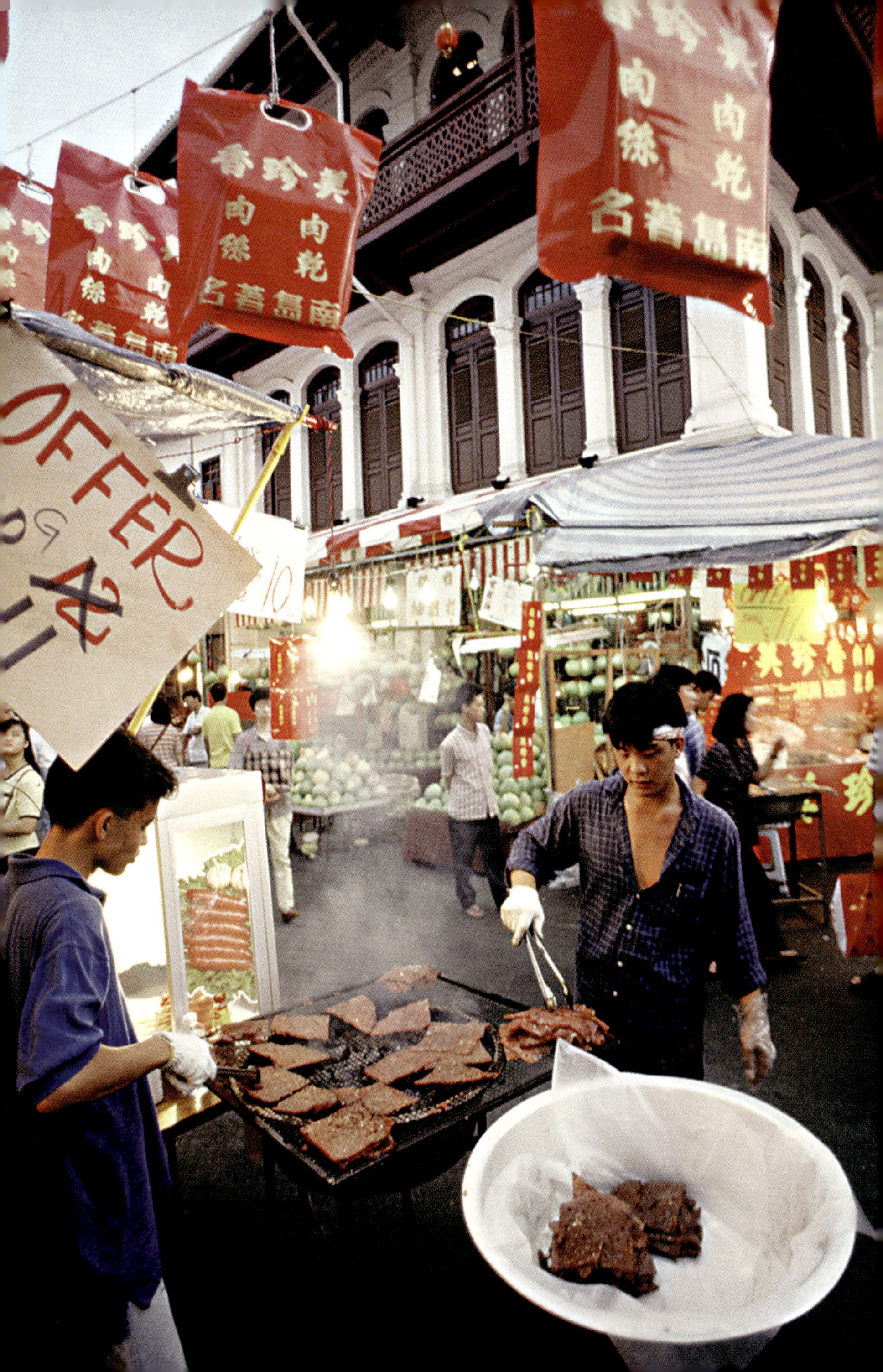
香珍美
肉絲
肉乾
名著島南
OFFER
10

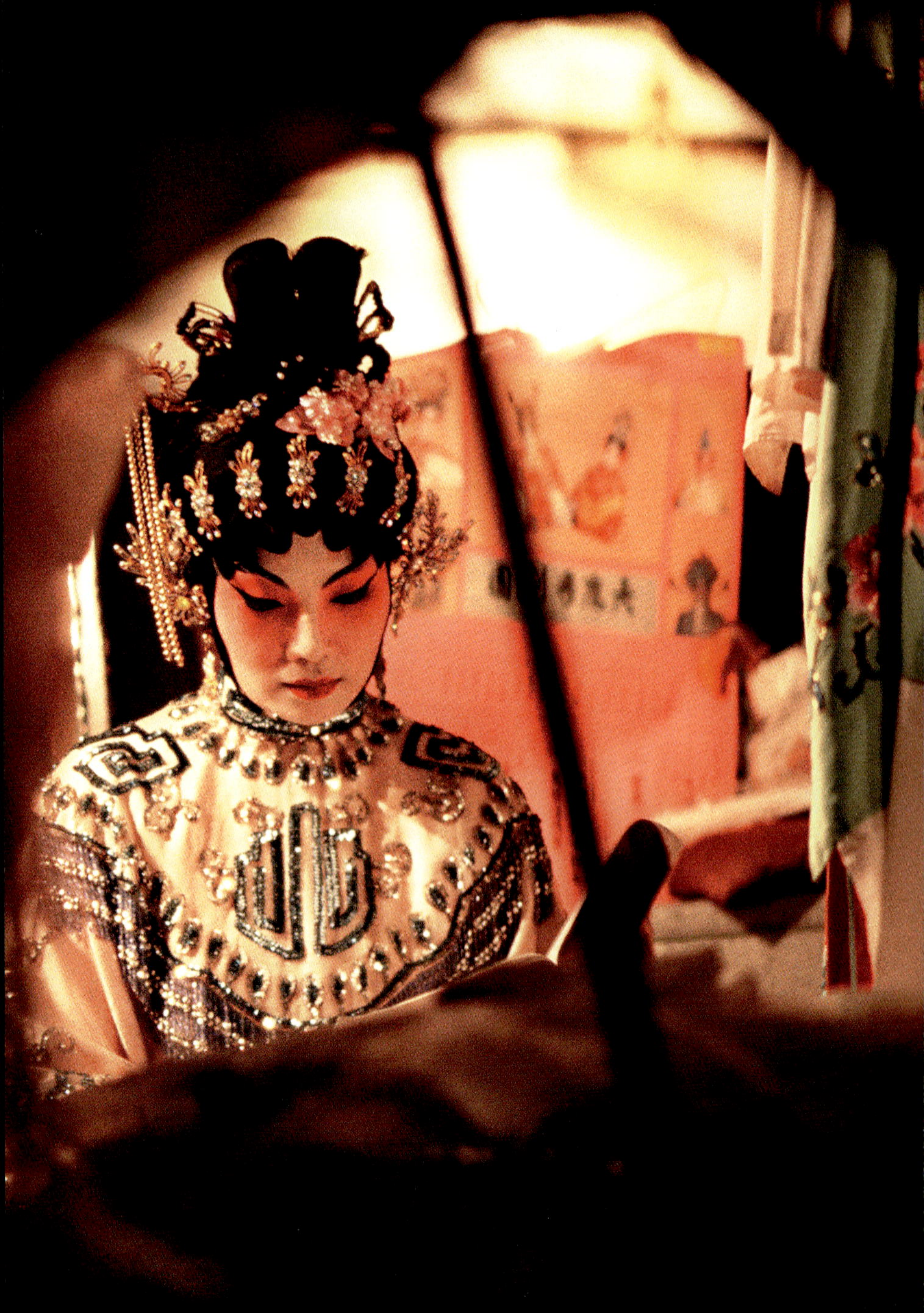

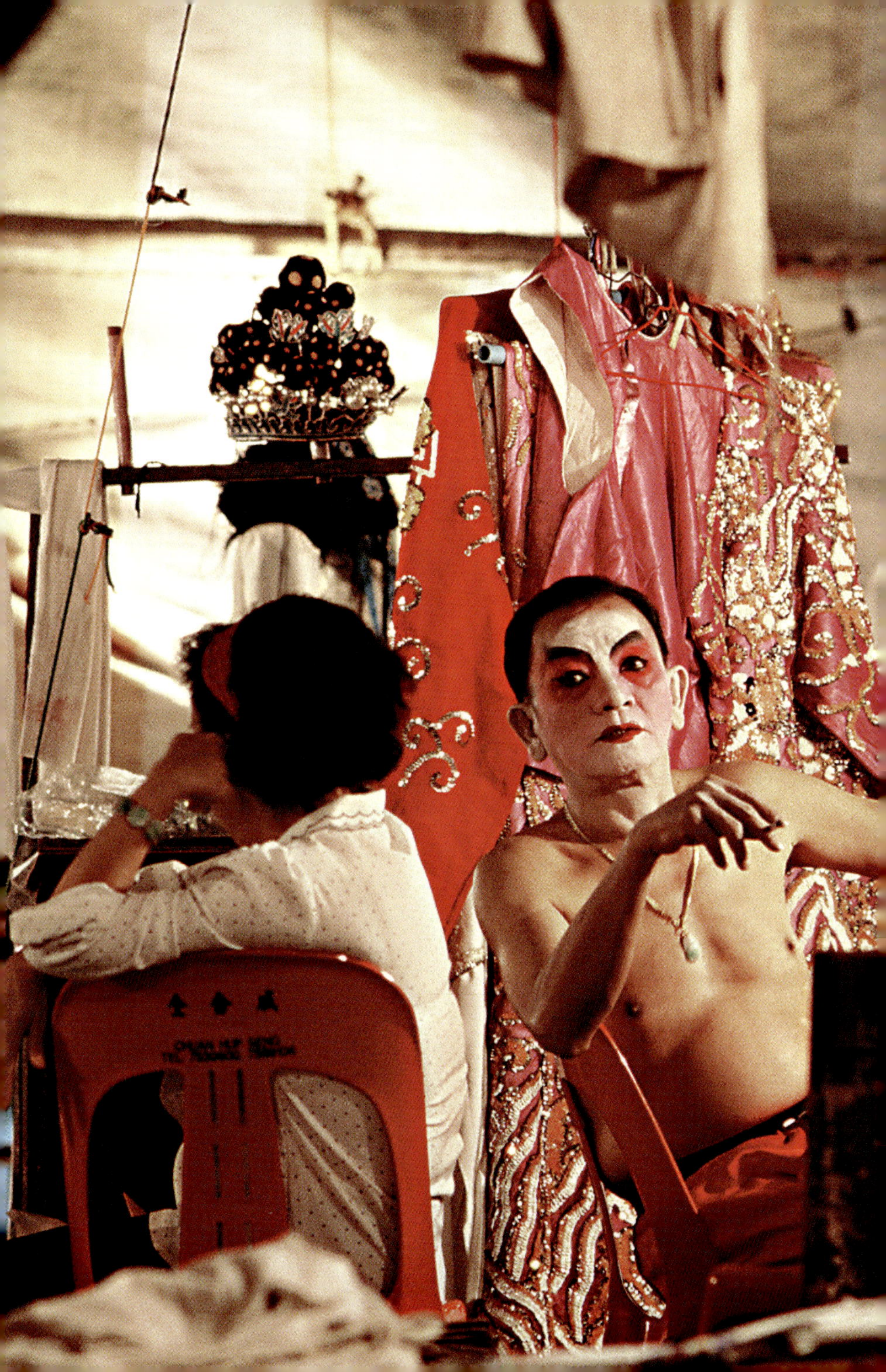

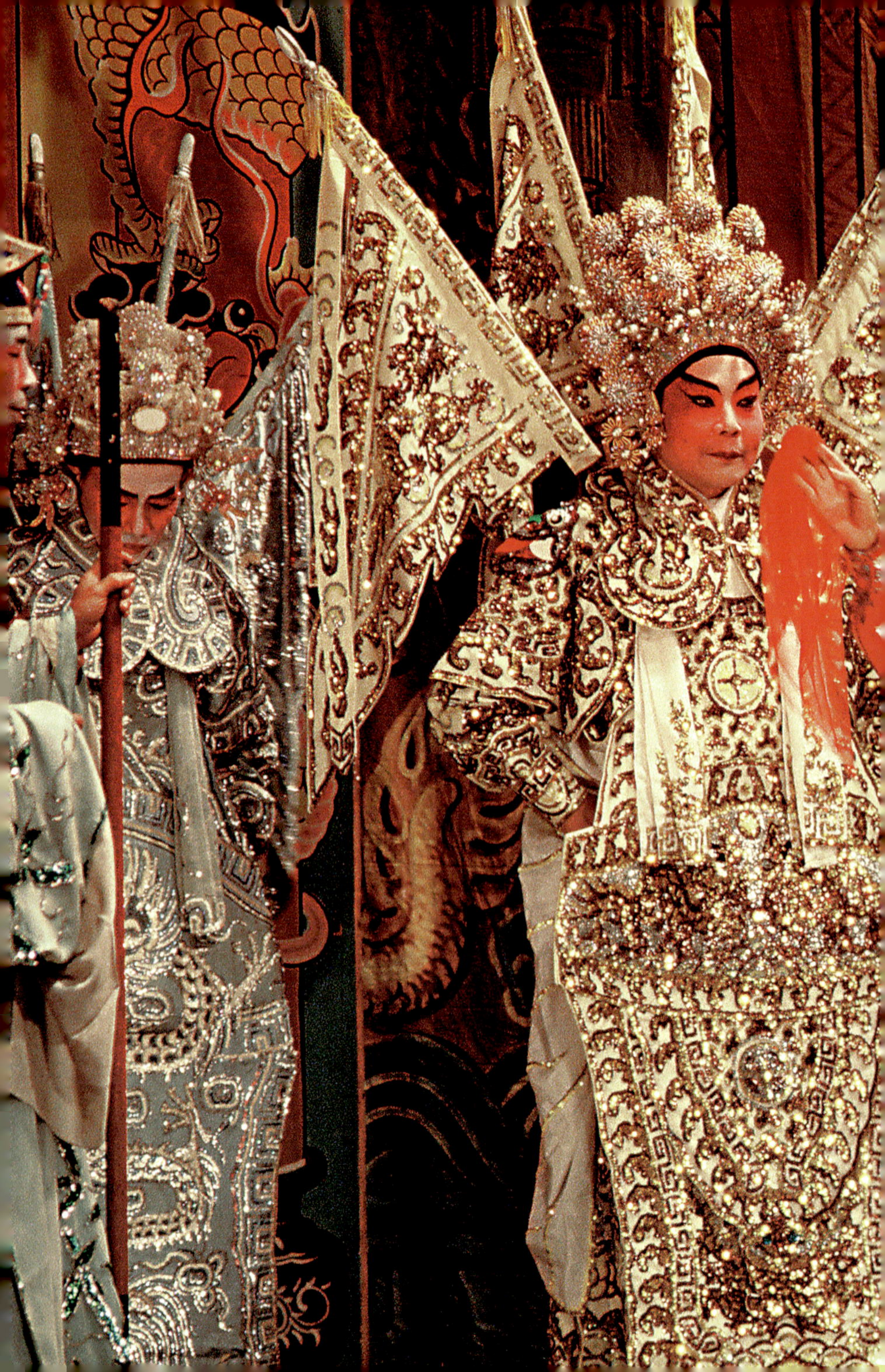

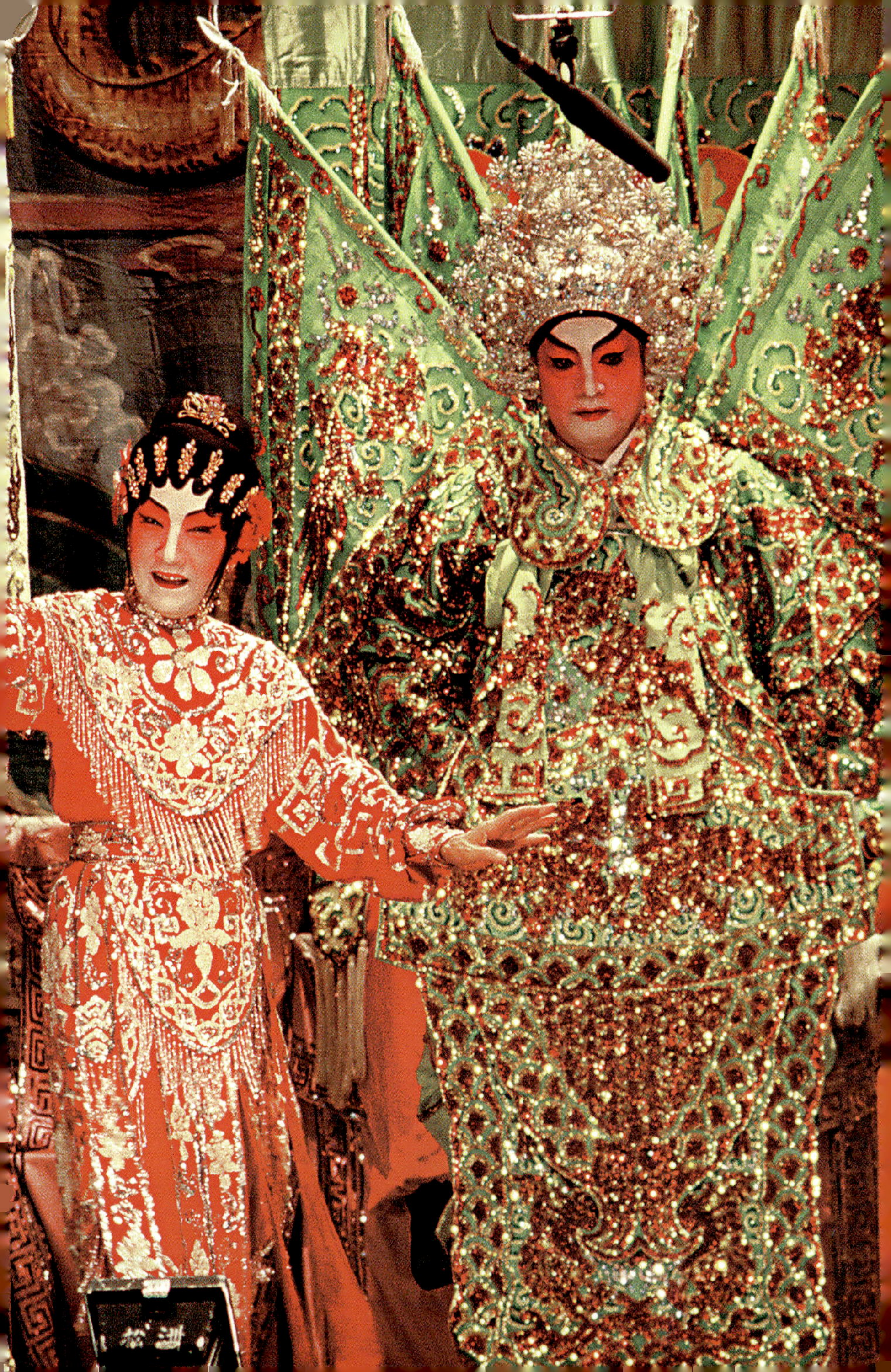

光被甲表

升堂

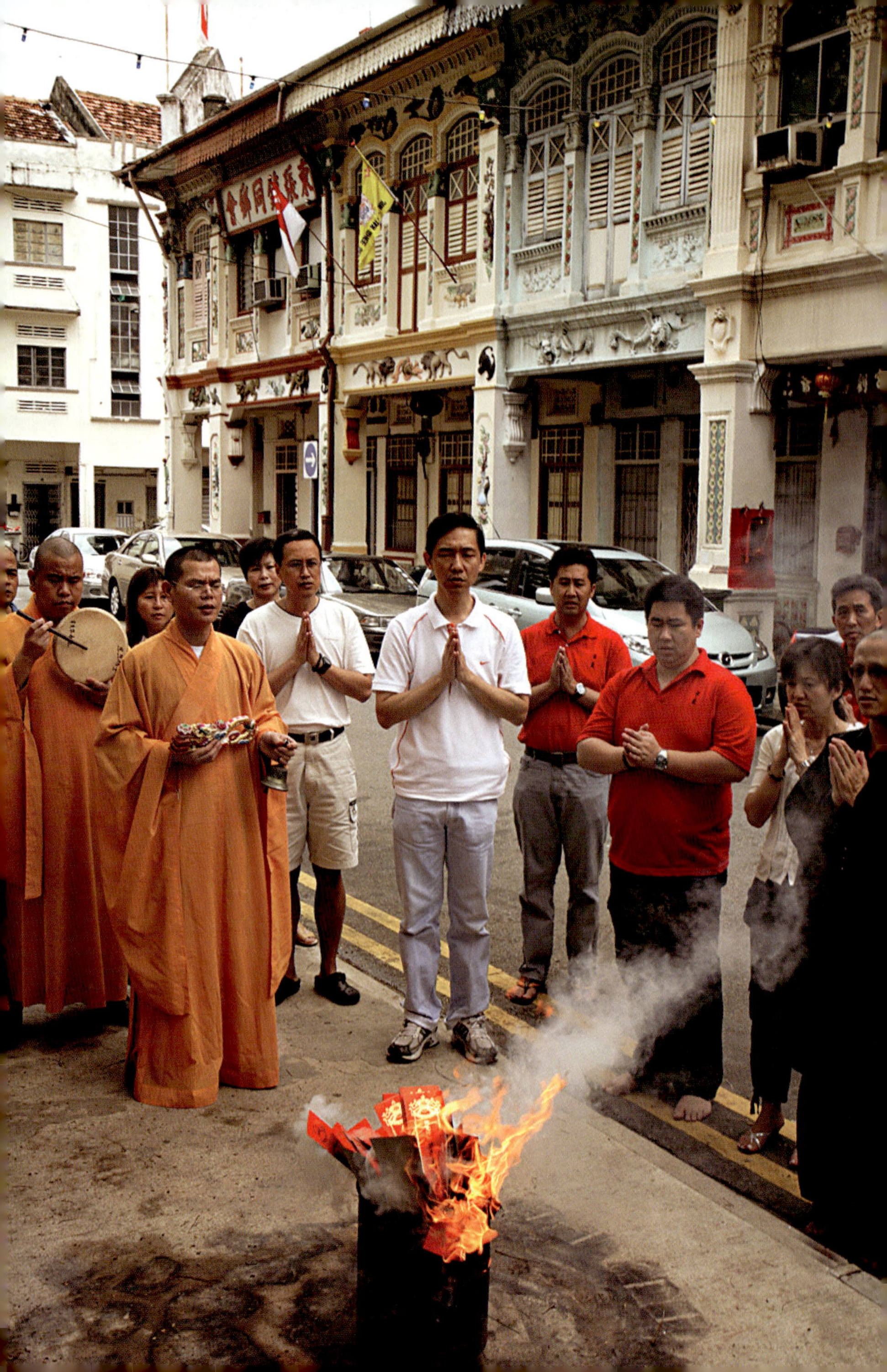

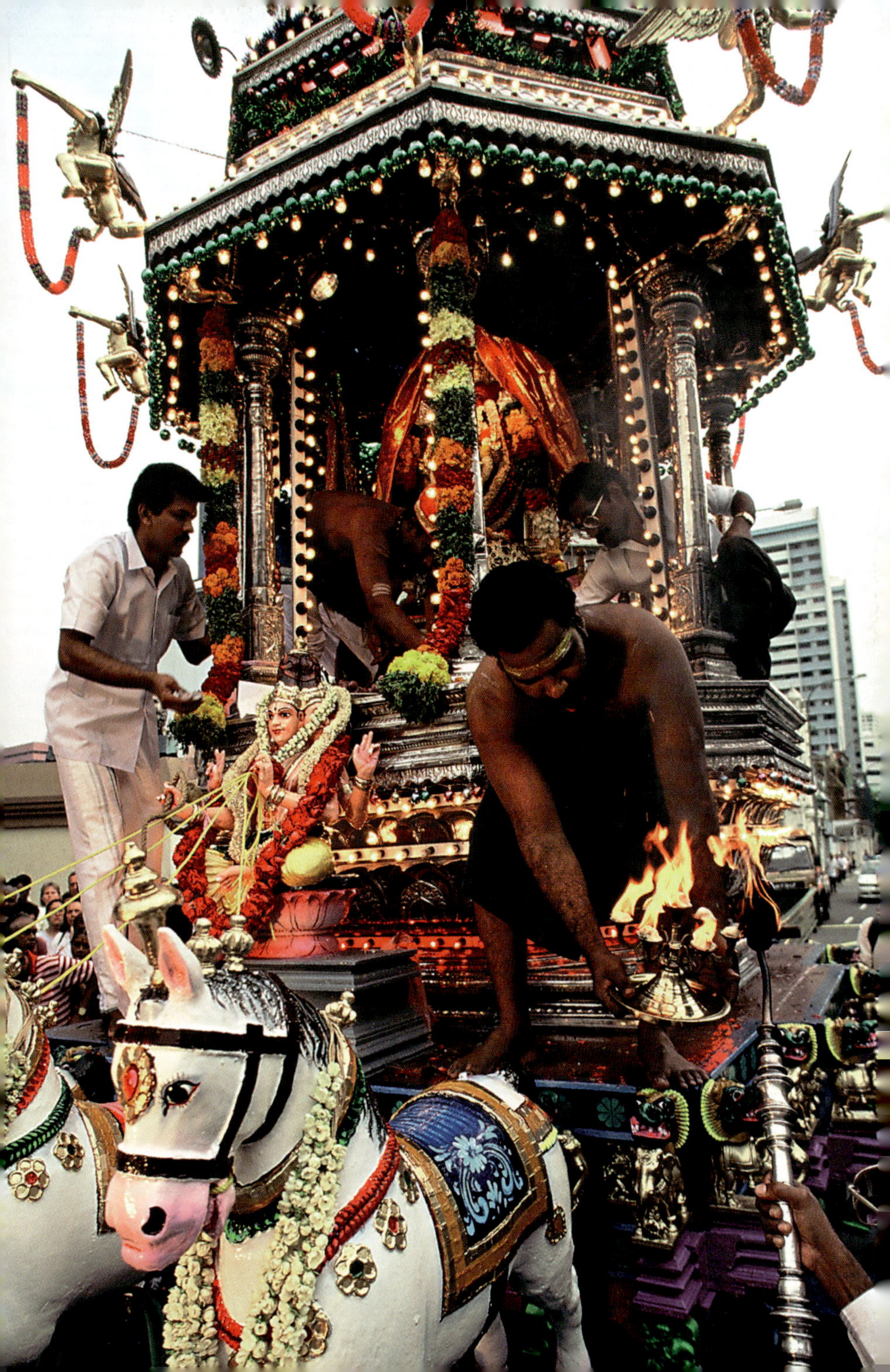

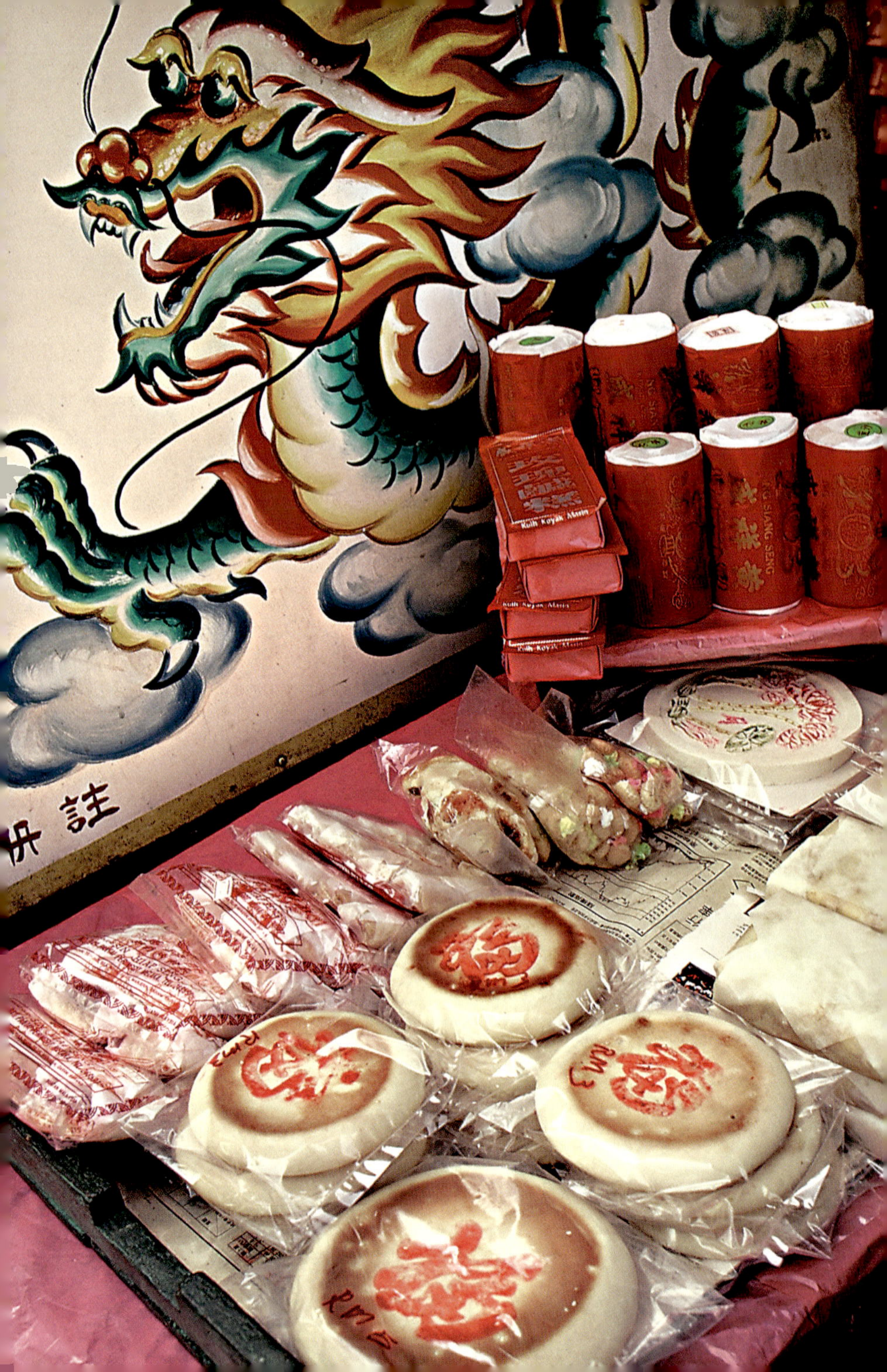
註
Kuih Koyak Masin
NG SIANG SENG

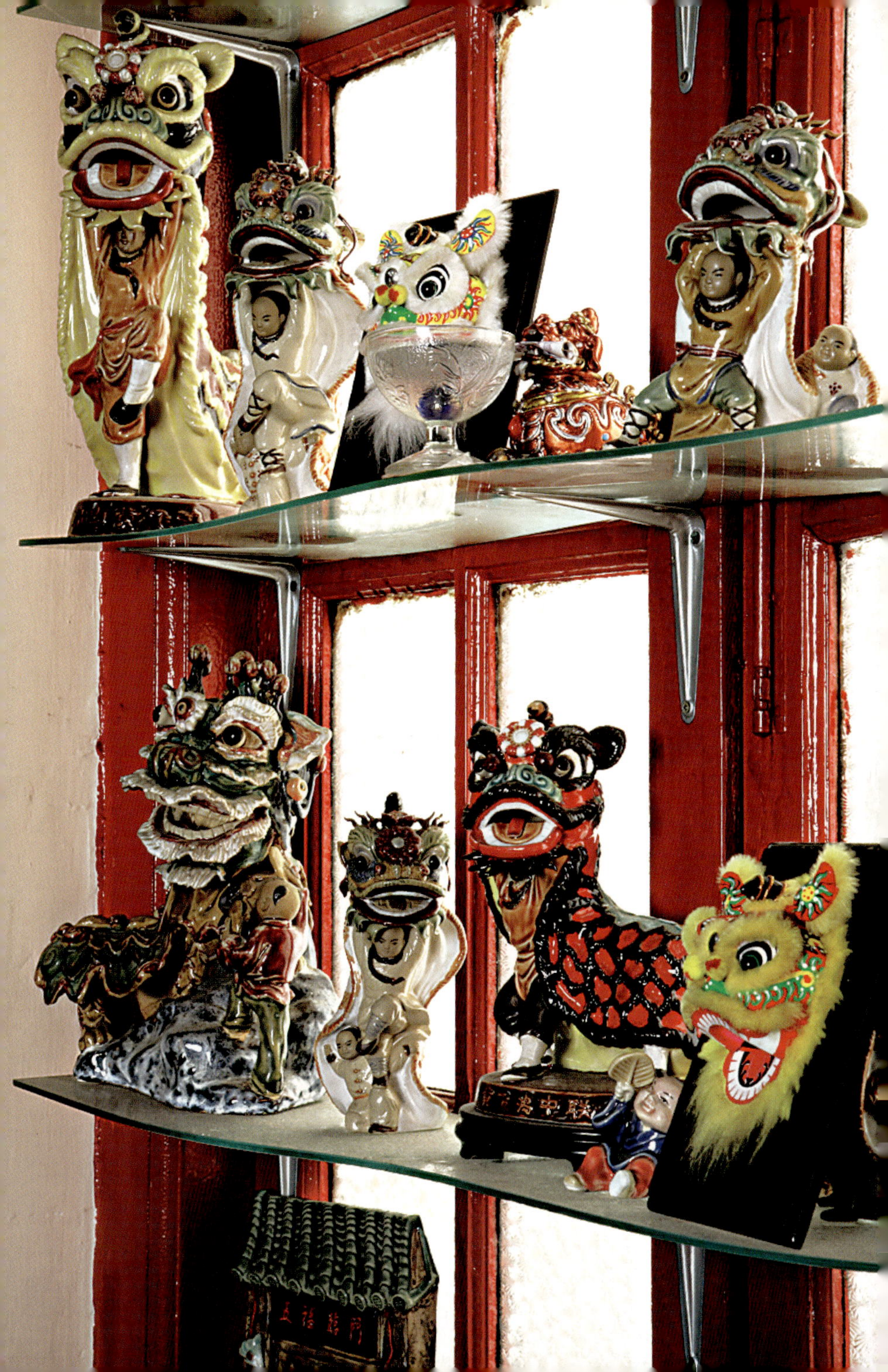

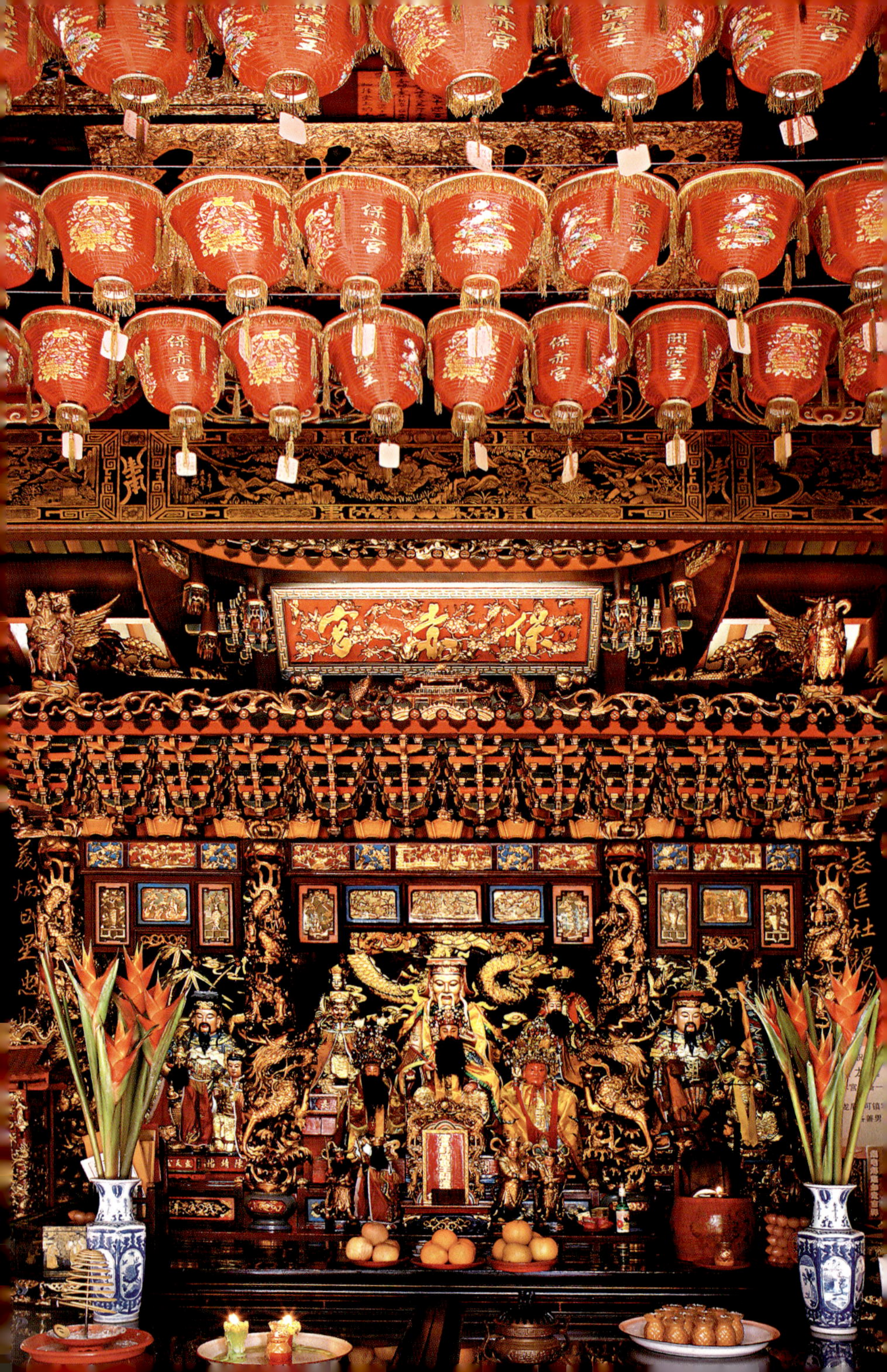

保赤宫
開漳聖王
保赤宫

ஶ்ரீ வடபத்ரா காளியம்மன் சந்நிதி
SRI VADAPATHIRA KALIAMMAN SANCTUM

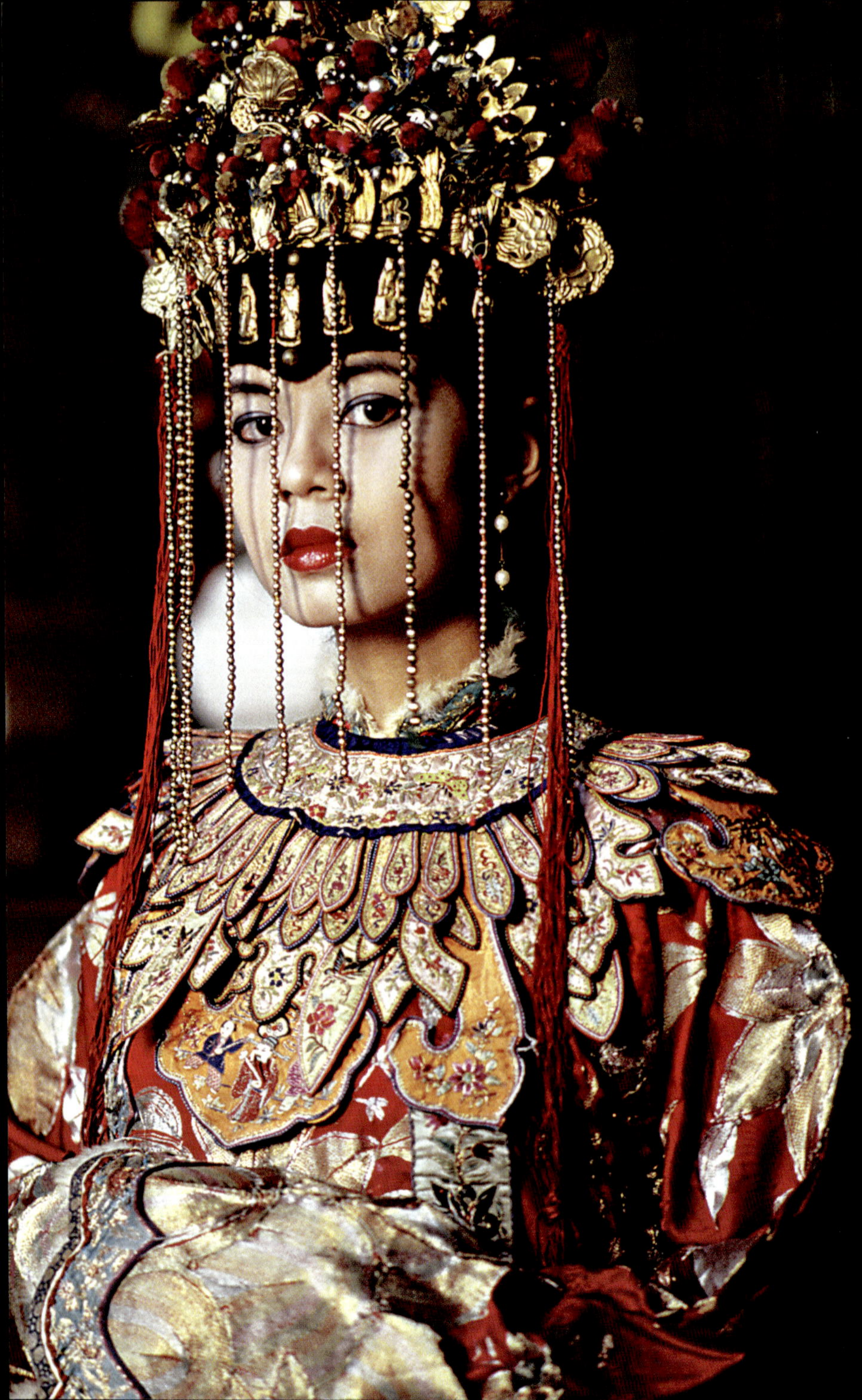

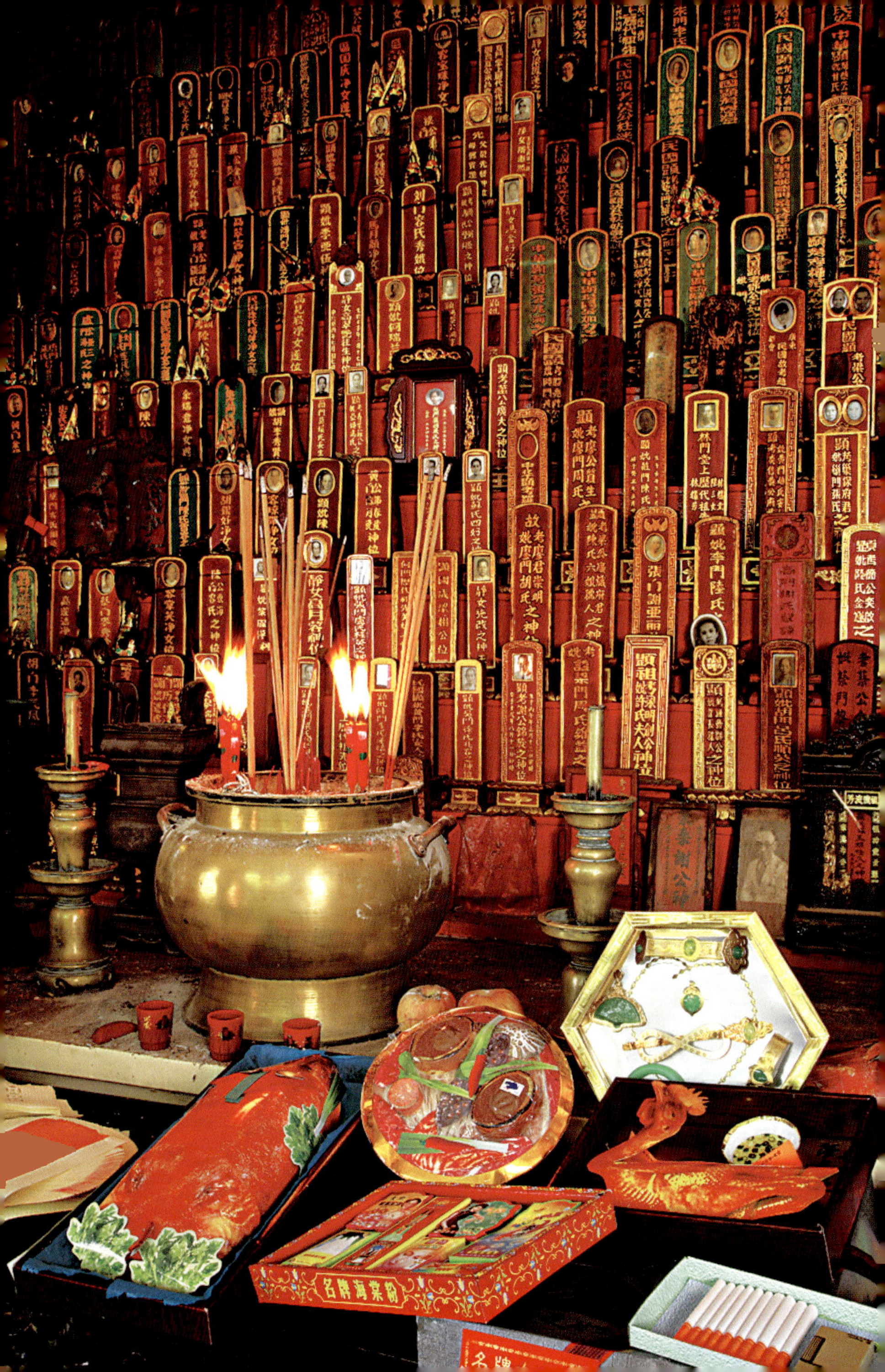

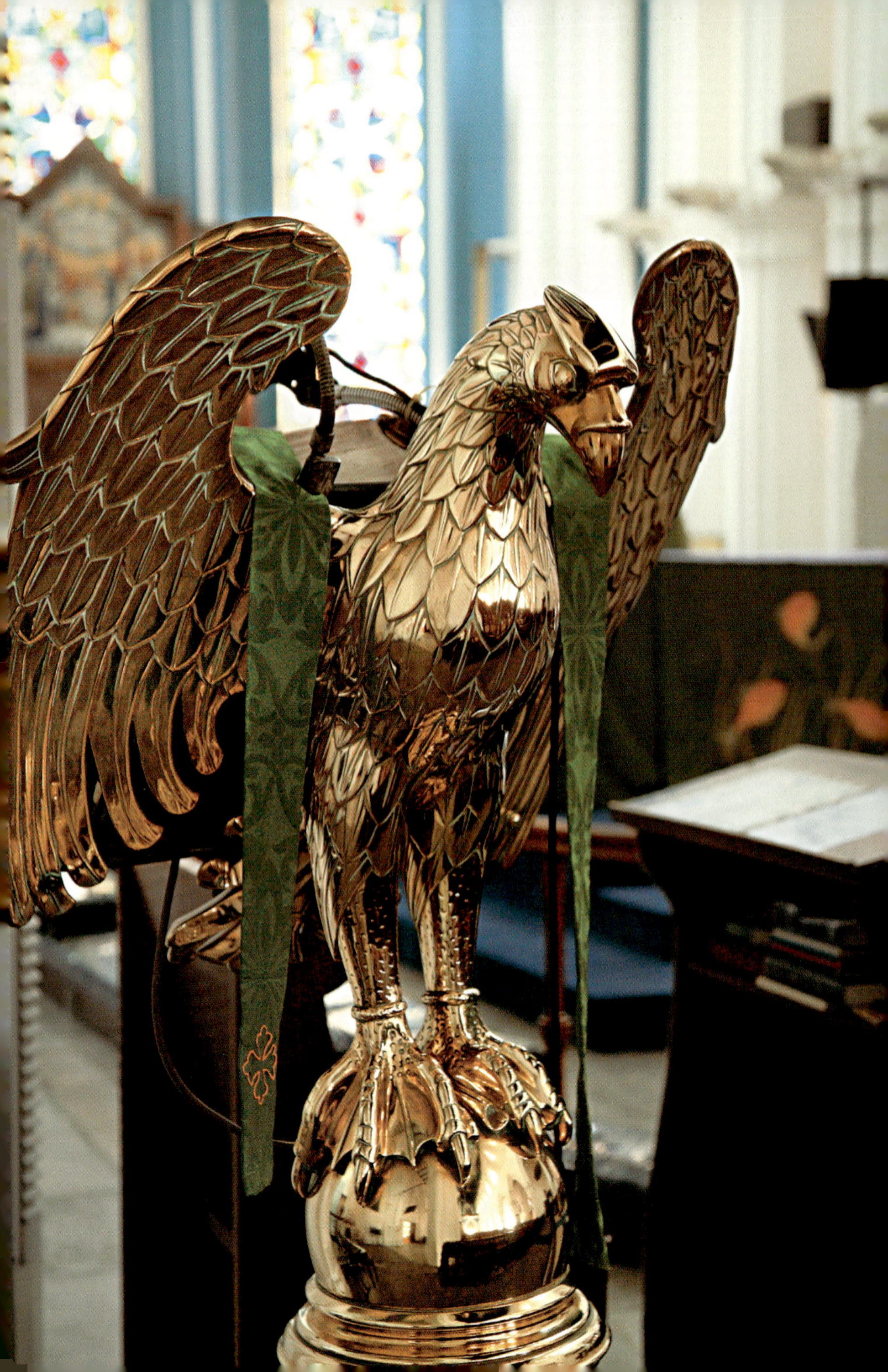

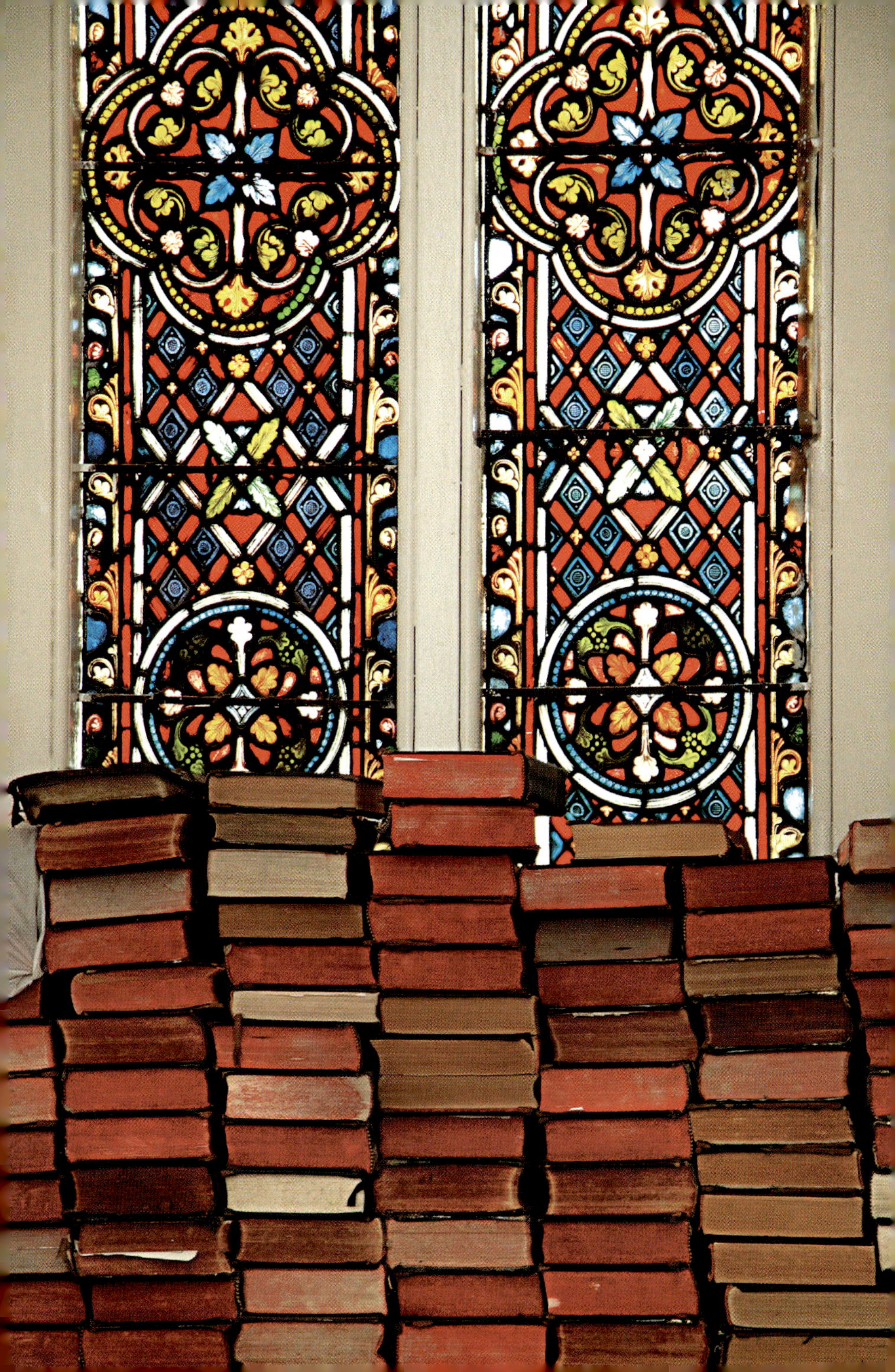

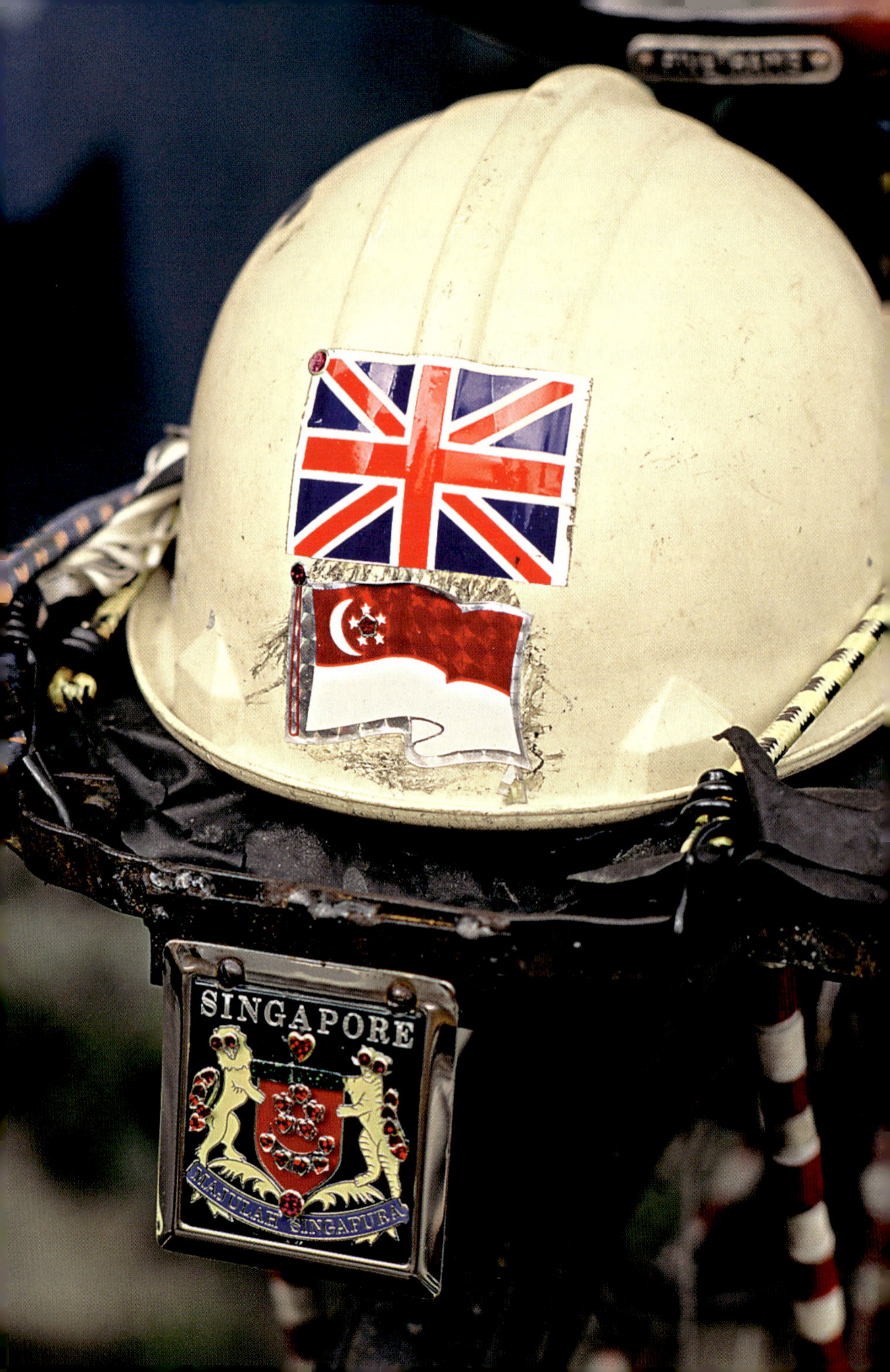
SINGAPORE
MAJULAH SINGAPURA

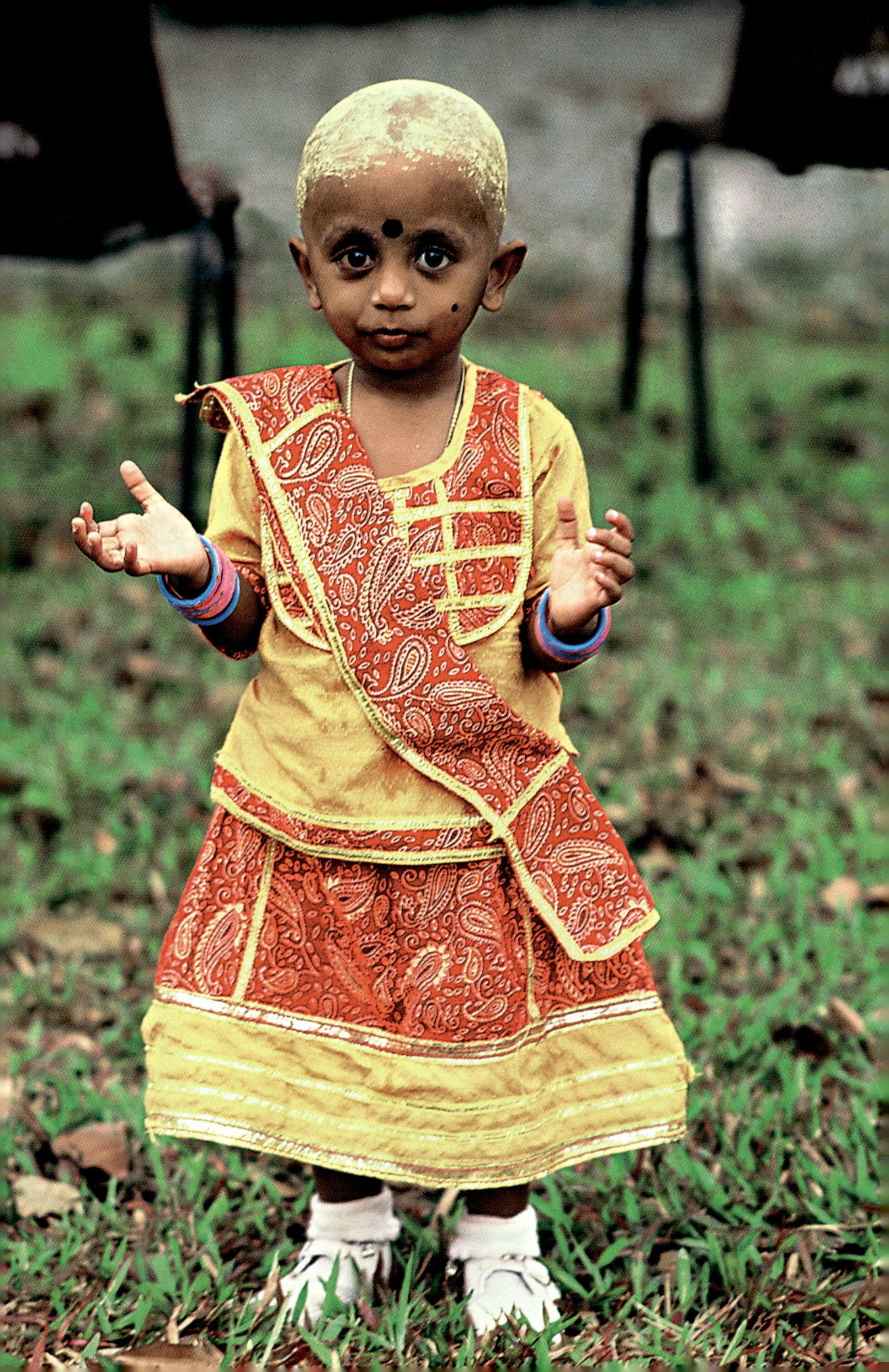

意 吉

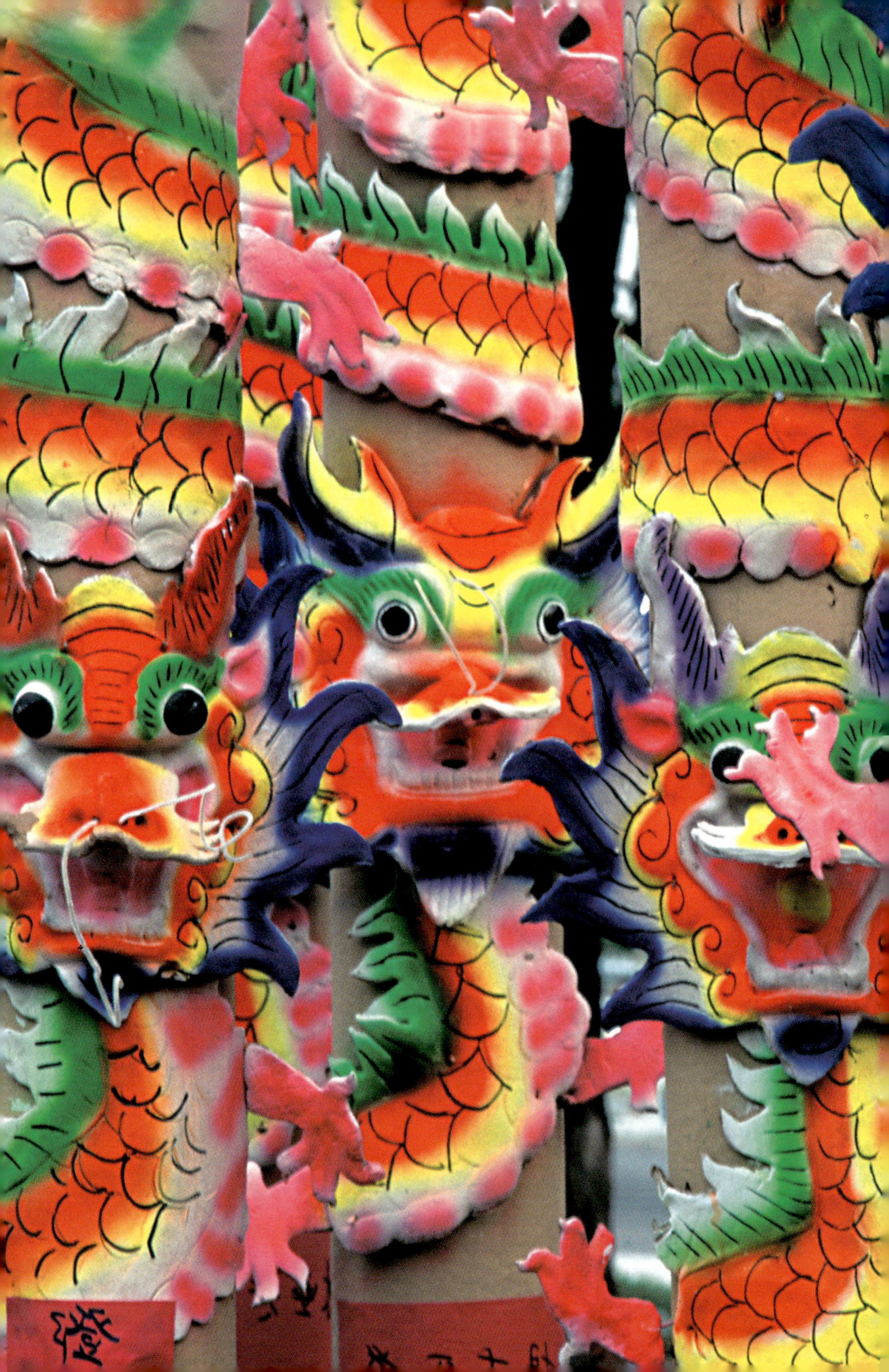

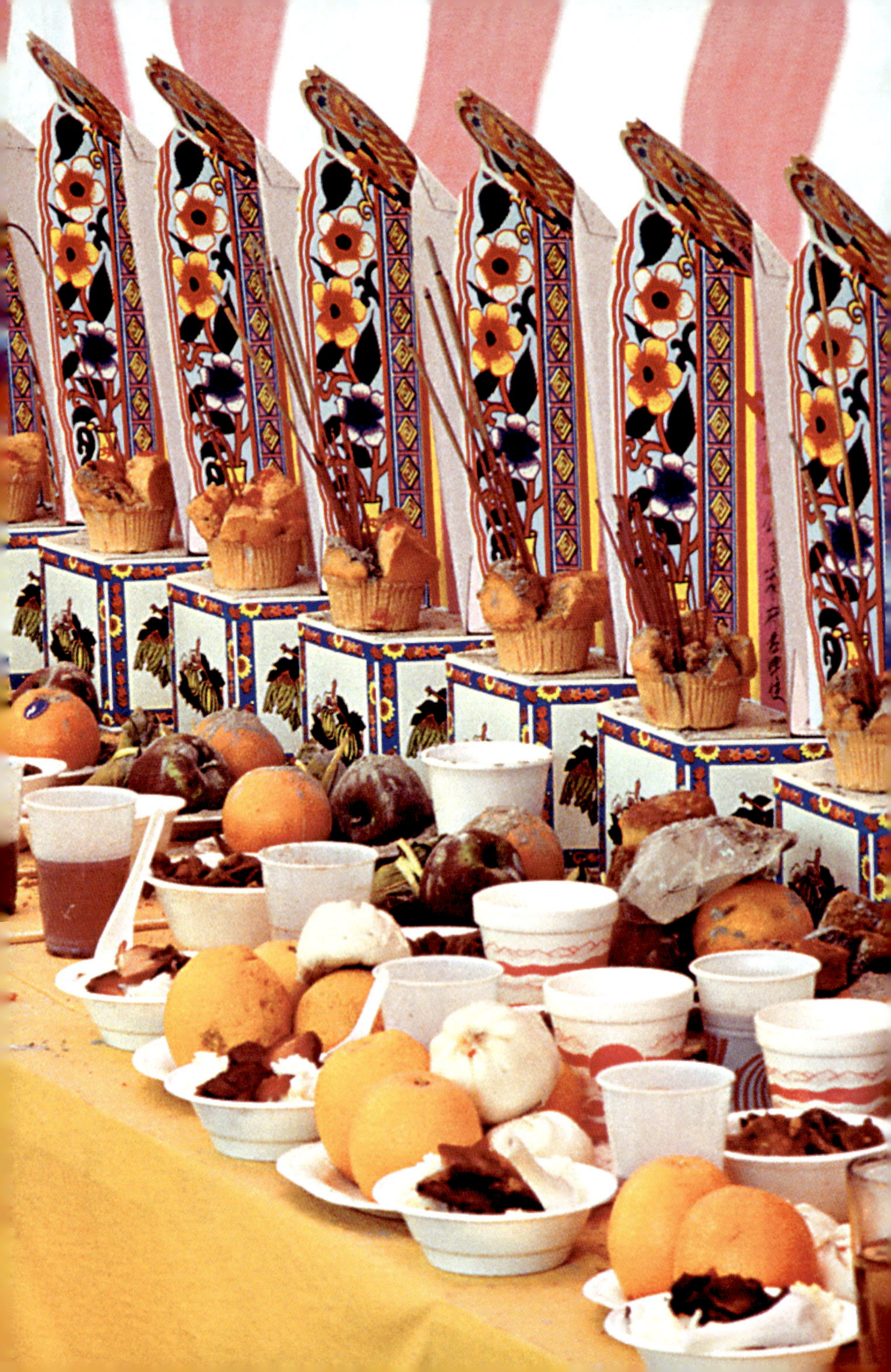

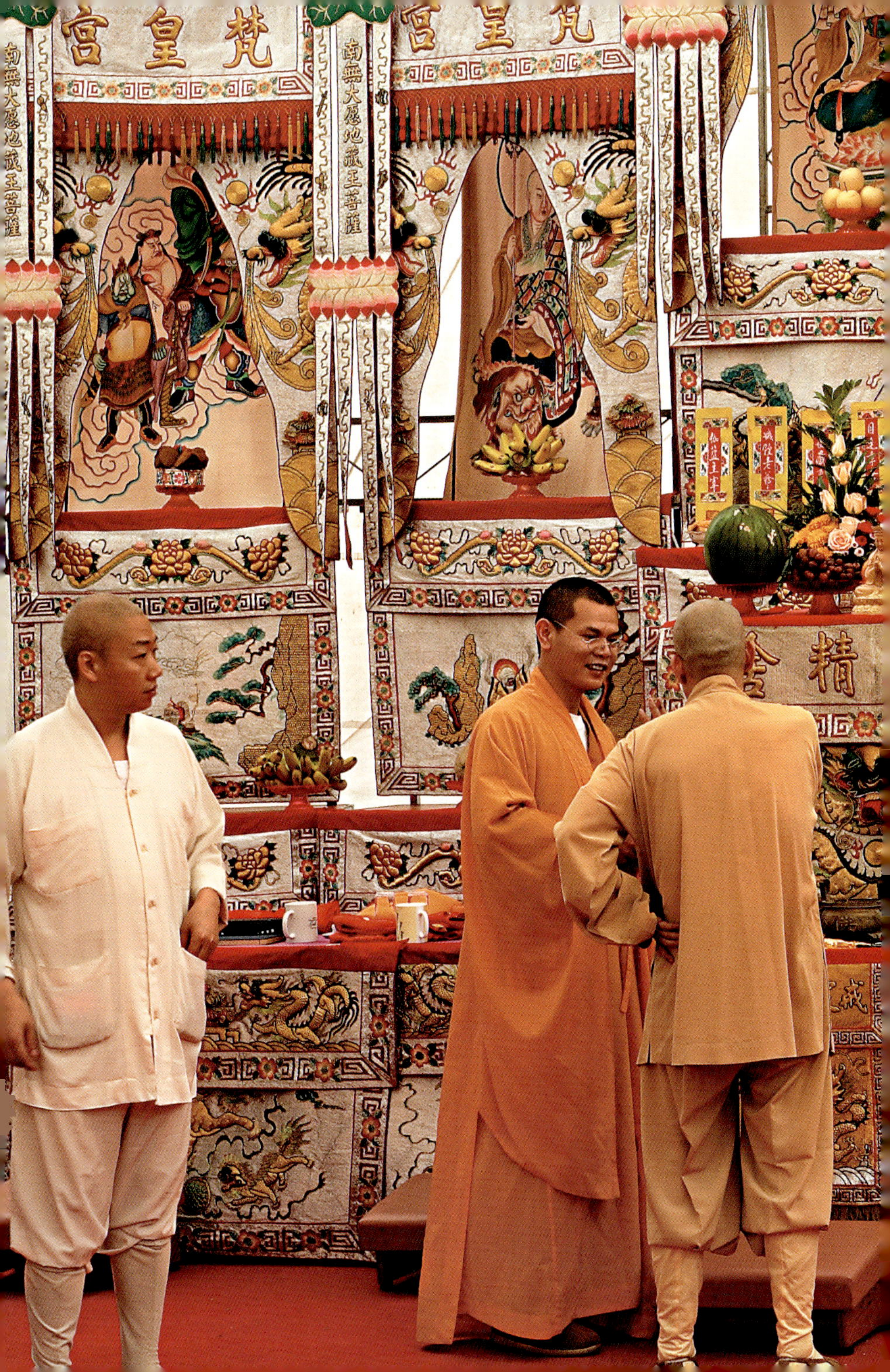

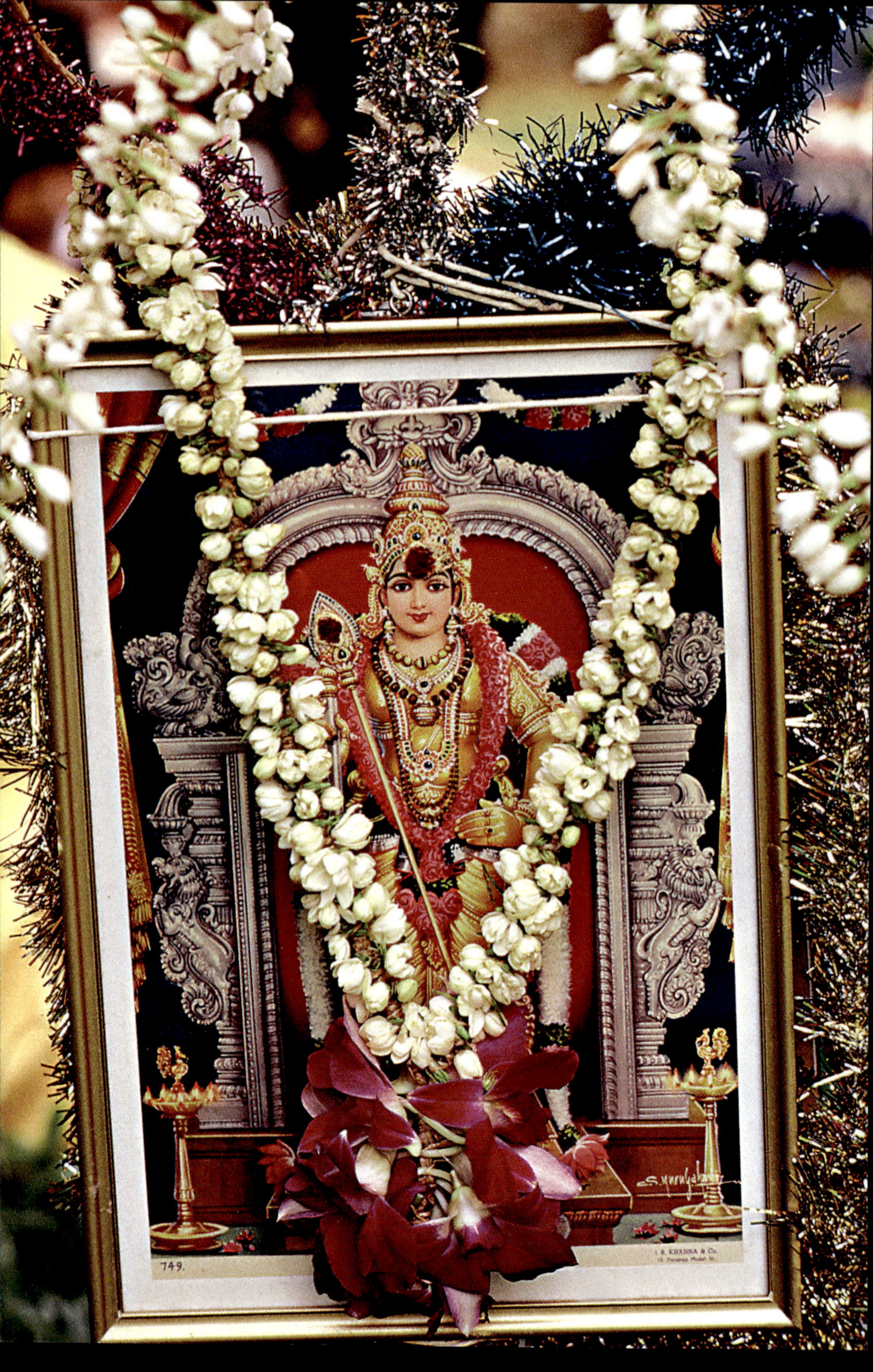
749
KHANNA & Co.

神光普照

迎祥

天官賜

天降財源
神賜安康寧

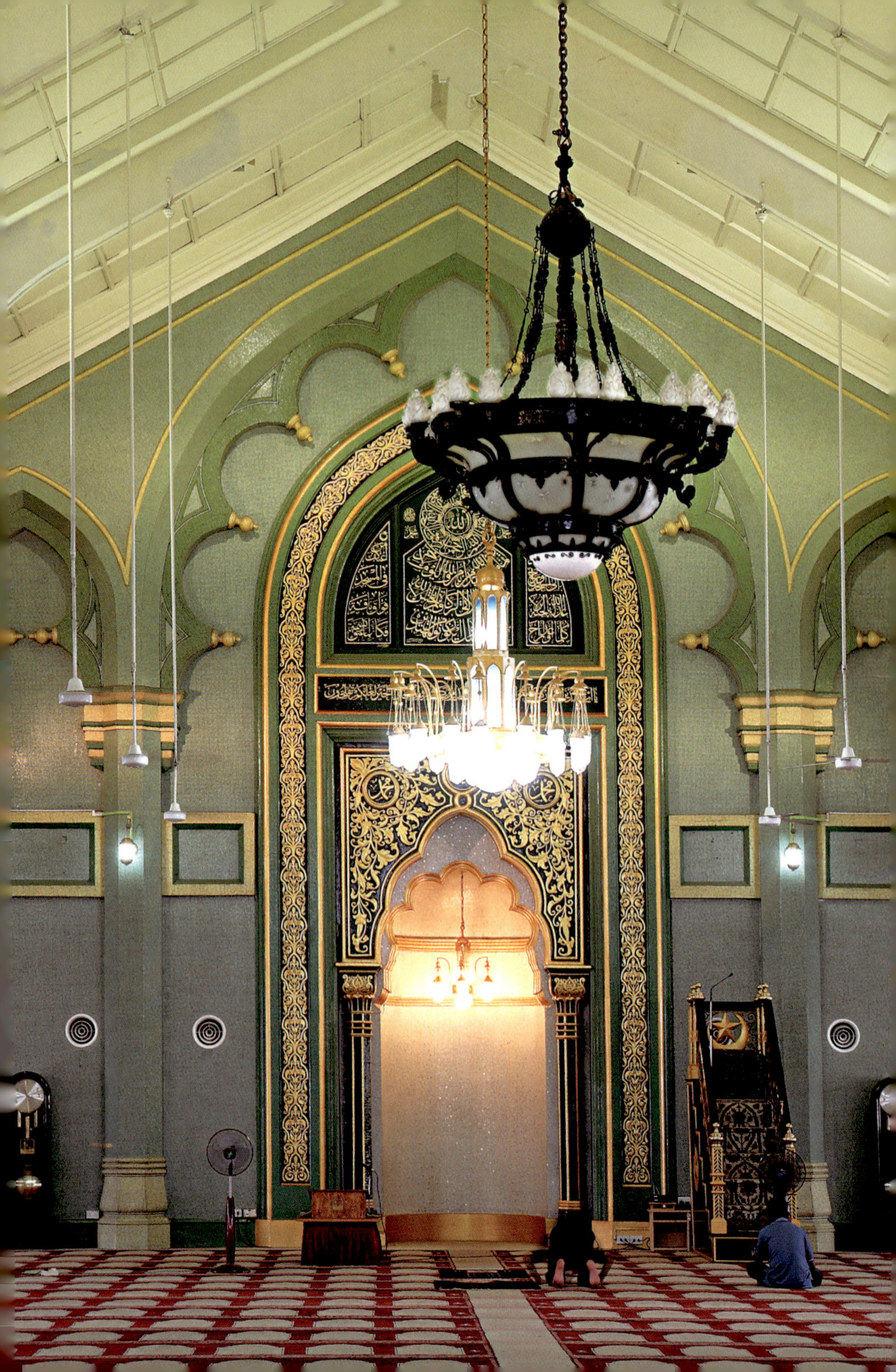

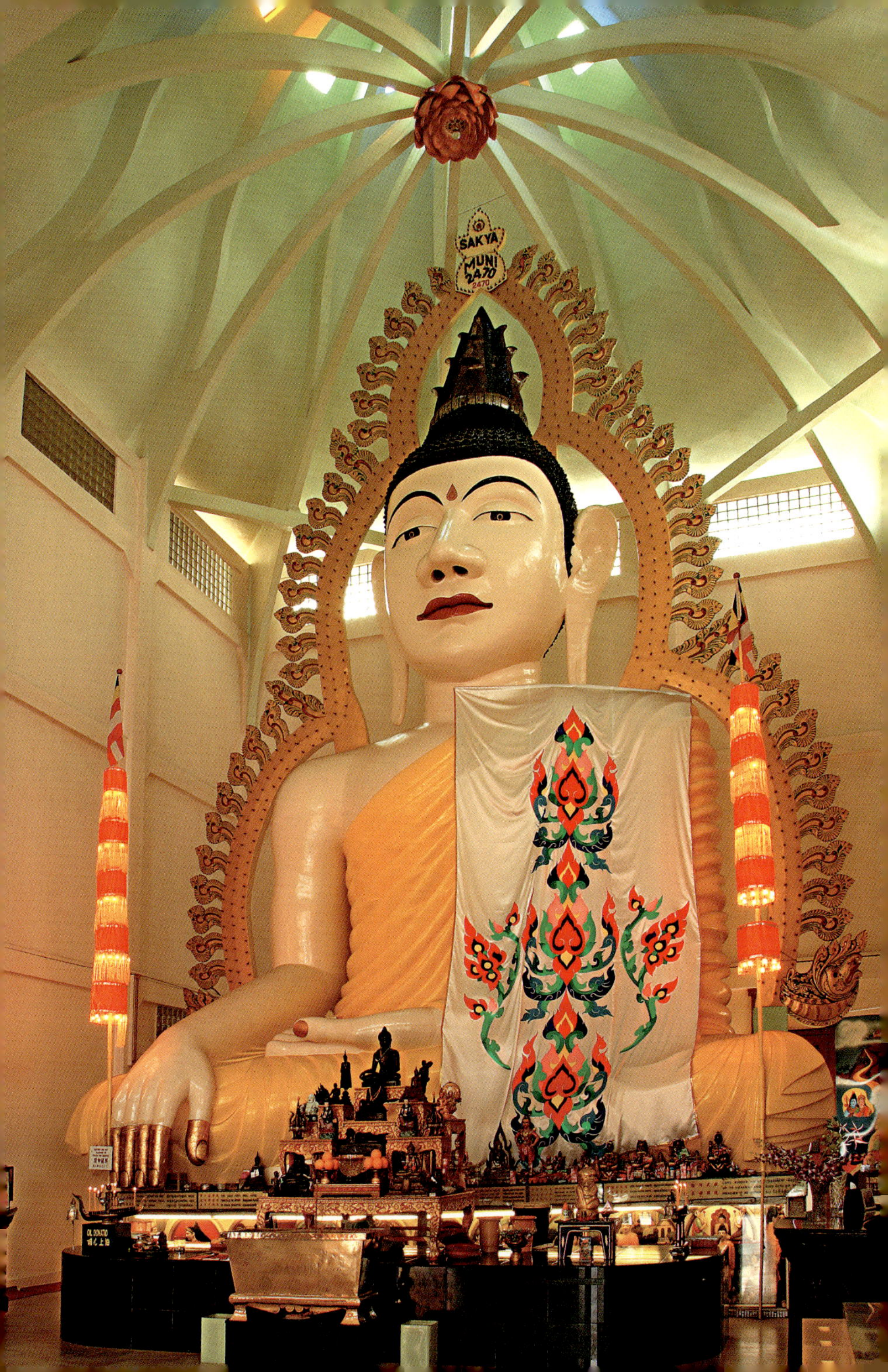
SAKYA
MUNI
2470
2470

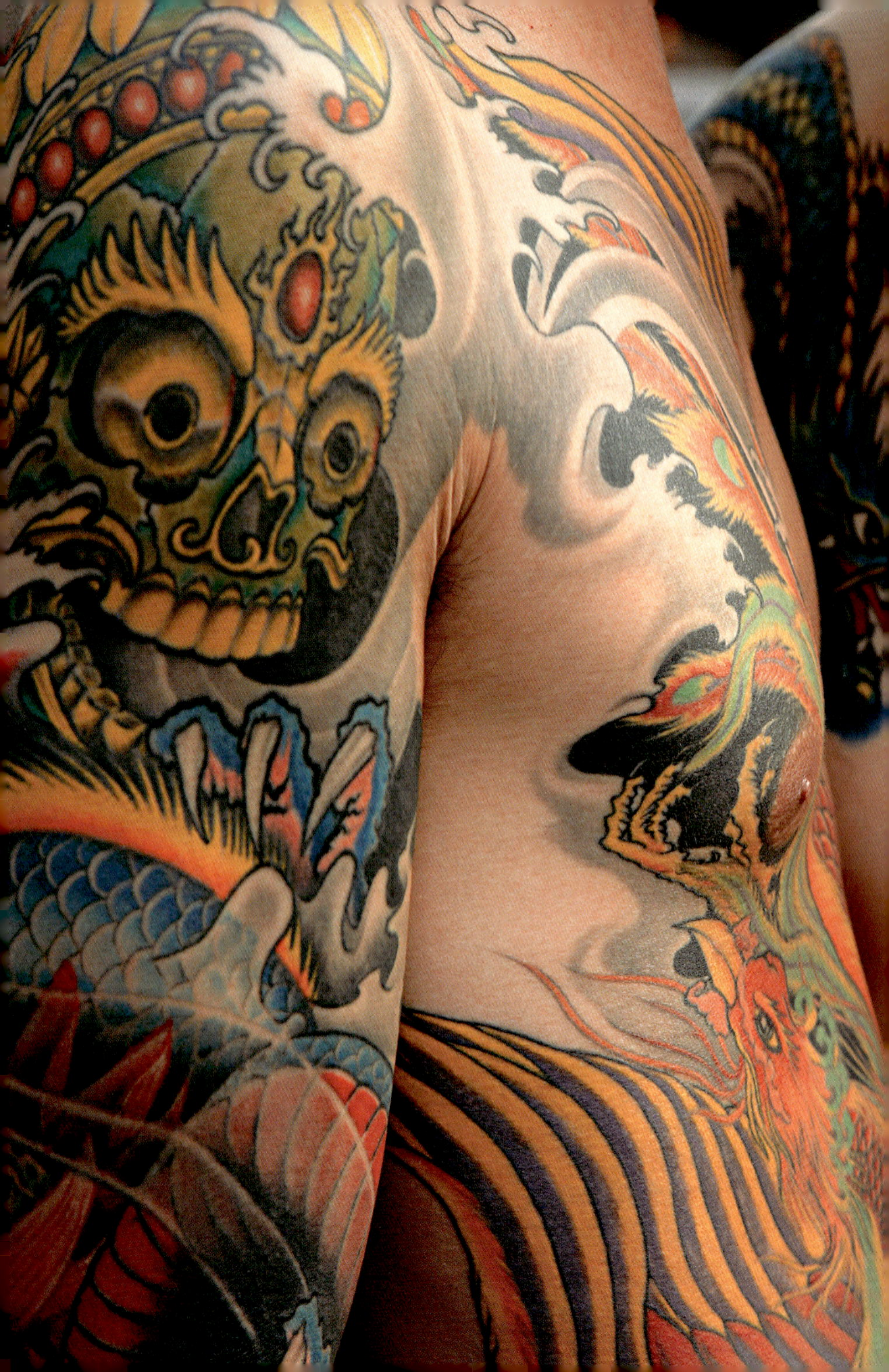

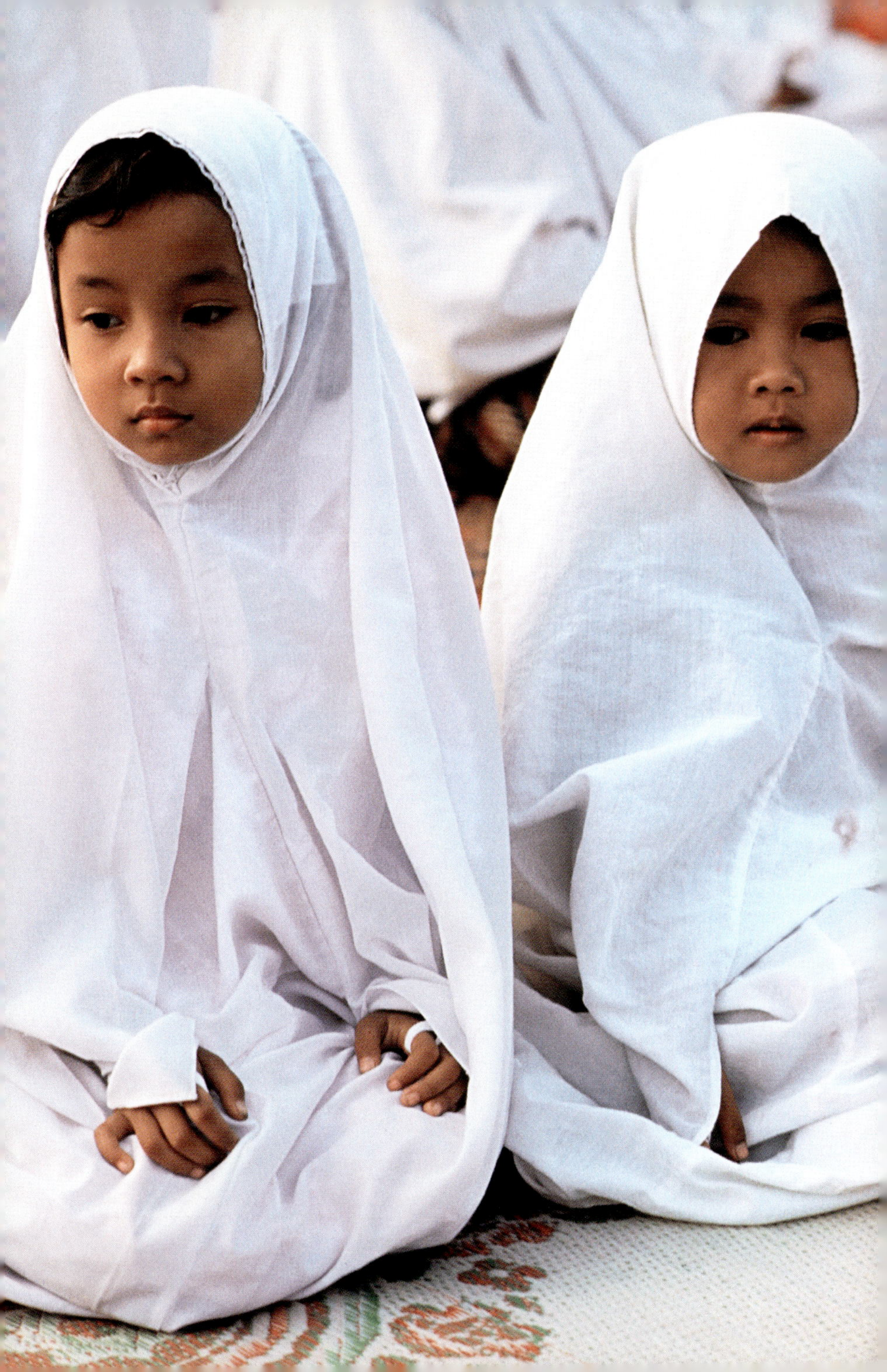

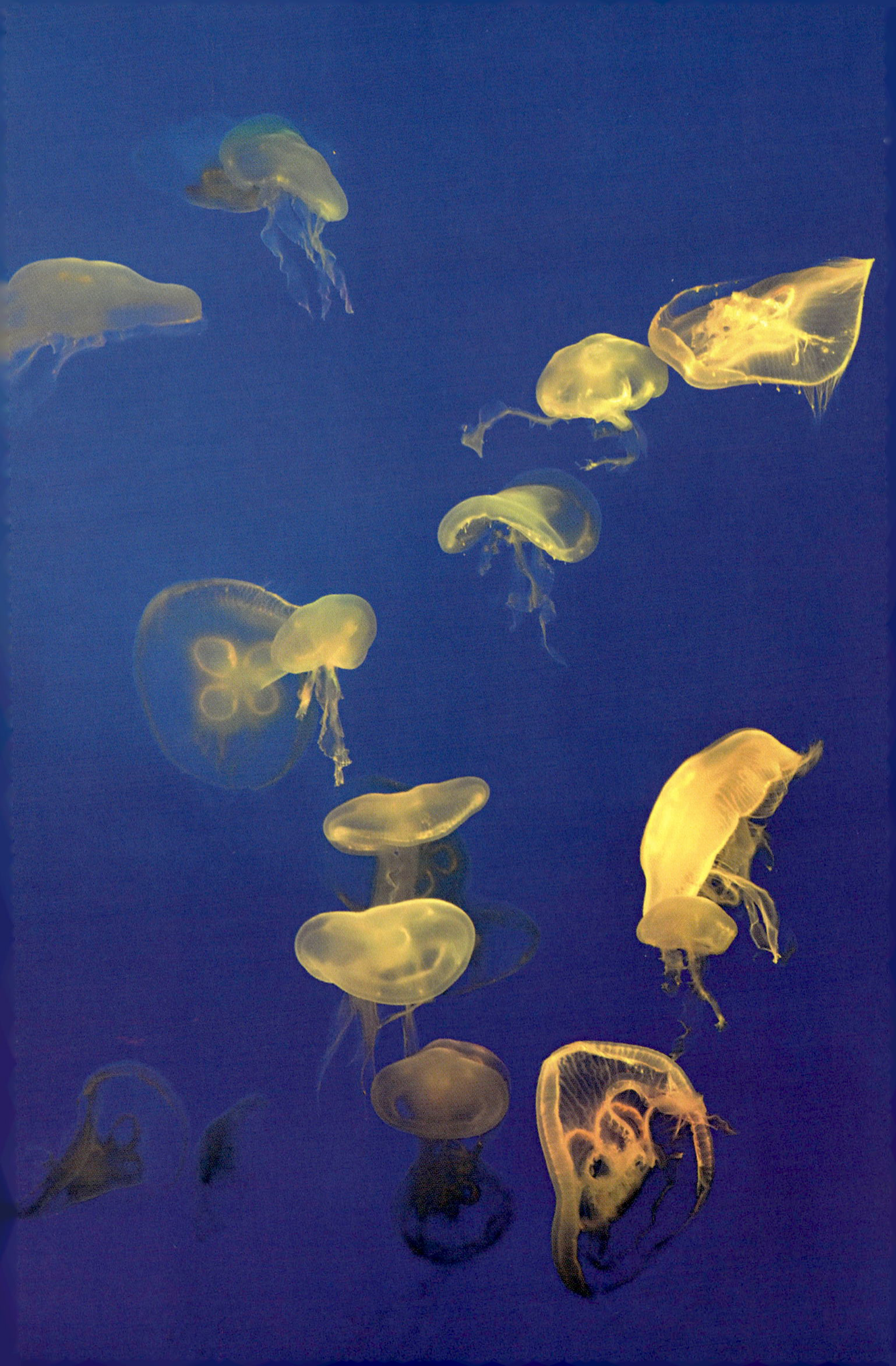

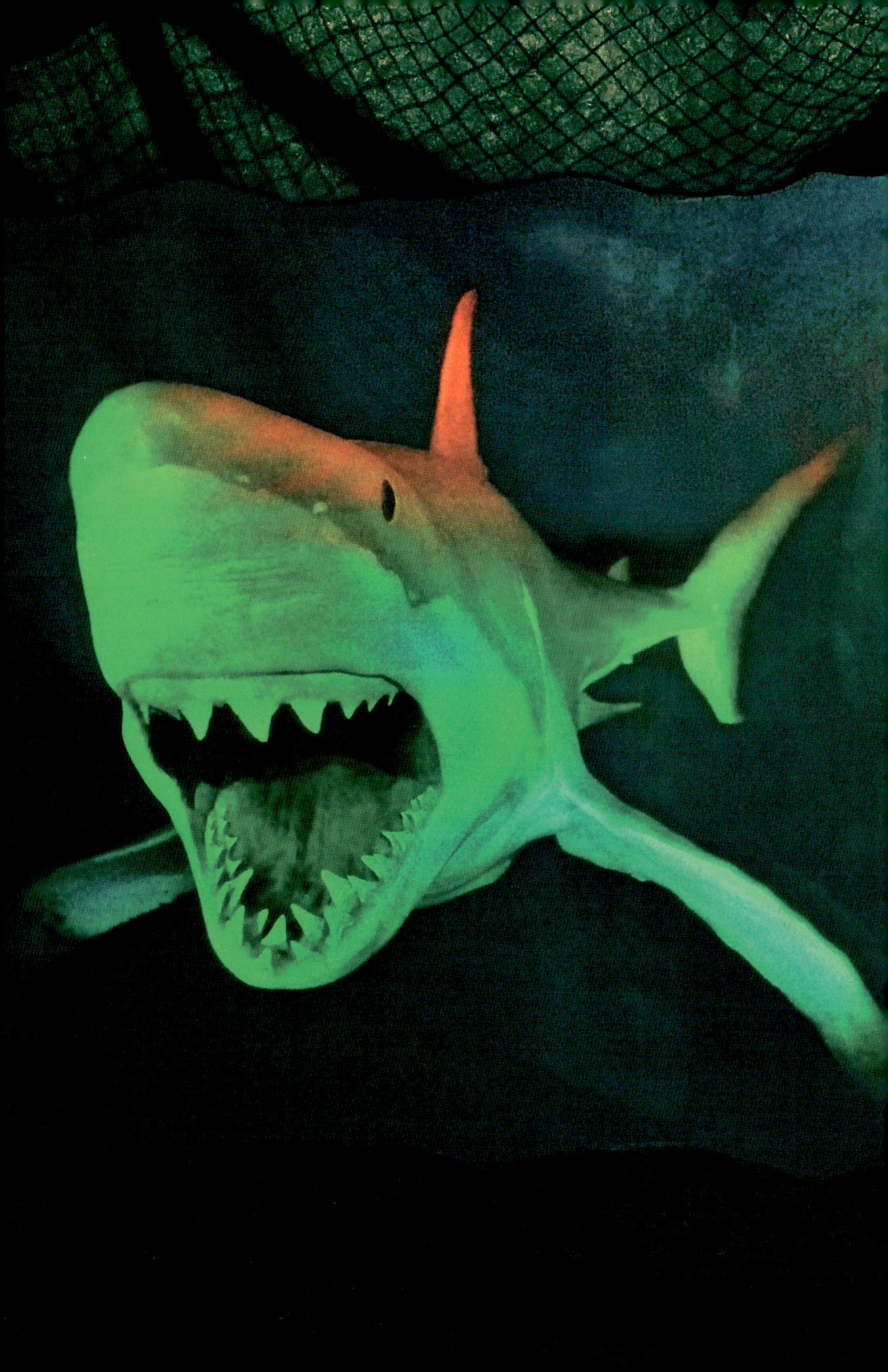

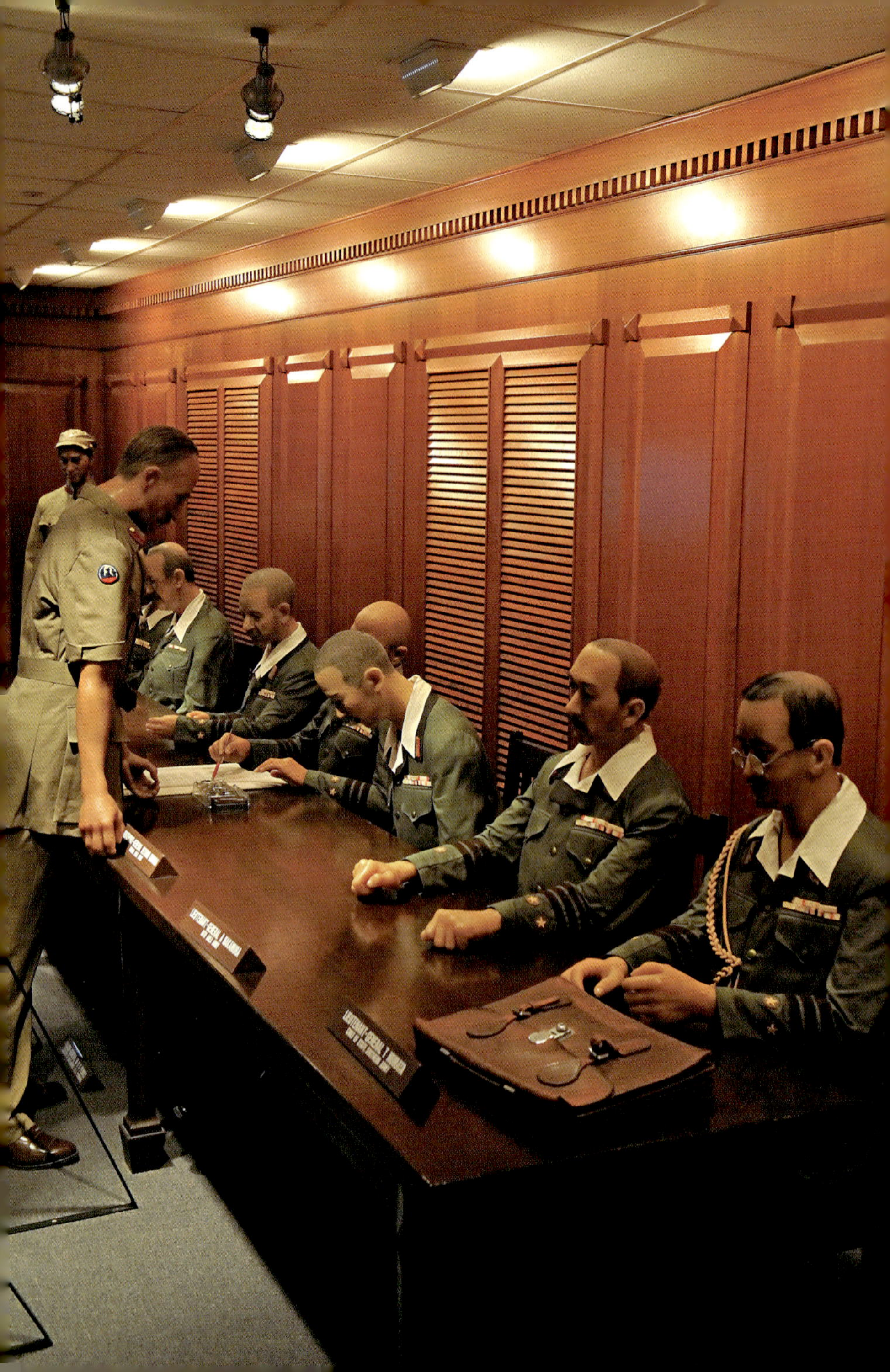
LIEUTENANT-GENERAL
LIEUTENANT-GENERAL

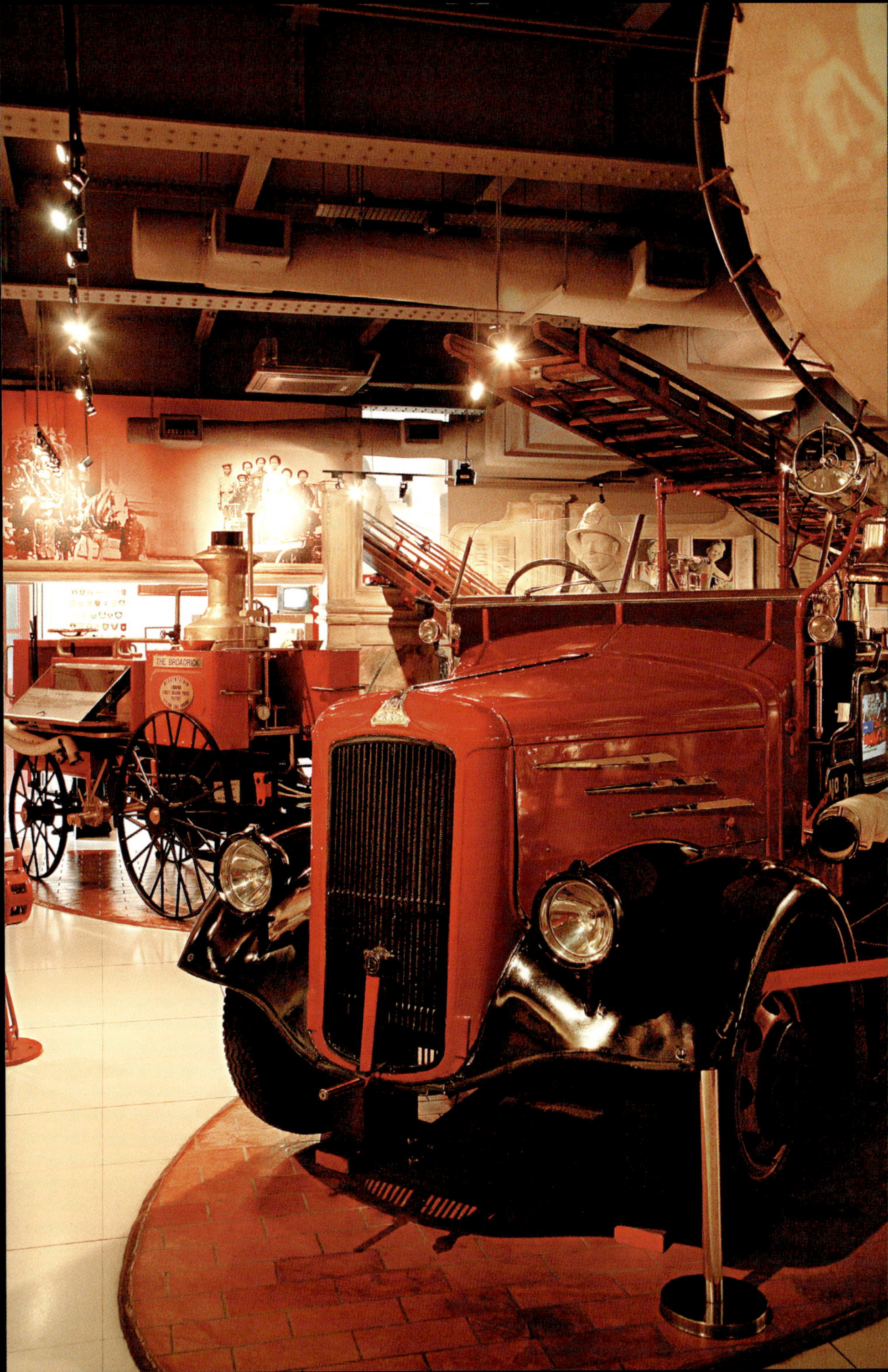
THE BROADRICK

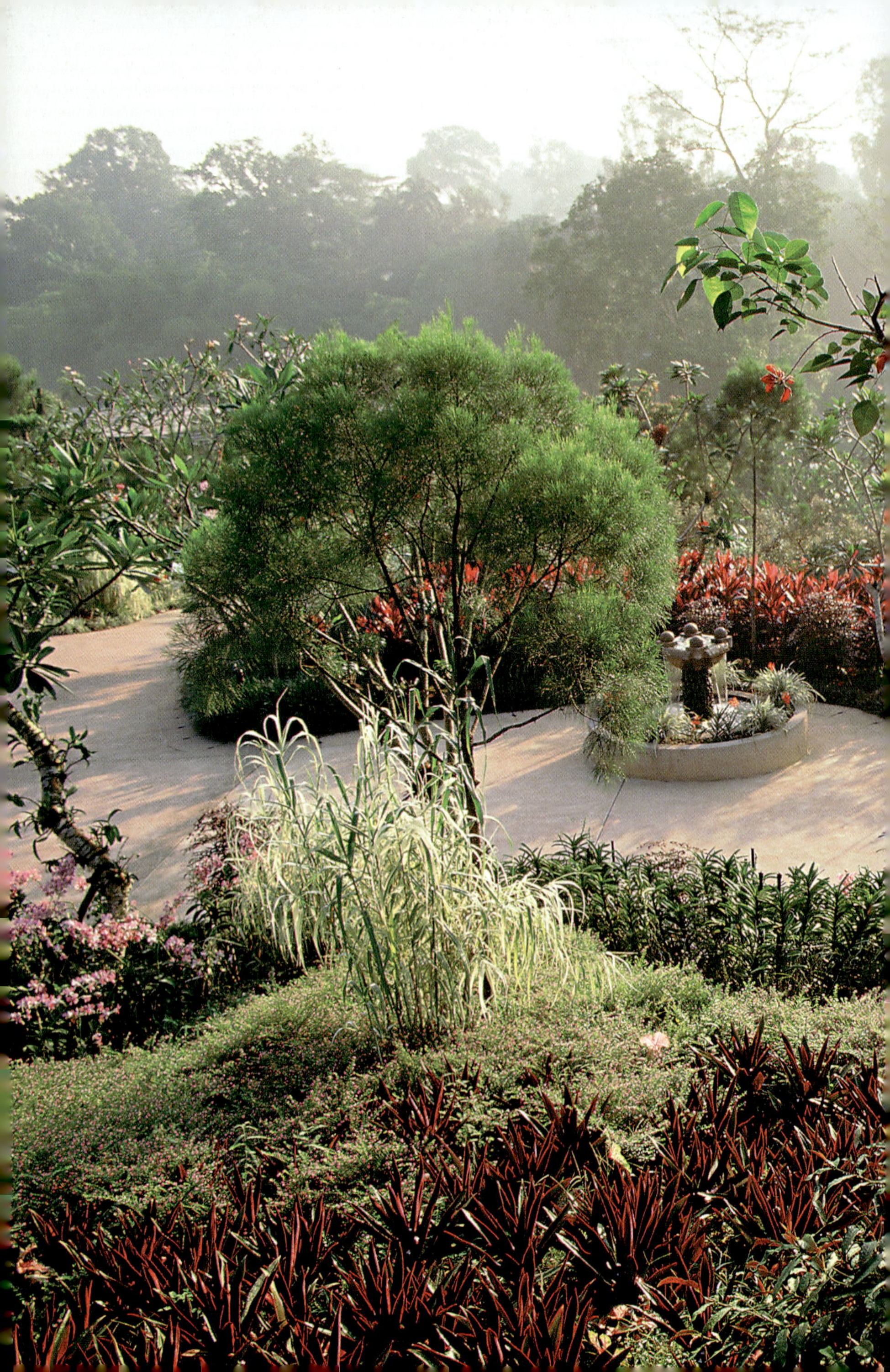

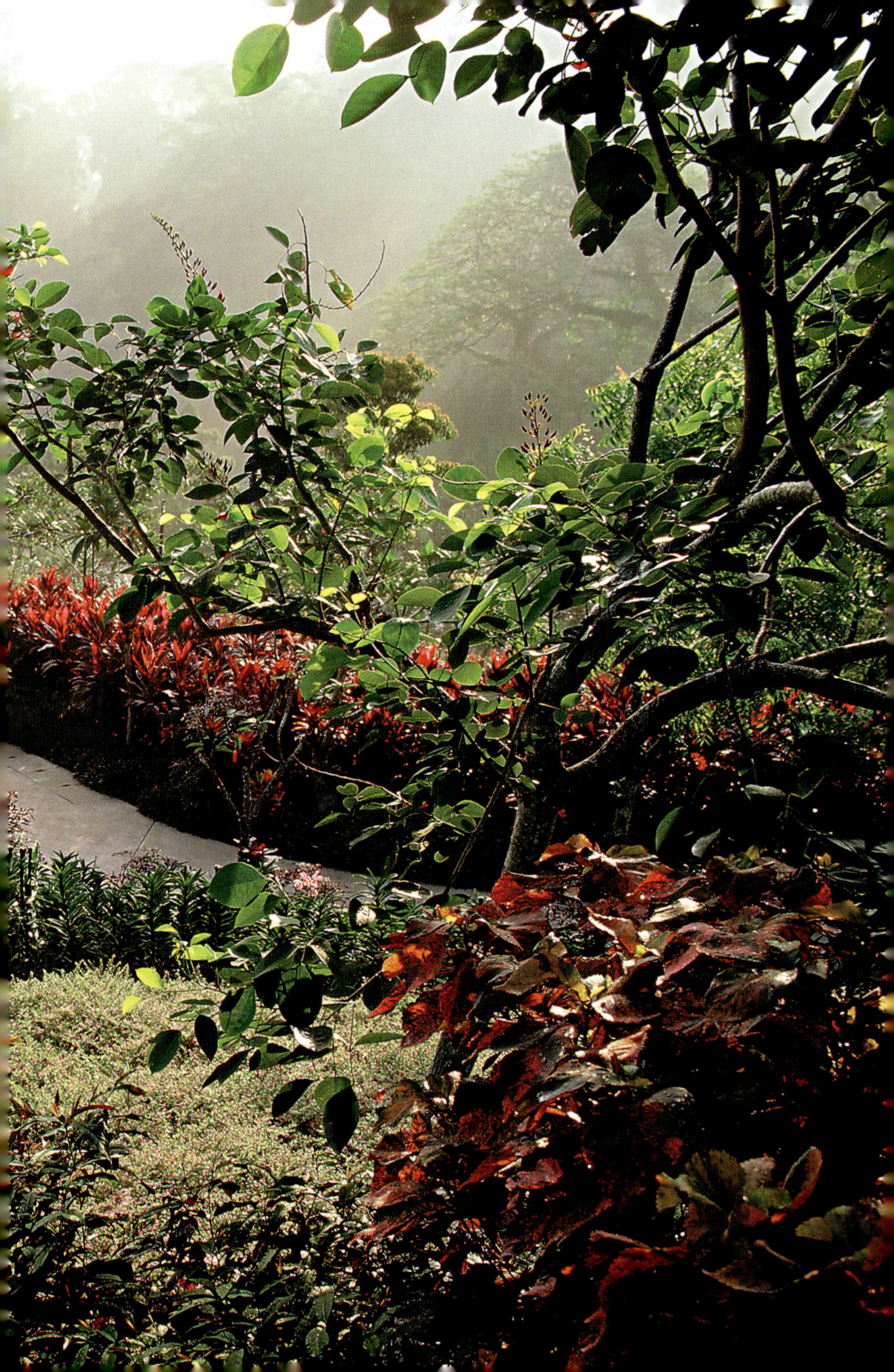

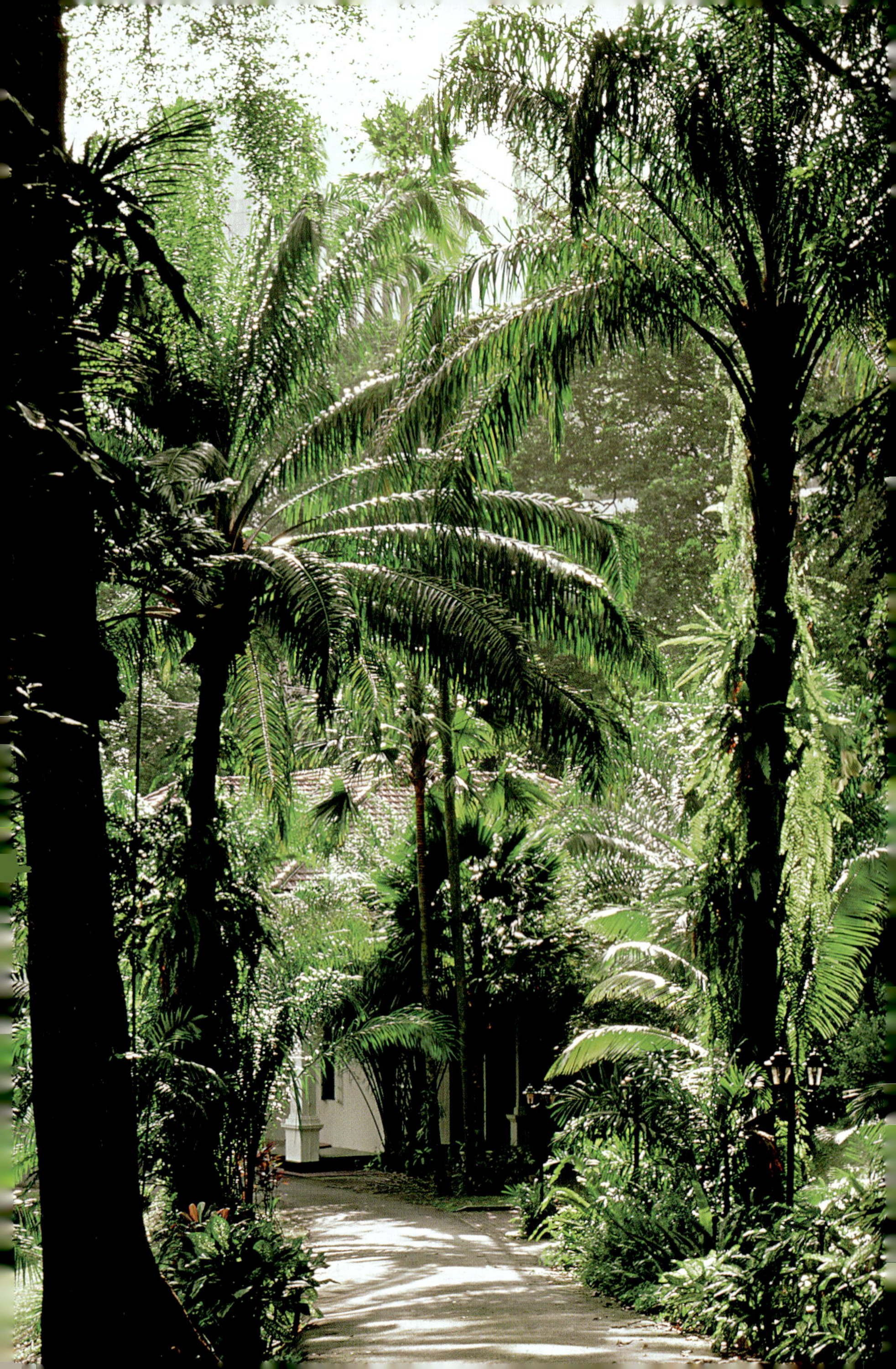

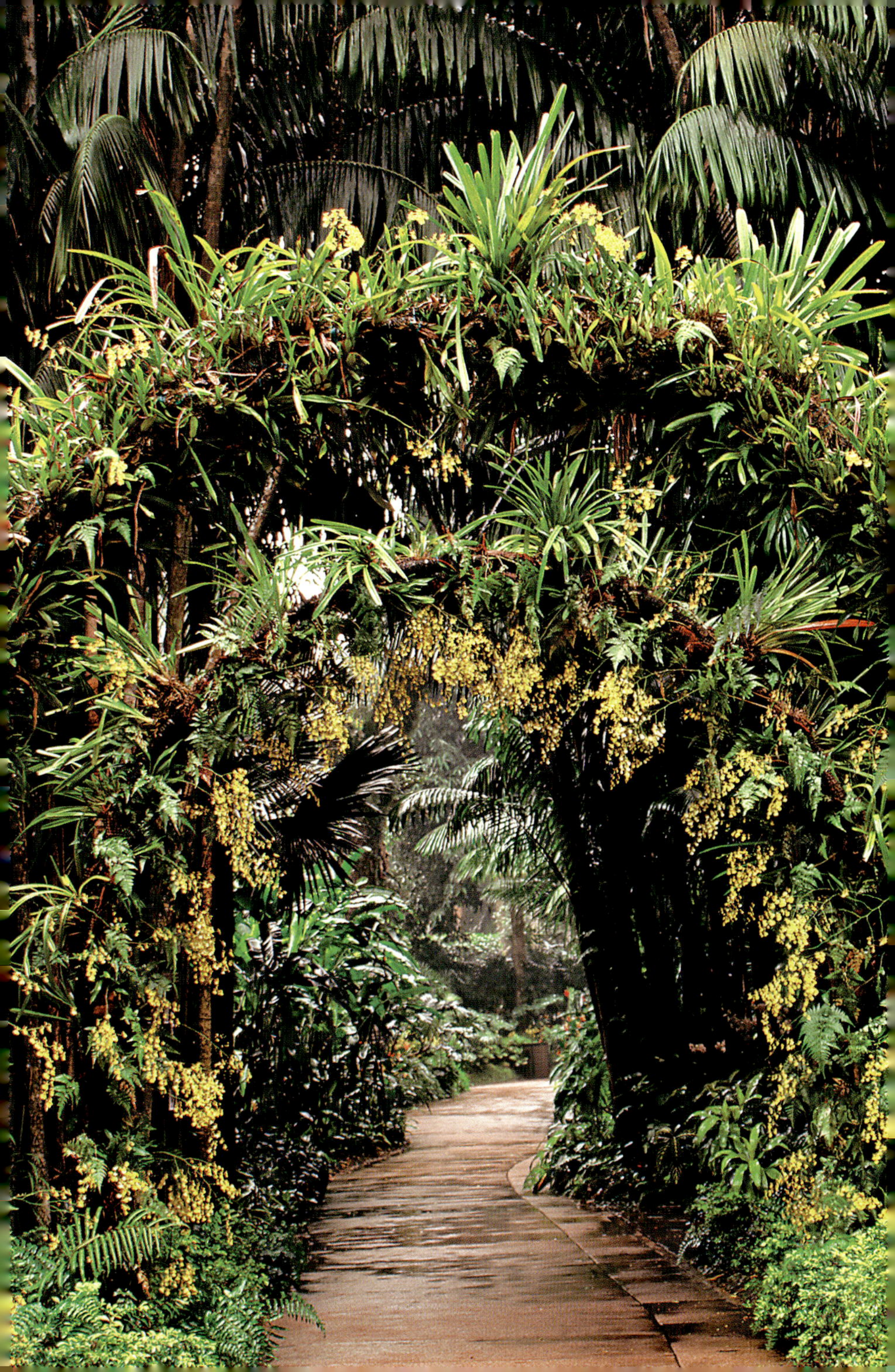

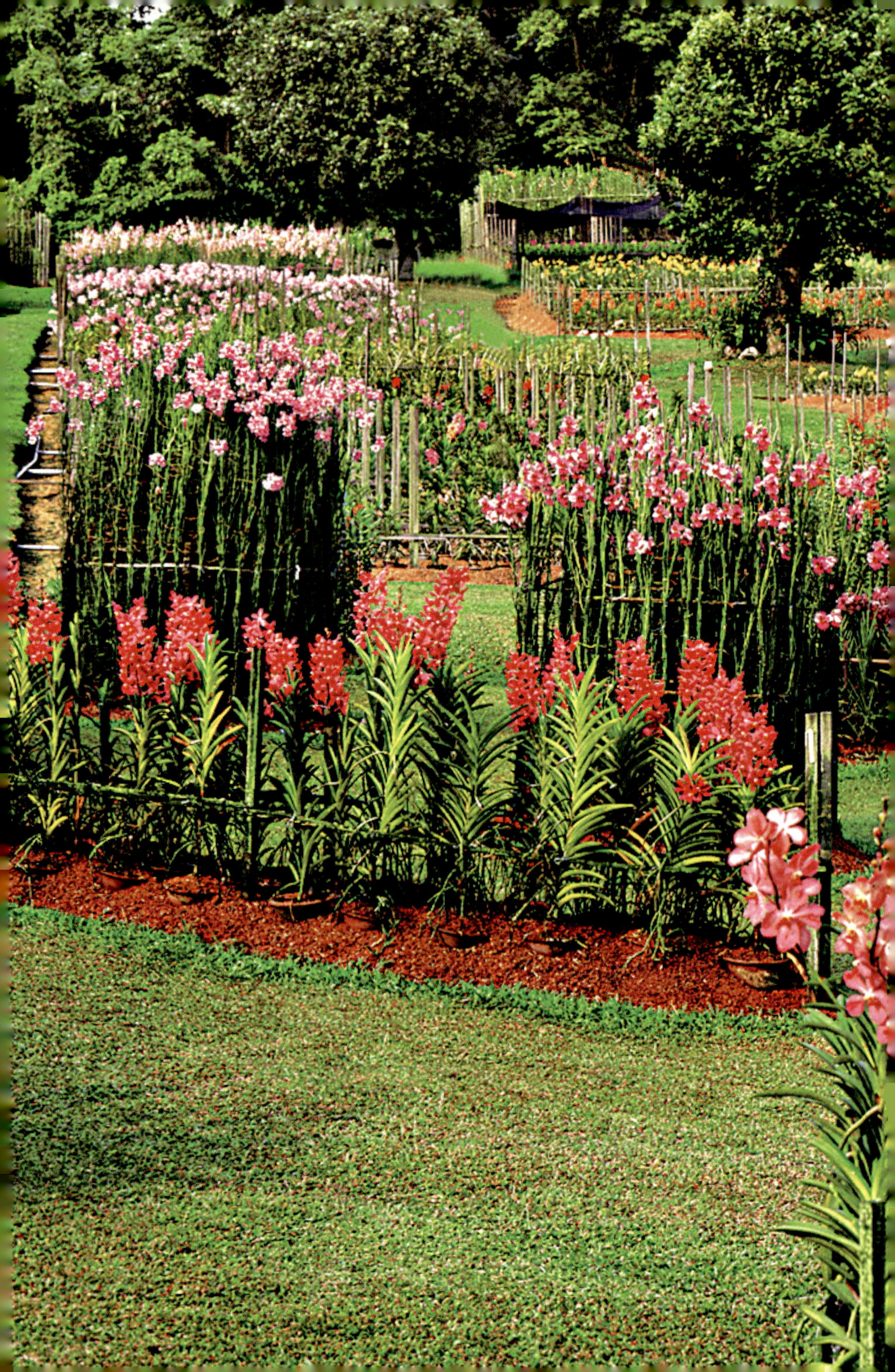

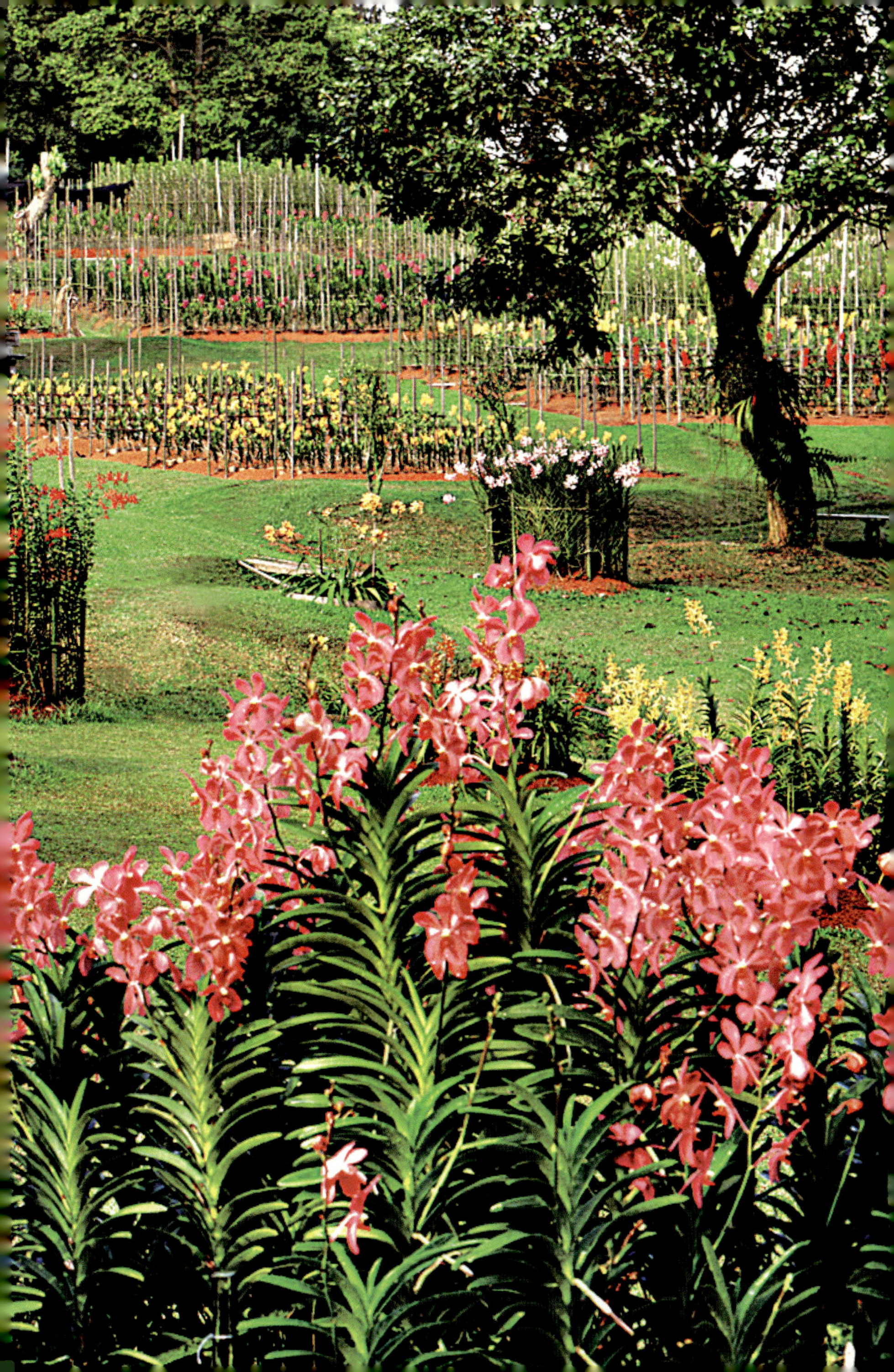

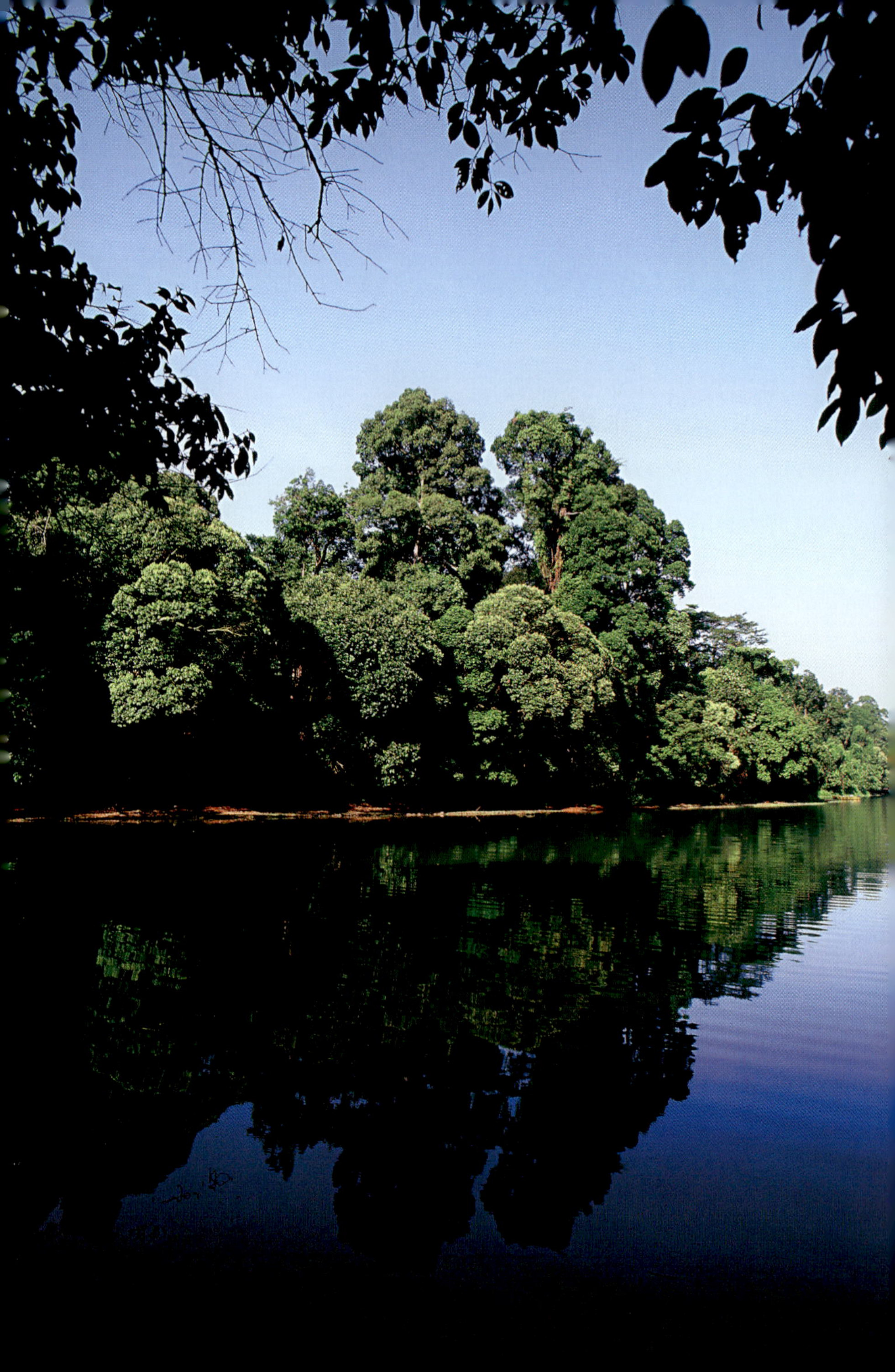

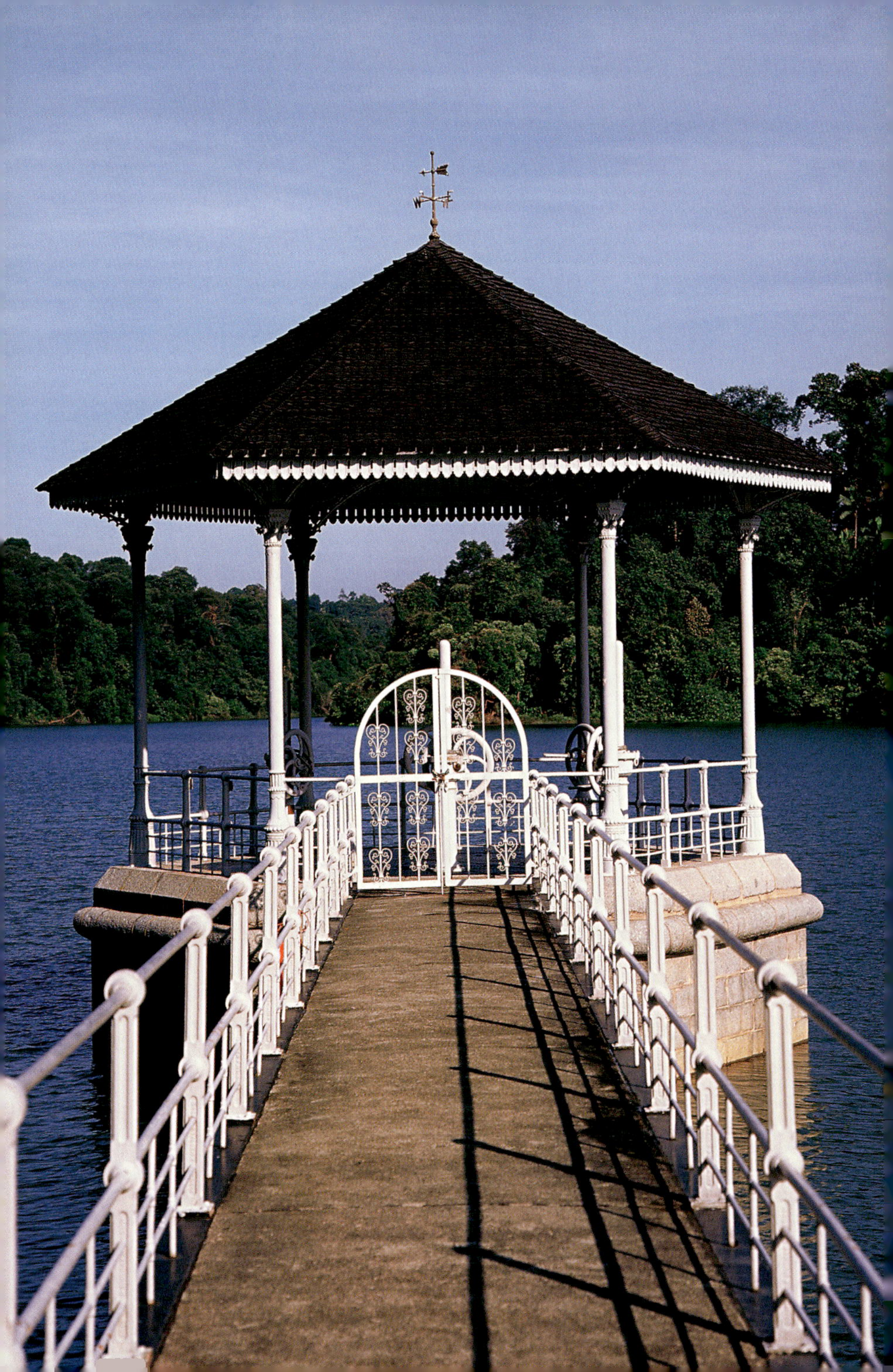

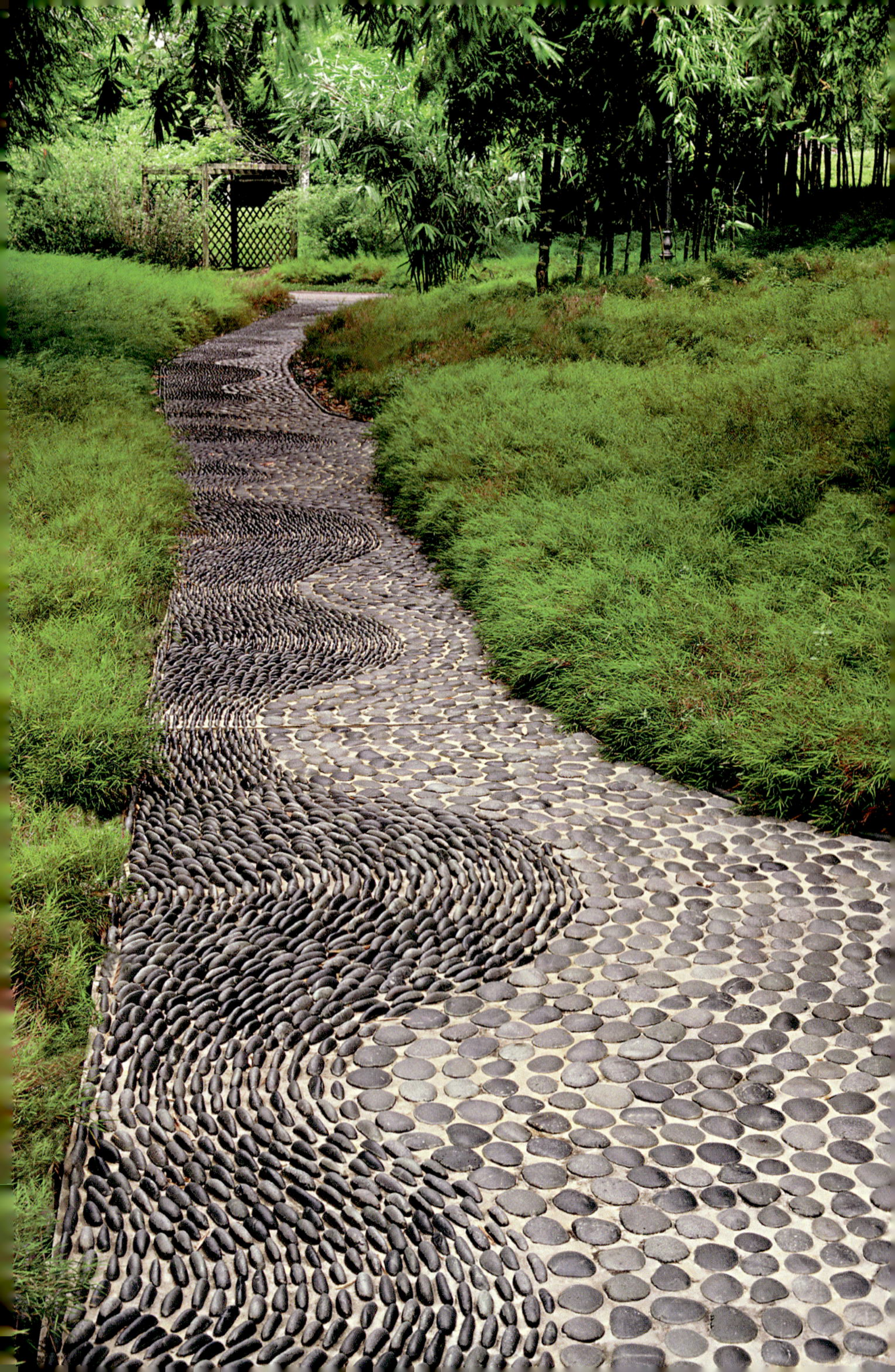

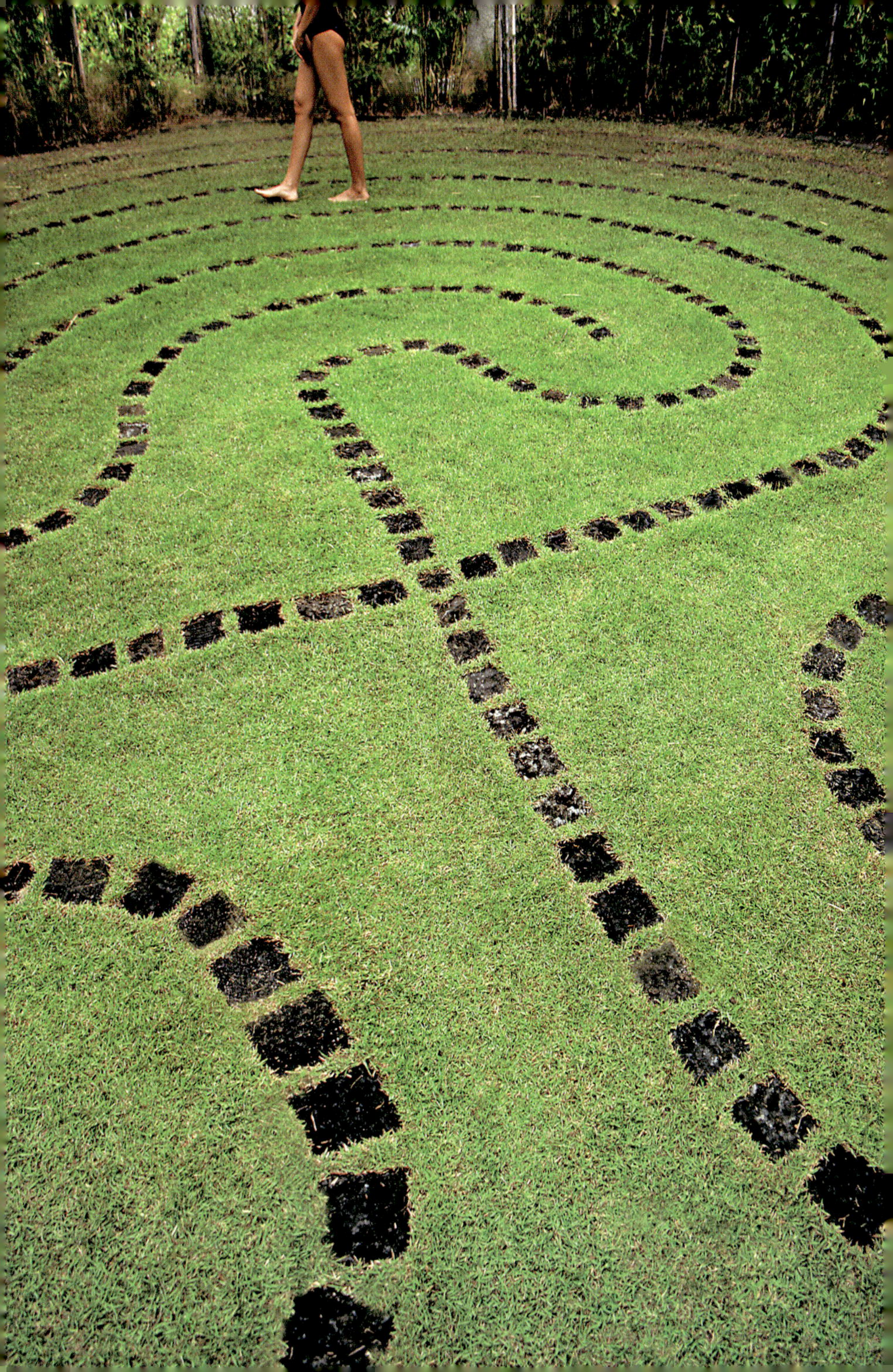

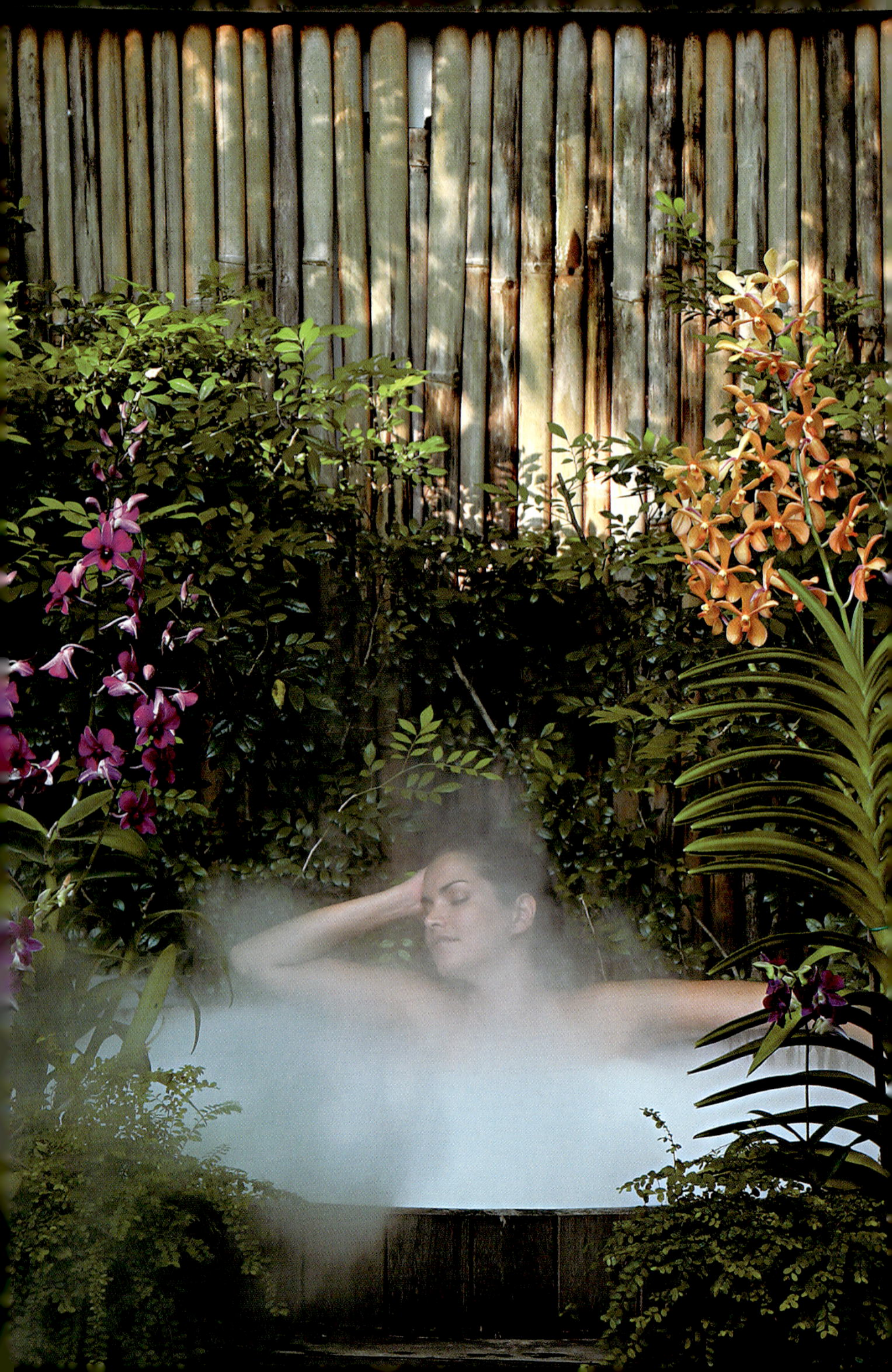

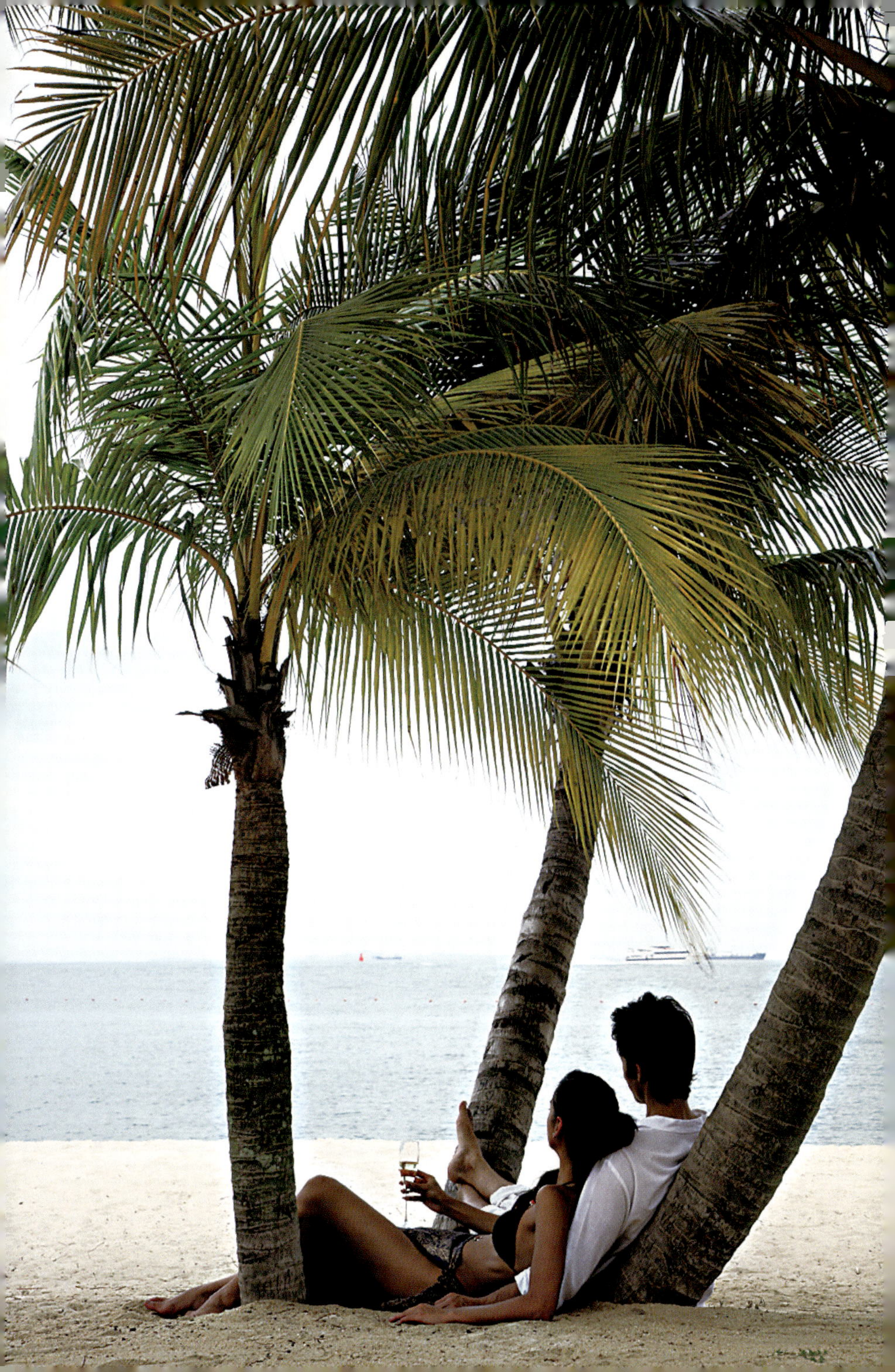

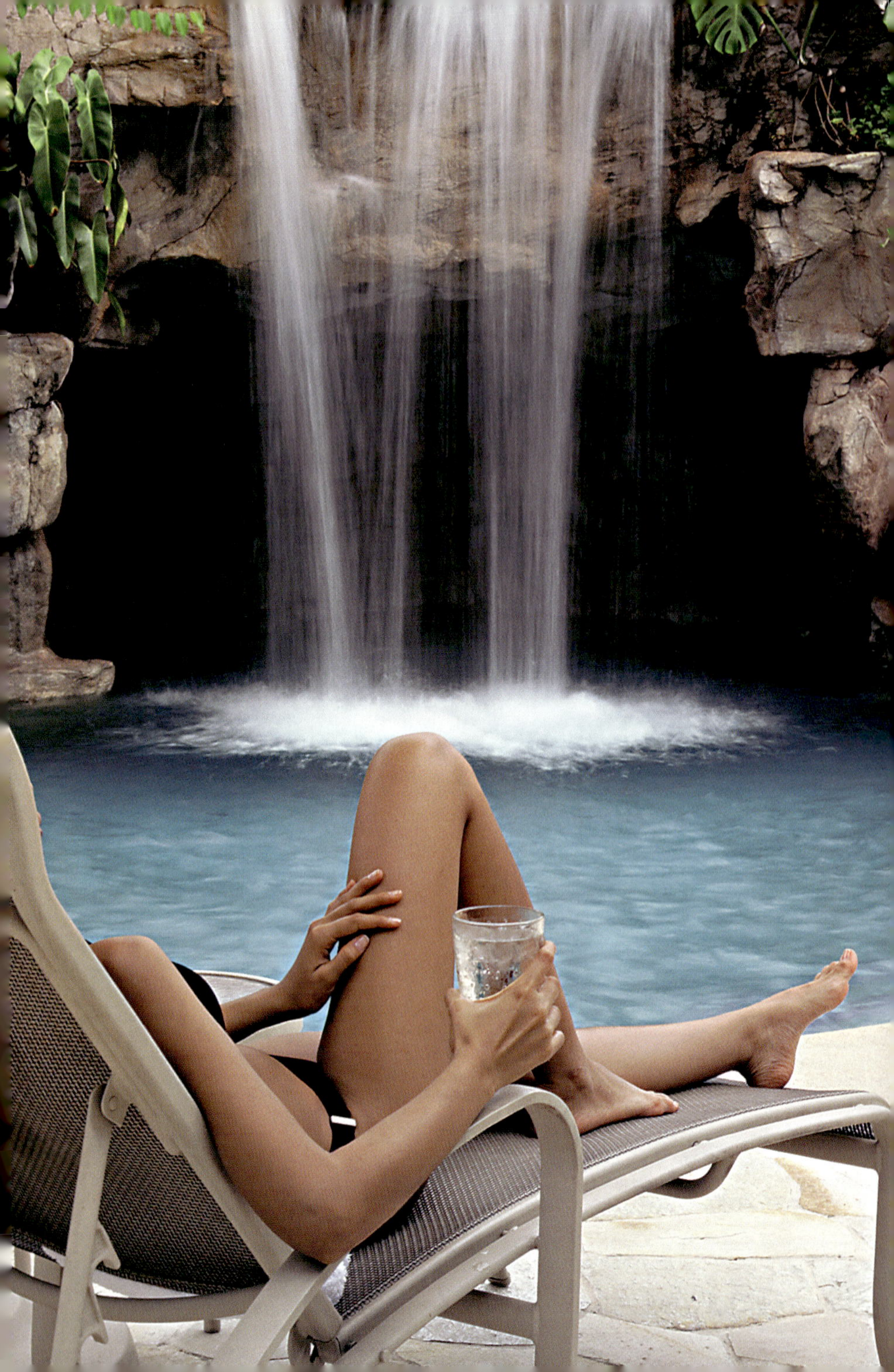

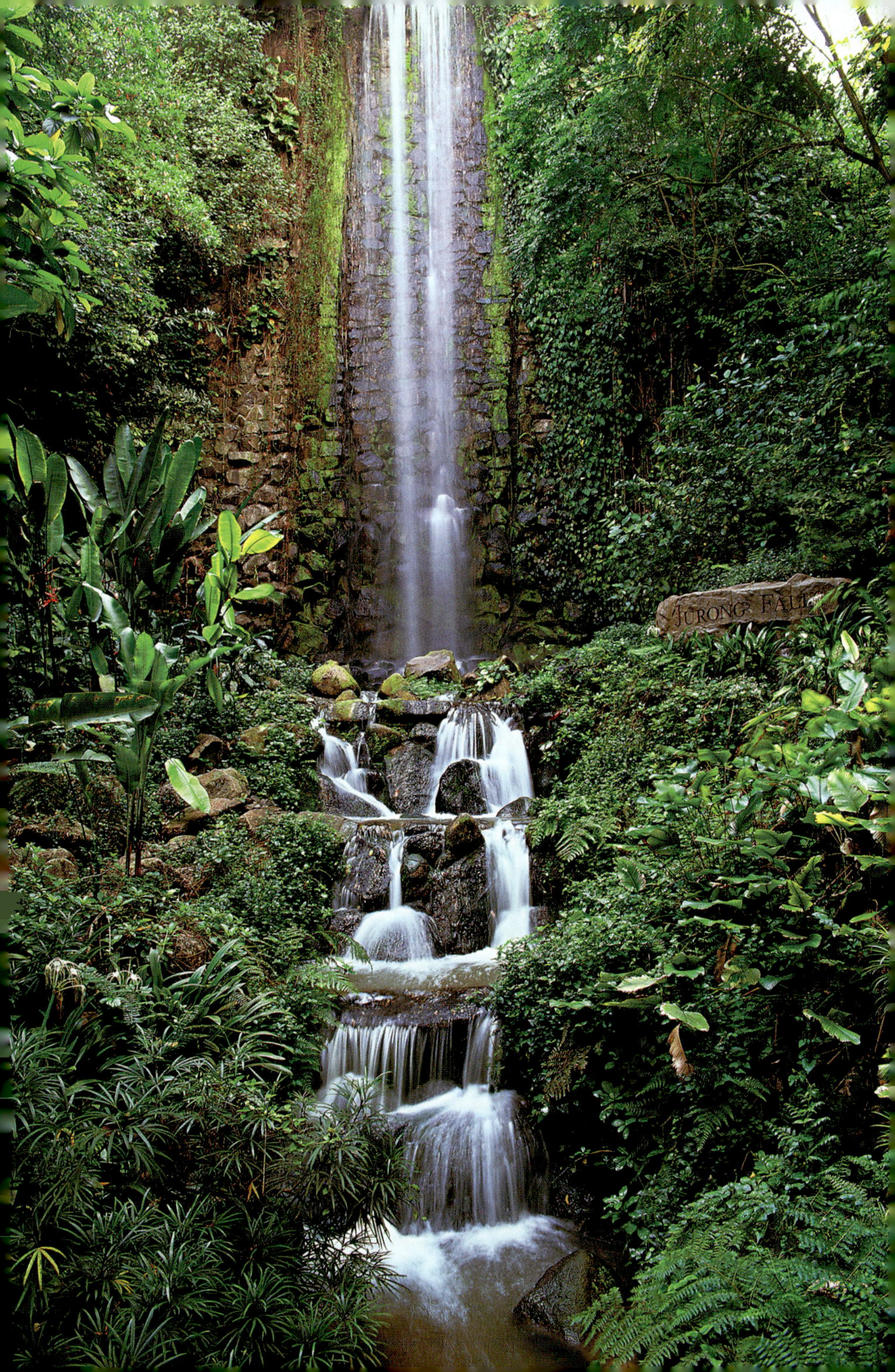
JURONG

10 An oil painting by artist A L Watson c. 1910 depicting a view of the Esplanade, a fashionable spot to take an evening stroll in colonial times. Today, much of this beach-front has been reclaimed for further development.

12–13 Views of Singapore town in 1973. On left are shophouses on Bugis Street, once famous, or infamous, as a gathering place for transexuals; on right, is the Singapore River with godowns and bumboats at Boat Quay.

14–15 1992 preceded the city-state's urban restoration programme. Here, Spottiswoode Park and Ann Siang Hill shophouses retain their colours (just!) and character, but are sadly decaying structurally. The one on right is now rebuilt.

16 Chinatown is home to many a memorabilia store, selling anything from tourist tat to antiques and artifacts. This Club Street emporium specialises in an eclectic mix of goods: old street signs, fading photos and wall clocks.

18–19 Tradition runs deep even in today's Chinese culture: here we see the elaborate inner courtyard of the Nanyang Sacred Union temple, founded in the 1930s, and a photo of an elderly Chinese man in funeral dress (1904).

20–21 When Stamford Raffles designed Chinatown, he stipulated that shophouses be fronted by a covered walkway not exceeding five feet in width. Here are two "five foot ways" on Blair and Duxton Roads.

22 Located between the docks and town, Tanjong Pagar Road has seen many incarnations: today, it's a hub of offices, restaurants and bridal attire shops. In the past, it was home to thousands of Chinese and Indian dock workers.

24–25 Emerald Hill and Blair Road are two fine examples of "gazetted" shophouse enclaves where historic preservation takes precedence over material development. Note the superb tiles on left and stucco detailing on right.

26 The Berjaya Duxton Hotel, aka the Duxton on Duxton Road, was one of Singapore's first boutique hotels when it opened its doors in the early 1990s. Made up from a row of converted shophouses, it houses elegant lodgings.

28–29 Typical Asian marble tables are accompanied by bentwood chairs (left) and rattan loungers (right) in a coffeehouse and residential terrace respectively. High ceilings, natural ventilation and tiled floors keep such spaces cool in the tropics.

30–31 Western and Asian styles are seen in the tiled scenes from Cantonese opera on the Majestic Theatre's facade and wall panels of Malay scenes in the Singapore Railway Station. Both are great examples of tropical deco.

32–33 Diversity in unity sums up this scenario: Imposing facades of the Sultan Mosque in Kampung Glam (left) and a Frank Brewer designed home inspired by the Arts and Crafts Movement (c. 1920s in Ridout Road).

34–35 Old colonial style doesn't go out of style in Singapore, despite many decades of independence: Dine in splendour in the Tiffin Room at Raffles Hotel, or cadge a coffee at the British Embassy residence in Nassim Road.

36–37 Eclectic East meets West in many a domestic interior: Buddhist statuary and Chinese cabinet in a living room on left and hand-painted wallpaper, English carpets and faux Chippendale furniture in the Duxton on right.

38–39 Modernist bold and beautiful are equally visible: On left, a table at the Cliff, a fine-dining restaurant designed by Yasuhiro Koichi, and, on right, a residential interior with Zhu Wei's impactful painting and Canta chair.

40–41 Both Chinese and Malays believe that fish bring prosperity and luck into a home, so a gift of goldfish or carp isn't uncommon. Ablutions performed on right at this glass basin give views of an outside pool with koi.

42–43 In Chinese culture, the colour red symbolizes prosperity, happiness and luck. Be it in the form of a plastic chair with offerings to the gods or a modernist lacquerware table setting, it is a ubiquitous sight all around the island.

44–45 Luxe looks with a fashion-forward aesthetic aren't uncommon in hotels and residences. Here, a glamorous bathroom at the New Majestic Hotel and a pristine bedroom designed by Karina Zabihi in a private home.

46–47 Bright, airy windows, be they in a modernist skyscraper or an Emerald Hill home, let in light and views in equal measure. Furniture is in keeping with the general aesthetic: modern cavalier (left) and traditional wooden (right).

48–49 Singapore's deep harbour is its raison d'etre. This harbour view is taken from the breezy balcony of a heritage "black-and-white" home on Bukit Chermin Road; a few such houses are conserved here.

50–51 Architectural styles vary from modern to classical, as exemplified by White House Park (2007) designed by Thai-Dutch architect Hans Breuer and the Istana (1869), the official residence and office of the President.

52–53 The interiors of the neo-Palladian Istana (translating as "palace" in Malay) feature statuesque columns, deep verandahs and louvred windows as well as a three-storey, 28-metre high tower block situated at its centre.

54 The Istana gardens occupy 106 acres in central Singapore on what was once a nutmeg plantation. Comprising a parade area, water gardens and a semi-formal cottage garden, as well as a nine-hole golf course, they are extensive.

56–57 Signs of the past are evident in built and natural heritage all over the island. Here, an ancient banyan tree spreads its arial roots, while the *porte-cochère* of a "black-and-white" mansion is surrounded by lush trees and vegetation.

58–59 Many old colonial homes remain, such as these two residences on Goodwood Hill. The one on right benefits from an add-on conservatory, while the other has been left intact with large verandah and an expanse of lawn.

60–61 Rain trees on an old plantation lane, Nassim Road, offer shade, while a pair of travellers' palms frames the entrance to a home on Goodwood Hill. Although native to Madagascar, this palm is now synonymous with Singapore.

62 Singapore's campaign to replace the *kampung* or village with mass public housing elevated people and architecture, materially and literally. The high-rise Rochor Centre towers are typical; note the bamboo poles bearing washing.

64–65 Modernisation from the 1950s onward found form in many infrastructure projects that included the building of offices, civic buildings, shopping malls, a comprehensive road and rail system as well as schools and universities.

66–67 New and old mingle in art and architecture as exemplified by these water towers at one of the gates leading to Far East Square and vivid Roy Lichenstein sculptures representing Chinese characters at the Millennium Walk complex.

68–69 Architecture as geometry: Built at a road junction on Circular Quay, this 1920s art deco era office is built in a wedge shape or triangular prism. Opposite is the glass cone of the postmodernist Wheelock Place (1996).

70–71 Shopping is one of Singapore's national obsessions—along with eating. Be it a cheap rack of shoes on Chinatown's Pagoda Street or a sleek stack of shops at Paragon mall is irrelevant: what's important is the act itself.

72–73 Little India's bargain basement stores have more than a passing resemblance to a bazaar in Bombay: Mementoes, trinkets, clothing, shoes, saris, silks and more are all to be found along its narrow streets and alleys.

74–75 Cheap and tacky, sophisticated and sleek —variety is the name of the shopping game in the city-state. Made in China or designed in Singapore? The photo on right shows modernist local designer store Song + Kelly.

76-77 Elegant eating, haute cuisine Eastern style with flavours for every palette. Try the Tiffin Curry Buffet, featuring traditional Indian specialities, at the famed Raffles Hotel or dip into a sophisticated Chinese feast to tantalize tastebuds.

78–79 Nobody needs an excuse to eat in Singapore and local delicacies such as laksa noodles with seafood (left) and Hainan chicken rice (right) are popular dishes, especially when elegantly served at Raffles Hotel.

80–81 Religious harmony is a given with an enviable "live and let live" attitude. A soaring *gopuram* at the Hindu Sri Mariamman temple (1910) is down the road from the Tang dynasty style Buddha Tooth Relic Temple (2007).

82–83 Lending a hand—or a back—a pal offers a seat to a participant in the Thaipusan ceremony. He'll carry this impaled *kavadi* on a 4-km journey of atonement, all the while watched by tourists, family and friends.

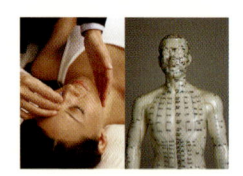

84–85 Traditional Chinese Medicine (TCM) flourishes in a population that is close to 75 percent Chinese. TCM clinics and Chinese medical halls offer therapies including acupuncture to free up blocked meridians and release flow of *qi*.

86–87 Body adornment or body piercing? Finery or frippery? Both utilise gold and silver, be it in the form of a manequin's brocade sari or a free spirit's use of face and ear ornamentation. Anything goes, as they say.

88–89 Chinese formal or disco attire? A rack of demure, but super sexy, cheongsams designed by Allan Chan vies for attention with a pair of dancing babes etched into the entrance of a bar in Serangoon Road.

90–91 The ancient art of calligraphy uses special brushes, ink chops and elaborately crafted paper. Also elaborate, but entirely natural, are these rocks: known as Chinese scholar's rocks, they were shown in literary studios in the past.

92–93 A Chinese *penjing* collection: similar to bonsai, tropical species are artfully trained to resemble mini temperate trees. More are displayed in the Suzhou Penjing Garden, a quiet spot with walled courts, gardens and moon gates.

94–95 Western remedies are often eschewed for medicinal herbs imported from China by diehard TCM afficionados; Chinese New Year is celebrated with traditional fodder in a night market set up in front of the old theatre.

96–97 Chinese opera performances at theatres, on makeshift stages and in public courtyards proliferate around Chinese New Year. Involving heavy costumes, masks and makeup, the musical drama originated in the 3rd century AD.

98 Beijing opera (*Jingù*) is a very popular form of traditional Chinese theatre. It combines music, vocals, mime and dance as well as acrobatics. It traces its roots to the late 18th century and uses highly embellished costumes.

100–101 The ornate Thiam Hock Keng temple (left) is Singapore's oldest Chinese temple (1839–42). It was built to service the Hokkien community. Leong San See Temple (right) was constructed in Chinese palace style (1913) and is Buddhist.

102–103 Auspicious red features prominently on the altar at Po Chiak Keng Temple, while the Sri Vadapathira Kaliamman Temple, a Tamil temple in Little India, is dedicated to the Goddess Kali. It began life in 1855.

104–105 A selection of mooncakes, the traditional food of the Mid-Autumn Festival held to celebrate the end of the harvest. Dancing lions, however, are more often seen at New Year; here, we see shelves containing lion ornaments.

106–107 Joss paper and prayer money, to provide the deceased with income in the afterlife, are burned at a Chinese funeral. On right, a chariot bearing a diety is attended to by Tamil priests during the Thaipusam procession.

108–109 Both weddings and funerals elicit involved customs and ceremonies: On left, a Peranakan bride suffers the burden of an ornate headress; on right, ancestors are venerated via "soul tablets", inscribed with their names, on the altar.

110–111 Christianity is the second most practiced religion in Singapore. St Andrew's Cathedral is the venue for Anglicans; its interior contains some memorable works of art as well as some beautiful stained glass windows.

112–113 Curious customs, such as donating hair to the temple (right) or riding a bicycle with a helmet that honours both Britain and Singapore (left) abound! It's the melting pot of both traditions and peoples that so appeals.

114–115 Pretty packaging adorns boxes of incense. Once a year, it's thought that ancestors return to their homes, hungry and ready to eat, so offerings of food and drink and lit incense are given to satisfy their needs.

116–117 Orange is the colour related to religion in Asia, be it in the fabric of a monk's robes (right) at a Chinese funeral or in a colourful display of food and drink offerings set out to appease hungry ghosts of ancestors (left).

118–119 Miniature shrines, photos of deities, offerings of incense and holy trees are found all over the city-state—on streets, in homes and in temples. Left depicts a picture of a garlanded Indian god, right a small Chinese altar.

120–121 The interiors of religious buildings are well tended and tranquil. On left, the cavernous prayer hall of Sultan Mosque; on right, a large hall with huge Buddha image in Sakaya Muni Buddha Gaya, a Thai Buddhist temple.

122–123 To reveal or to conceal? Body art or body hidden? There's seemingly no logic to the plethora of attitudes and mores amongst the population. A man displays all, while two girls remain covered at a madrasah school.

124–125 Asia's largest tropical oceanarium, Underwater World, on Sentosa Island, showcases some 2,500 marine life from 250 species. Over 20 million visitors have viewed its jellyfish and dramatic shark hologram.

126–127 Singapore has some fascinating museums, including Sentosa's Images of Singapore depicting historical scenes such as the end of World War II. Right is an exhibit at the Civil Defence Gallery Museum in an old fire station.

128 The tropics provide fertile ground for gardens, and Singapore's Botanic Gardens, founded in 1859 as a recreational park, are no exception. Laid out by a local nutmeg planter, they remain more or less unchanged today.

130–131 Singapore is most associated with palms and orchids, the latter being the national flower. Here a row of palms lines a driveway, while an arch of yellow Oncidiums brings colour to the Botanic Gardens.

132 The Mandai Orchid Gardens, set up by Lee Kim Hong and John Laycock in 1950, have been influential in both the propogation of new orchid hybrids and the introduction of unusual ornamental plants.

134–135 Over 100 hectares of primary forest flourishes in the Central Catchment Nature Reserve, especially around MacRitchie resevoir. Here rubber trees are to be found as well as this Victorian decorative cast iron pavilion.

136–137 Soothing the spirit as well as energising the body, gardens provide respite in the built-up city. A reflexology path in the Botanic Gardens is much used, while a meditation path at the Sentosa Spa gives calm and quiet.

138–139 Serenity is to be found in both the built and natural environment: Sentosa island, in the south, is known for its beaches, recreation and quiet areas. Left shows a Jacuzzi as Spa Botanica; right a beautiful beach.

140–141 Surrounded by water and the recipient of extreme tropical downpours, water is central to Singapore life. Here, we see a couple of created waterfalls: at a garden spa and in a massive aviary at the Jurong Bird Park.

Singapore Panoramas

Clarke Quay: Taking its name from Sir Andrew Clarke, Singapore's second governor, who was a major force in positioning Singapore as a major port in the late 1800s, Clarke Quay bustles especially at night. Many of the original buildings—old godowns and warehouses—have been restored and transformed into lively bars, restaurants and retail stores.

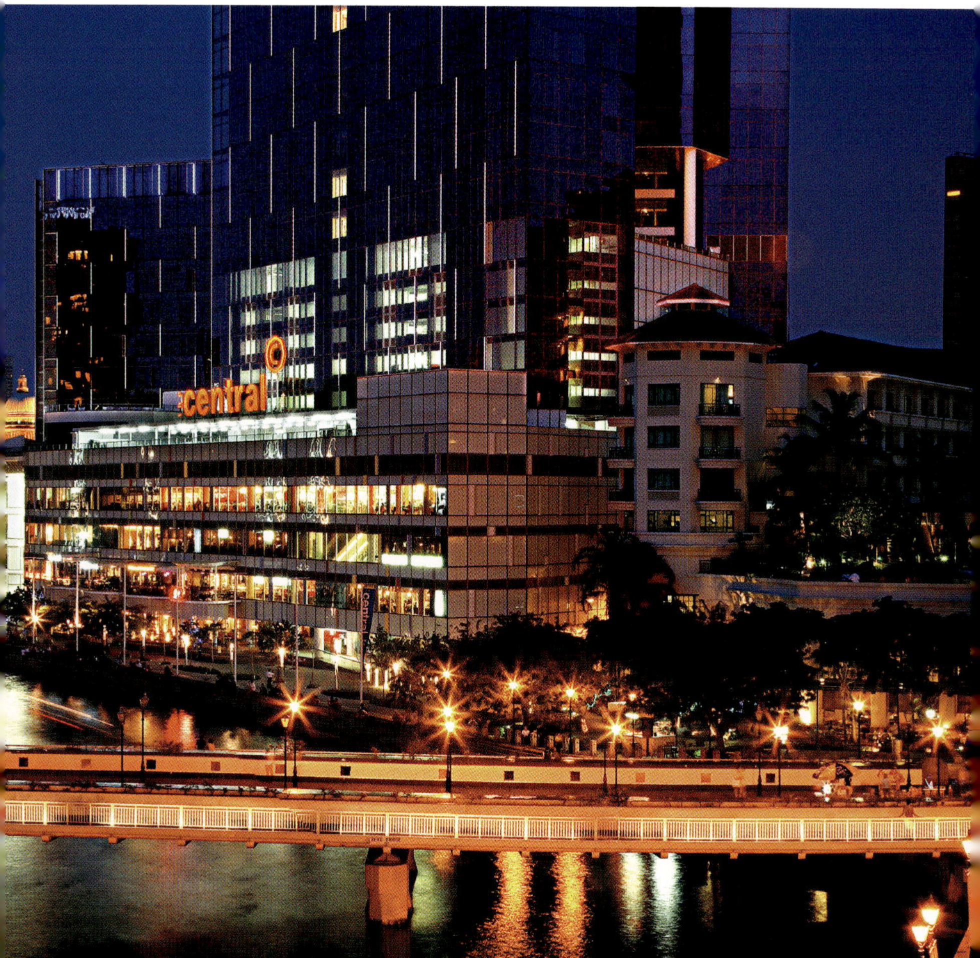
central

Singapore River: This shot of the Singapore River shows how past and present exist harmoniously in the city-state. In foreground, we see a number of colonial buildings including the old Parliament and Victoria theatre, whilst across the river rise the skyscrapers of the Central Business District, lined with low-rise godowns on Boat Quay.

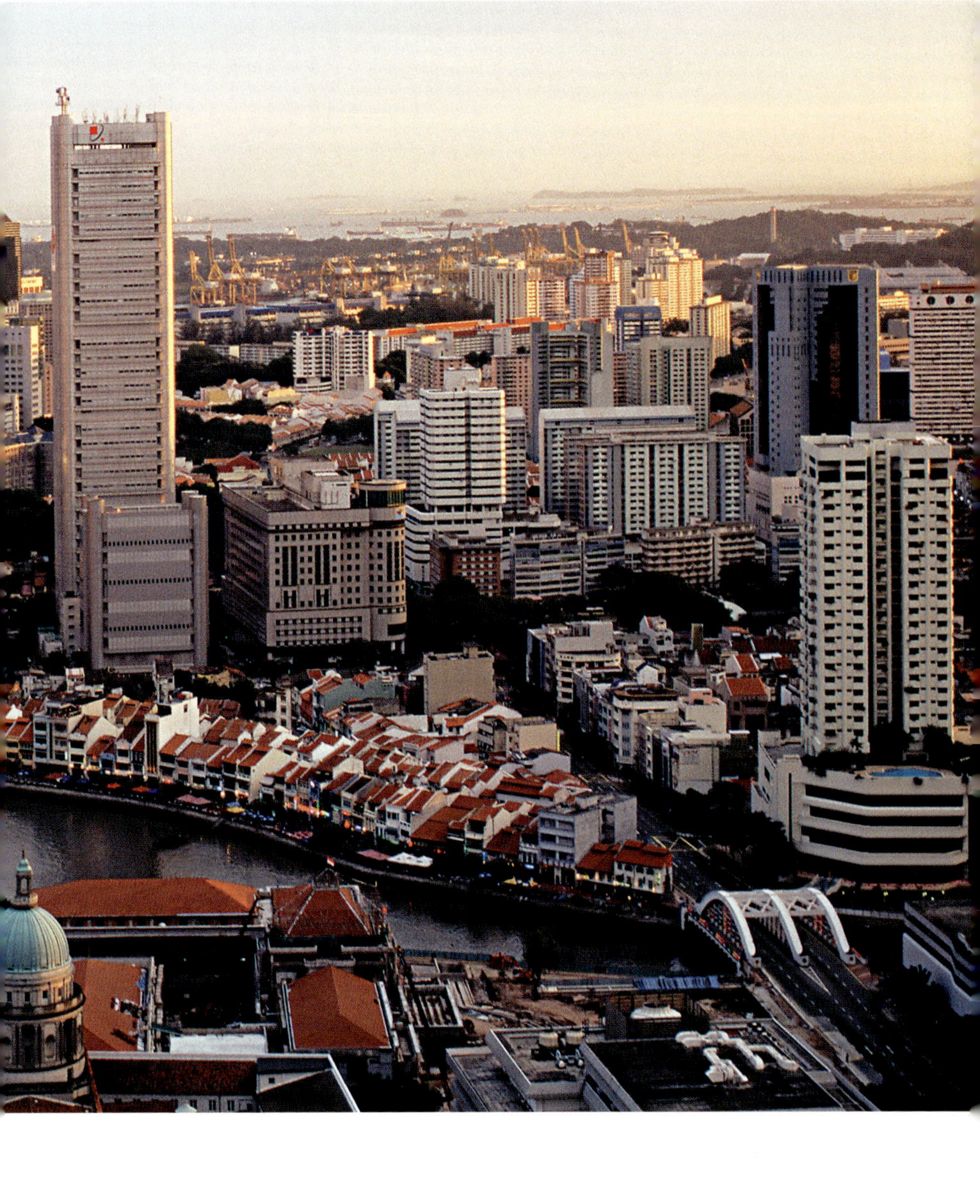

Kampung Glam: Named after the *gelam* tree which was prevalent in the area, Kampung Glam was the historic seat of old Malay royalty in Singapore. Today its meticulously restored architecture lies adjacent a more modern part of the city-state: here we find the Singapore Flyer, views to the harbour and Central Business District behind.

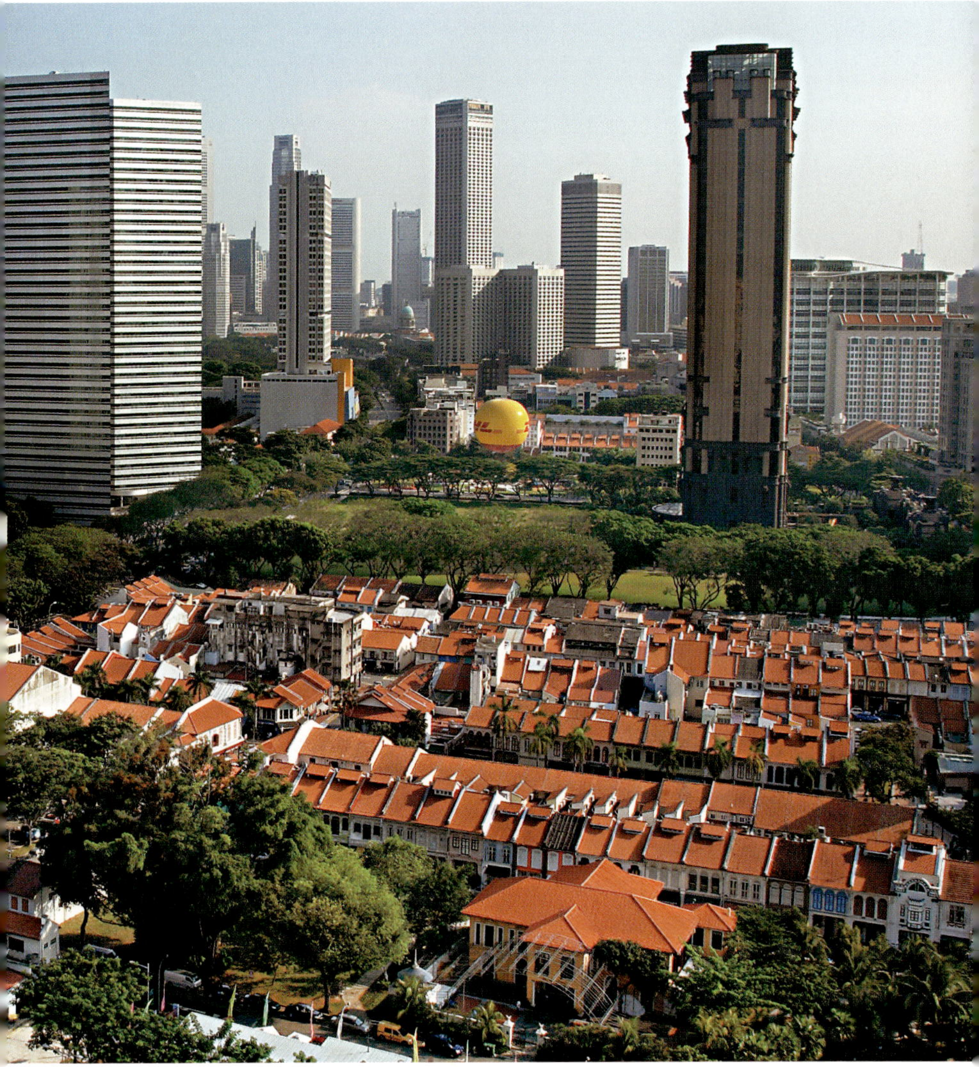

Koon Seng Road: One of Singapore's strengths lies in its commitment to architectural and cultural preservation. These residential terraces from the 1920s or '30s are an eclectic mix of Eastern and Western styles: Doric columns, classical emblature and pilasters sit side by side with bas reliefs depicting Chinese zodiac animals, bat shaped vents and *pintu pagar* doors.

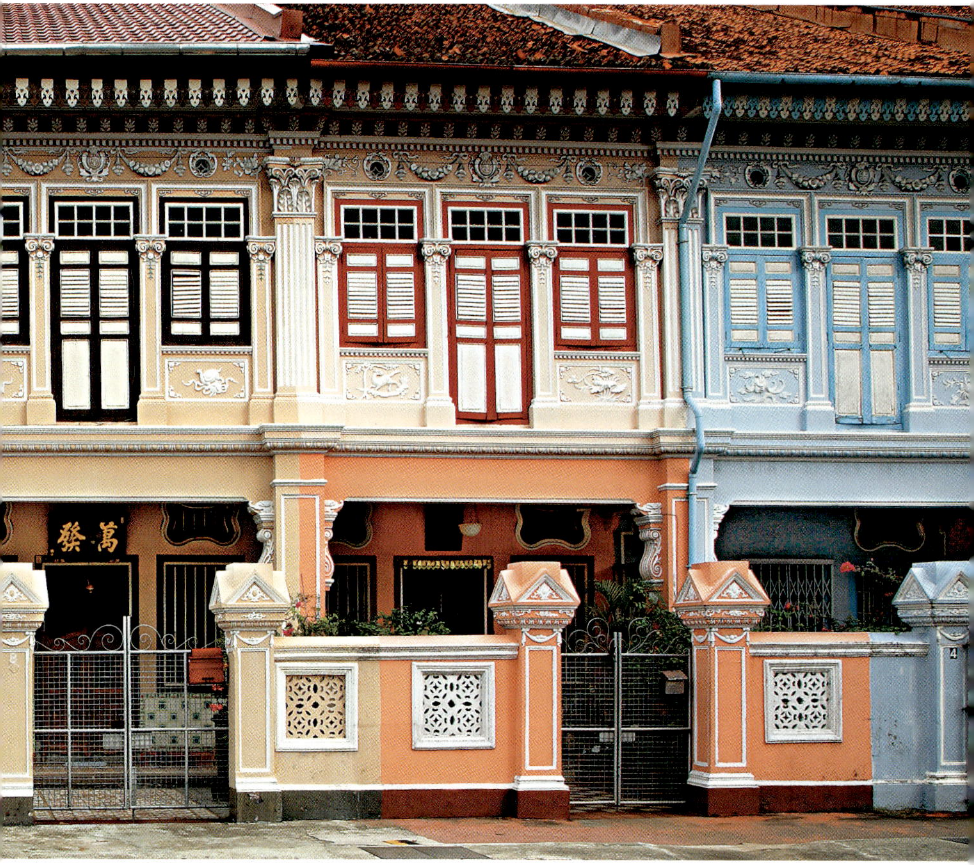
萬發
4

The Symbol of Singapore: Half lion, half mermaid, the so-called "merlion" is the Tourist Board symbol of Singapore. This statue sits at the mouth of the Singapore River, welcoming visitors to the city-state. Behind is the elegant Anderson Bridge (1910), named after Sir John Anderson, a previous governor. It was built to ease the congested Cavanagh Bridge (see overleaf).

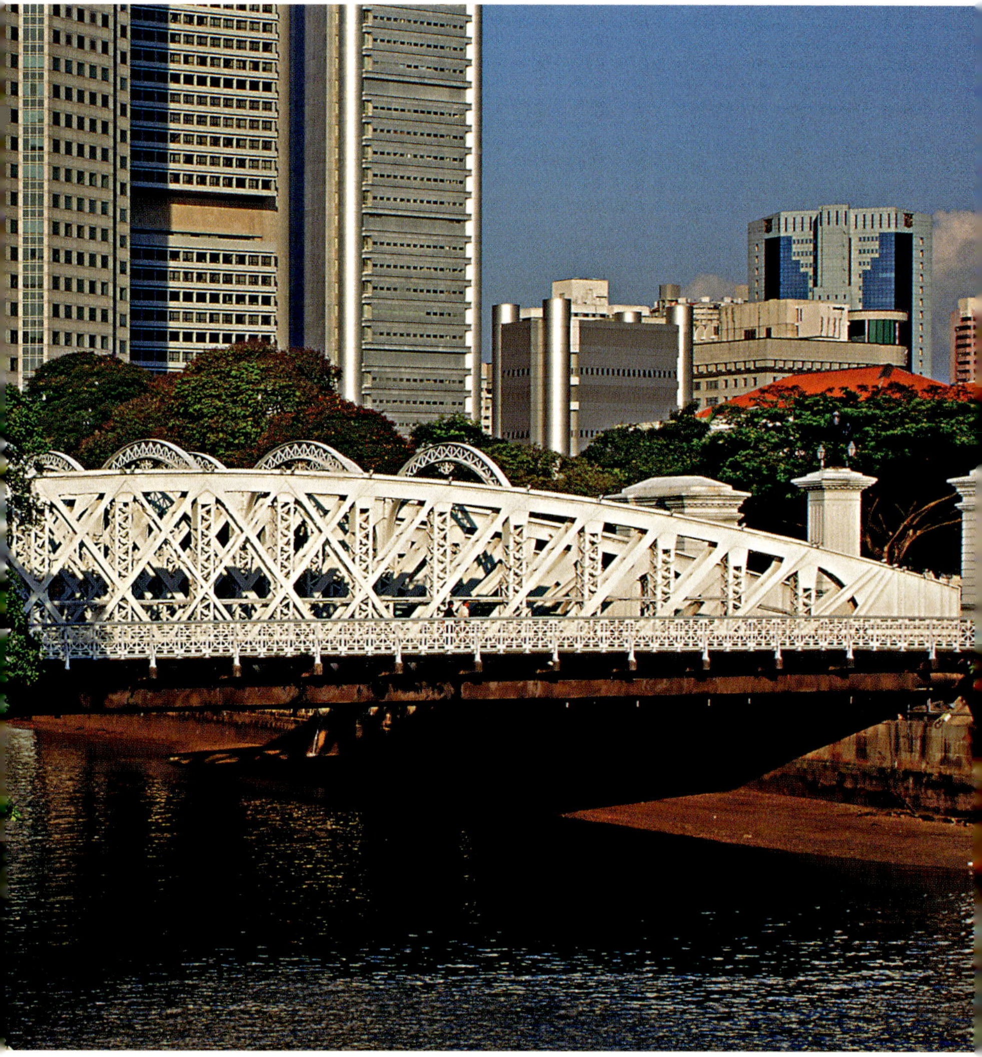

POLICE NOTICE
CAVENAGH BRIDGE
THE USE OF THIS BRIDGE IS PROHIBITED TO ANY VEHICLE OF WHICH THE LADEN WEIGHT EXCEEDS 3 CWT. AND TO ALL CATTLE AND HORSES.

BY ORDER
CHIEF POLICE OFFICER.